PRACTICING THE PROCESS

A BASIC TEXT

PRACTICING THE PROCESS

A BASIC TEXT

MARLENE MARTIN
Monterey Peninsula College

SCOTT, FORESMAN AND COMPANY
Glenview, Illinois   Boston   London

One thing that is always with the writer—no matter how long he has written or how good he is—is the continous process of learning how to write.

Flannery O'Connor

Acknowledgments are listed on page 335, which constitutes a legal extension of the copyright page.

Library of Congress Cataloging-in-Publication Data

Martin, Marlene,
   Practicing the process : a basic text / Marlene Martin.
      p.   cm.
   ISBN 0-673-18759-4
   1. English language—Rhetoric. 2. English language-
   -Grammar—   I. Title.
   PE1408.M38664 1989   88-28603
   808′.042—dc19   CIP

1 2 3 4 5 6–MVN–94 93 92 91 90 89

PREFACE

Kermit Frog is approaching middle age. What does that have to do with a college composition textbook? Plenty. Like Kermit, today's students have grown up in a world that says, "Let me entertain you." They have been bombarded with entertainment from the time they learned—with the Count—to count. Especially for basic students, a solid page of words is not attention-catching. While a text needs to present important information, it also needs to interest and motivate students. It needs to be broken up by illustrations and thoughtful questions and exercises.

Practicing the Process is designed to interest and instruct students who need to focus on formulating, organizing, and developing shorter themes before going on to more advanced compositions.

Although writing involves several separate activities, students tend to think primarily in terms of one: their weaknesses with mechanics. This is not surprising, of course, because many students are convinced they really have nothing important to say. By demonstrating how to use several methods for generating ideas, this text helps students discover they have a good deal to say. Without this confidence, they lack motivation to learn the necessary rhetorical and mechanical skills necessary to make them competent writers.

Students too often see composition as a task alien to their real world. They do not think of writing as something that will help them focus, plan, and organize their thoughts and, therefore, their lives. This text motivates students by showing them that the great value of writing clearly is not simply the final composition such writing produces but the insights the author gets in the writing process. Furthermore, the text illustrates that such clear thinking and writing will help students in their personal, academic, and professional lives.

To help students benefit in these three facets of their lives, the assignments and sample essays in this text move in a natural progression from the writers' personal worlds, through their home and family, to school and community, and finally to the larger world. Once students learn to write concrete, unified essays, they apply these skills to writing tasks they will face outside the composition classroom—such tasks as writing essay exams, research papers, and business letters.

This text uses short sample essays that are relevant to today's students. Each chapter contains samples of good professional and student writing as well as a flawed student essay on which students can hone their proofreading and revision skills. Correcting both the mechanical errors and the rhetorical weaknesses allows students to see for themselves the impact of writing weaknesses. Furthermore it allows them to use the concepts they have just studied and to see for themselves that clear thinking breeds clear writing just as muddled thinking breeds sentence fragments, run-on sentences, and incoherent paragraphs.

To help students correct mechanical errors, a standard correction symbol list appears on the inside back cover. The rules governing mechanical skills and practice exercises using these skills are included in the last section of the text.

A number of people deserve recognition for their help with *Practicing the Process*. The hours I spent on the text helped usher my husband John and sons Ian and Andrew into a Brave New World where feminist values live. My family has learned to wash clothes, shop for groceries, and microwave a frozen entrée.

Although I have taught composition classes for nearly twenty-five years, in writing this text I found that there was a great deal I needed to learn. Among those whose suggestions were very helpful were Elsie Galbreath Haley of Metropolitan State College, C. Jeriel Howard of Northeastern Illinois University, Steven Lynn, University of South Carolina, and John Markley of San Diego City College. In addition to writing the instructor's manual, Maureen Girard of Monterey Peninsula College has provided valuable suggestions and encouragement. Shirley Fischer has proved a helpful and enthusiastic proofreader.

This text has benefited especially from the insight and advice of two outstanding instructors: Duncan Carter of Portland State University and Virginia W. Stone of Pacific Grove High School and Monterey Peninsula College.

Scott Foresman editors Anne Smith, Patricia Rossi, and Kay Bartolo contributed many hours of valuable advice.

Monterey Peninsula College librarians Mary Anne Teed, Topsey Smalley, Bernadine Abbott, and Julia Batchev were wonderfully efficient and cheerful about finding the information I needed.

My high school teachers Irene Cook and the late Eloise Smallwood inspired me with their contagious enthusiasm for language. Without the initial inspiration and ideas furnished by Bertha Hutchins, I would not have attempted this book.

The hundreds of students who used this text in its formative stages deserve credit for their patience, enthusiasm, and encouragement. The student essays are indeed the stars of this text. It is to my students I dedicate this book.

MARLENE MARTIN

TABLE OF CONTENTS

THE FINAL TOUCH: A HANDBOOK

MECHANICAL ITEMS

THE SENTENCE

PUNCTUATION AND CAPITALIZATION

VERBS

PRONOUNS

MODIFYING PHRASES

STYLE

DICTION AND SPELLING

WORD PROBLEMS

PRACTICING THE PROCESS

A BASIC TEXT

1 WHY WRITE?

Drawing by Chas. Adams; © 1982. *The New Yorker Magazine, Inc.*

When someone reads what you write, he or she is in your power. The trick, then, is to use that power effectively.

Louis I. Middleman, **In Short**

CONCEPTS TO LEARN

- The importance of learning to write well

- The writing skills you will need personally, academically, and professionally

---

FOR THOUGHT AND DISCUSSION

1. To what child's rhyme does the cartoon which opens the chapter allude?
2. The rhyme for the cartoon has three versions. Why would multiple versions of the same rhyme exist? Remember that for most of its history, few English speakers could read or write.

Calvin C. Hernton is a contemporary poet who teaches Afro American Literature at Oberlin College. A former social worker, Hernton says he has "an almost too human concern for humanity." Hernton expresses his concerns about himself and his fellow human beings by writing about his thoughts experiences—subject matter that range from being a black male in contemporary America to the problems caused by war, hatred, and racism. Hernton's wide range of subjects includes watching people scurry about with umbrellas up after the rain had stopped and his fears about flying in airplanes. In other words, Hernton uses his writing to express his ideas about being a unique human being.

The Distant Drum

I am not a metaphor or symbol.
This you hear is not the wind in the trees,
Nor a cat being maimed in the street.
It is I being maimed in the street.
It is I who weep, laugh, feel pain or joy.
I speak this because I exist.
This is my voice.
These words are my words, my mouth
Speaks them, my hand writes—
I am a poet.
It is my fist you hear beating
Against your ear.

Calvin C. Hernton

FOR THOUGHT AND DISCUSSION

1. What does Hernton mean by the first four lines?
2. Why does Hernton want to communicate with others?
3. According to the last line, how badly does Hernton want to communicate his ideas?
4. Suggest some examples of the specific concerns Hernton might have about events occurring in our world.

THE BEST OF POINTS AND THE WORST OF POINTS

The cartoon and poem which begin the chapter illustrate important points about writing. At worst, when we don't write our ideas, they get lost. At best, when we don't write ideas—or we don't follow rules in writing—our ideas change as they are repeated.

The Story of the English Language

Until William Caxton brought the printing press to England in 1476, the English language, itself, changed rapidly. To give you an idea of how quickly English changed before the printing press, read the following sample of *Beowulf* in Old English, which was spoken when French-speaking King William the Conqueror invaded England in 1066:

> *Oft Scyld Scefing sceathena threatum,*
> *monegum mægthum meodosetla ofteah,*
> *egsode eorlas, syththan ærest wearth*
> *feasceaft funden; he thæs frofre gebad,*

As you can see, to understand *Beowulf* we would have to study Old English just as we would study a foreign language. Translated, the Old English is the following:

> Often did Scyld Scefing and his warriors deprive his foes of their very mead-benches, and strike terror into the Heruli people.

The French Connection

With a French-speaking king and few books to standardize the language, English changed enormously during the next three centuries. By the late 1300s the language developed into what is now called Middle English. The following lines which open Chaucer's *Canterbury Tales* exemplify Middle English.

> Whan that Aprill with his shoures soote
> The droghte of March hath perced to the roote . . .

Understanding directions to the nearest McDonald's would have been a little easier in the Middle English of 1390 than it was in the Old

English of 1100. In Middle English, however, you might misunderstand enough words to wind up at the Ritz instead of at the Golden
Arches. Translated into semi-modern English, Chaucer was saying:

> When in April the sweet showers fall
> And pierce the drought of March to the root . . .

Rule Britannia: The Triumph of Modern English

By the time Shakespeare was born in 1564, the printing press had
begun to standardize English, and it has changed comparatively little
since then. In *As You Like It*, we understand what Jaques means when
he talks of "the whining school boy, with his satchel and shining
morning face, creeping like [a] snail unwilling to school." (In fact, on
a few occasions we may have made our own way to class at a snail's
pace.)

SO WHAT?

What does all this have to do with learning to write? Plenty. The written word gives our language and our world greater stability. When our
thoughts are properly written, they communicate over great distances
and through the centuries.

In the five hundred years since printing presses started rolling, the
amount and importance of printed material in our world has snow-
balled. During almost every minute of the day we are surrounded by
writing. In our homes cereal boxes, package directions, newspapers,
magazines, and clothing labels all bombard us with the written word.
At work the bombardment becomes a barrage of memos, letters,
directions, and reports.

Write On

Researchers have found that the higher our incomes are and the more
promotions we earn at work the more reading and writing we do. One
survey of college-educated people showed they spend an average of
twenty-three percent of their working time writing. Even engineers—
famous for their desire to flee from college writing courses—spend a
quarter of their working time writing. What's more, these figures are
low because those surveyed tended to report their actual time writing, not the prewriting activities which, as later chapters will show,
are essential to the writing process.

The Future: Where the Jobs Are

Forecasters predict an increase in dependence on the written word.
According to General Motors, the auto industry's ratio of nontechni-
cal to technical jobs was 5.6 to 1 in 1981. By 1990 it will be 1 to 1. In
1981, one million word processors were used to organize information.
By 1990 there will be twenty million word processors in use. Rabbits
could scarcely do better. According to the Department of Labor, forty-

five million people worked at generating information in 1980. By 1990 that number will grow to fifty-five million, an astounding statistic when you realize that fifty-five million will be one-quarter of the entire population of the United States. Words, then, are where the jobs are—and will be.

When Language Fails

The Challenger Space Shuttle disaster of January 28, 1986 is a dramatic illustration of the importance of the written word. The Presidential commission appointed to investigate this tragedy had to sift through more than 140,000 pages of documents and listen to transcripts and other information to reach the following conclusion:

> If the decision makers had known all of the facts, it is highly unlikely that they would have decided to launch 51-L.

In part, the Challenger crew died because those who knew the shuttle was unsafe did not convincingly communicate the danger to those who ordered its launch on that icy winter morning.

The Big Boss

Uncle Sam employs one of the largest work forces in the world, and his communications problems are not limited to space programs—as anyone who has plowed through a tax form will confirm. The following excerpt from Lieutenant Colonel Charles G. Cavanaugh, Jr.'s article for Army officers explains the importance of the written word as the United States Army prepares soldiers for today's trenches.

Vocabulary   NCOIC: Noncommissioned Office-in-Charge

THE WRITE WAY TO DO IT
Lt. Col. Charles G. Cavanaugh, Jr.

The commander sends the paper back for the fourth time with a less-than-courteous note "suggesting" a need for clarity. The corporal on a field problem scratches his head, stops training and heads for a field phone to ring up the first sergeant and "politely" ask what he really means by his scribbled note.

Both soldiers are wasting time. Both have delayed a decision. Both understand the problem: "If they can't write it clearly, how am I supposed to know what's going on?" Napoleon once said that an army moves on its stomach. That's probably true. But another essential for a modern army is communication—written and oral.

Like it or lump it, today's Army relies on paperwork. Whether it is a sophisticated argument for presentation to a congressional committee or a simple training memo for a rifle range NCOIC, most of what the Army does is fueled by words on paper. The Army's not doing that well, so it has started an ambitious program to help solve the problem.

"Gen. Maxwell Thurman, the vice-chief of staff, started the ball rolling on the program," said Lt. Col. William A. McIntosh. "He saw the need, and he has the horsepower." McIntosh is a permanent professor of English at West Point and has a doctoral degree from the University of Virginia. He developed the program's initial phases. . . .

"We discovered that soldiers at all levels need to communicate better in writing and that there is no way on earth the Army can truly educate every member.

"We had to select reasonable training objectives and accurate diagnostic tools, and realized that a lecture format would not work. Our whole program, at each level, will be performance-oriented," he added. . . .

McIntosh said a major aim of the program is to correctly identify soldiers' weaknesses. "Testing is critical," he continued, "because many people don't know they have weaknesses and need help. . . .

["The students] must learn to communicate their ideas if they are to advance. They must learn to be clear and concise if they are to lead effectively. That's what this program is all about," he said. . . .

First to participate in the new program will be soldiers who will receive sixteen hours of instruction designed to meet a standard which states: "Effective writing is writing that can be understood in a single rapid reading and is generally free of errors in grammar, mechanics, and usage. . . .

Chambers concurred, "It's not so important that an Army officer know the difference between a gerund and a participle. It is important he be able to write coherently," he said. . . .

"The course is performance-oriented," McIntosh emphasized. "This is hands-on stuff, not lectures that students absorb by osmosis. Soldiers taking the writing course will do plenty of writing, and the instructors will do plenty of grading. There is no way to sidestep in this course. . . . "

This is an exciting and worthwhile program. Everyone who comes in contact with the program should be better because of it. . . . The Army wants and deserves professionals who can use their talents to the fullest."

FOR THOUGHT AND DISCUSSION

1. Why is the military going to the effort and expense of teaching soldiers to write more clearly and coherently?
2. What problems could occur because of a misunderstanding in a military memo?
3. What does McIntosh mean when he says his program is "performance-oriented"?

When Words = Dollars

Sylvia Porter is a columnist who writes about a favorite topic for many of us: money. In the following column she discusses the relationship between money and writing in the business world.

MANAGERS NEED TO WRITE WELL
Sylvia Porter

Do you spend up to 40 percent of your time writing reports, memos, correspondences, and instructions? Do any of your employees? Then you have on your staff what amounts to professional writers who, to be successful, must communicate effectively with many different audiences.

Yet sloppy, incoherent, vague, or simply dull writing clogs thousands of typewriters and word processors across the land.

I know. As a recipient of hundreds of press releases, memos, and letters each week, I can testify that a startling total—many from prestigious companies—are incomprehensible. The result: Many wind up in my wastebasket unread.

Surely they represent a waste of some highly paid employees' time. These letters and press releases are not what employers want to pay for.

No one really knows how much poor writing costs businesses. Clearly, the obvious answer is "a lot."

One observer has estimated that more than one-third of business letters do nothing more than seek clarification of earlier correspondence. So why don't people say what they mean the first time around?

Middle managers get most of the writing assignments in American business and, consequently, commit many, if not most, of the writing errors, according to Maryann V. Piotrowski, of Corporate Writing Consultants in Cambridge, Massachusetts, and author of "Re:Writing," a monthly newsletter.

"Most writing by top management is short and to the point," she told my research associate, Ellen Hermanson. "These people don't have to impress anyone."

But at lower levels, employees want to wow their bosses, look good, and advance. All too often, however, they stumble and muff their basic task: to communicate.

It is astonishing that few in business ever receive the kind of instruction necessary to help cure the plague of bad writing. . . .

"The hours spent on teaching employees to write well will be repaid," Ms. Piotrowski emphasizes.

Time wasted on poor writing is time lost to the company. Effective communication is, indeed, ultimately a question of cost.

And since so many managers spend so much time writing, it becomes a time management issue, as well. . . .

Many executives claim they have too much work to do to revise a mere letter or report.

How silly. Do you want to risk giving the impression that you can't think straight? Spending the extra time to clarify your thinking—and writing—pays off.

FOR THOUGHT AND DISCUSSION

1. What level of workers get most writing assignments?
2. According to one observer, what percent of business letters simply explain previous letters?
3. At the end of her column, what three errors does Porter warn writers to avoid?
4. How can people learn to avoid "sloppy, incoherent, vague, or simply dull writing"?

The Write Stuff for Business

What types of writing do businesses need? While the following does not list every possible kind of business writing, it includes the most common types:

Business letters
Proposals
Memos
Reports
Instructions
Formal documents
Summaries
Legal briefs

Certainly the academic world also requires a good deal of writing. For example, a survey conducted of majors as diverse as architecture, business, nursing, and forestry indicated a need for the following kinds of writing:

Short answer tests
Essay tests
Journals
Letters
Lab write-ups
Project descriptions or abstracts
Research papers
Critical papers

Not only your work-a-day and school worlds benefit from improved writing skills. By learning to organize and express your ideas clearly, you will better understand the ideas and issues about which you write.

According to C. Day Lewis, an Irish-born, English poet and detective author, "We do not write in order to be understood; we write in order to understand." Granted, we sometimes already know exactly what we want to say when we sit down to write. The more complicated the issue, however, the stronger the chance that we will come to understand our ideas better as we develop and organize them while writing.

PREWRITING EXERCISE ONE
Back to Work

Let's take a few minutes to see how writing affects your life.

"All right," you say. "Improving my writing skills is important. So tell me how to write better."

Improving your writing skills, just like improving any other skill, will demand your total involvement. Would you want to fly in a plane piloted by someone who had read books and attended lectures about piloting but had not actually practiced in a plane—without you in it? Similarly, you can not learn to write simply by reading about writing and listening to your instructor. You must believe that good writing skills will be useful, and then you must use what you are learning; you must write.

1. Make lists of the types of writing you will need personally, professionally, and academically.
2. Once you have made the lists, share your answers with your classmates. As they read their lists, add their relevant ideas to your own lists.

PREWRITING EXERCISE TWO
Thinking of You

The first step in the Army's writing program was to test soldiers' writing skills. Take a few minutes to assess your own writing strengths and weaknesses, using the following five steps:

1. List the six writing skills you need to work on most. Begin by naming your writing strengths and your writing weaknesses.
2. Go back and decide which strengths and weaknesses belong in the top six.
3. Rate these strengths and weaknesses 1–6, with the greatest strength and most serious weakness being number 1.
4. Share your lists with your classmates and then compile class lists.
5. Separate both of the class lists into the following two lists: those that involve the mechanics of writing, such as punctuation and grammar, and those that involve generating and organizing ideas.

IT TAKES TWO TO TANGO—AND WRITE

Writing requires two very different kinds of activities. One activity is learning and then applying the mechanical rules such as punctuation, spelling, and capitalization. The other activity is deciding what we want to say. If we worry about mechanics when we are trying to generate ideas, our flow of ideas will be sidetracked.

The purpose of writing is to clarify for ourselves what we think and then to communicate that thought to others. Just determining our views on a subject takes a good deal of concentration. If we worry about mechanical rules at the same time, we become less efficient at both processes, and we miss the satisfaction of exploring our ideas in depth.

Because writers need to separate idea-generating from mechanics, this book covers these two processes in separate sections. "The Final Touch: A Handbook" at the end of the text is a summary of mechanical rules. The rest of *Practicing the Process: A Basic Text* will help you generate and organize your ideas.

The Good News

You will be pleased to learn that, unlike having your wisdom teeth extracted or your fingernails pulled off one by one, writing can and *should* be a nonthreatening, enjoyable process. When you see an assignment only as an unpleasant task you must do for someone else, you will suffer as you write—and so will your writing.

Russell Baker, a successful newspaper columnist, describes his reaction to a writing assignment from his student days in the following selection from his autobiography *Growing Up*.

GROWING UP
Russell Baker

Late in the year we tackled the informal essay. "The essay, don't you see, is the . . . " My mind went numb. Of all forms of writing, none seemed so boring as the essay. Naturally we would have to write informal essays. Mr. Fleagle distributed a homework sheet offering us a choice of topics. None was quite so simpleminded as "What I Did on My Summer Vacation," but most seemed to be almost as dull. I took the list home and dawdled until the night before the essay was due. Sprawled on the sofa, I finally faced up to the grim task, took the list out of my notebook, and scanned it. The topic on which my eye stopped was "The Art of Eating Spaghetti."

This title produced an extraordinary sequence of mental images. Surging up out of the depths of memory came a vivid recollection of a night in Belleville when all of us were seated around the supper table—Uncle Allen, my mother, Uncle Charlie, Doris, Uncle Hal—and Aunt Pat served spaghetti for supper. Spaghetti was an exotic treat in those days. Neither Doris nor I had ever eaten spaghetti, and none of the adults had enough experience to be good at it. All the good humor of Uncle Allen's house reawoke in my mind as I recalled the laughing arguments we had that night about the socially respectable method for moving spaghetti from plate to mouth.

Suddenly I wanted to write about that, about the warmth and good feeling of it, but I wanted to put it down simply for my own joy, not for Mr. Fleagle. It was a moment I wanted to recapture and hold for myself. I wanted to relive the pleasure of an evening at New Street. To write it as I wanted, however, would violate all the rules of formal composition I'd learned in school, and Mr. Fleagle would surely give it a failing grade. Never mind. I would write something else for Mr. Fleagle after I had written this thing for myself.

When I finished it the night was half gone and there was no time left to compose a proper, respectable essay for Mr. Fleagle. There was no choice next morning but to turn in my private reminiscence of Belleville. Two days passed before Mr. Fleagle returned the graded papers, and he returned everyone's but mine. I was bracing myself for a command to report to Mr. Fleagle immediately after school for discipline when I saw him lift my paper from his desk and rap for the class's attention.

"Now, boys," he said, "I want to read you an essay. This is titled 'The Art of Eating Spaghetti.'"

And he started to read. My words! He was reading *my words* out loud to the entire class. What's more, the entire class was listening. Listening attentively. Then somebody laughed, then the entire class was laughing, and not in contempt and ridicule, but with openhearted enjoyment. Even Mr. Fleagle stopped two or three times to repress a small prim smile.

FOR THOUGHT AND DISCUSSION

1. Why did Russell Baker say most informal essay subjects are "simple-minded" and "dull"?
2. What made Baker change his mind?
3. How was Baker's attitude toward writing his spaghetti essay different from his usual attitude in writing an essay?
4. What made the essay such a success that Mr. Fleagle read it to the class?

PRACTICE MAKES PERFECTIBLE

Like Russell Baker, you, too, can come up with worthwhile, enjoyable subjects that make you want to write for yourself and not just for the Mr. Fleagles of your life. The following writing exercise will help you explore three methods to come up with your own "Spaghetti Essay" idea.

WRITING ASSIGNMENT
Using What You Have Learned

Write an essay of approximately two hundred words about your experiences with or expectations about writing. Concentrate on writing as a *process*. Instead of being concerned only with the end product—the essay you hand in—you will study and practice the steps that will help you to get to that end product: a clearly stated and logically and concretely developed essay. While you will study prewriting techniques in greater detail later, begin with a quick look at three prewriting methods that will help you in the writing process.

Before you write—in what is called "prewriting," you must examine your thoughts and feelings about a subject. Like Russell Baker, you may decide to describe a significant past experience with writing. On the other hand, you might want to focus on the way writing better will help your career.

Before you begin your actual essay, jo down all the ideas that occur to you about writing for your personal, professional, or academic life. Don't worry about whether or not these ideas seem silly or irrelevant. If they pop into your mind, trap them on paper. It is vital for you to be uncritical of your ideas when you are prewriting. In addition, during prewriting, you must ignore concerns about writing mechanics. Don't worry. We will concentrate on catching up with your errors later.

To help inspire ideas try one or more of the following methods:

1. Clustering.

    a. In the center of your paper write *writing*.
    b. Circle this word.
    c. As a related idea occurs to you, jot it down and circle it.
    d. If one idea leads to another, write the new idea under the idea that inspired it. Connect related ideas with lines.
    e. After a few minutes of clustering, many people suddenly understand what they want to say about writing.
    f. Write the essay inspired by your clustering.
    g. "Writing: Here I Go Again?" The essay inspired by the clustering in Figure 1.1, appears on page 16 in the "Student Star Essays: The Polished Product" section at the end of the chapter.

2. Brainstorming.

    a. Make a list of ideas that occur to you as you examine your thoughts and feelings concerning writing.

FIGURE 1.1   A Clustering Sample

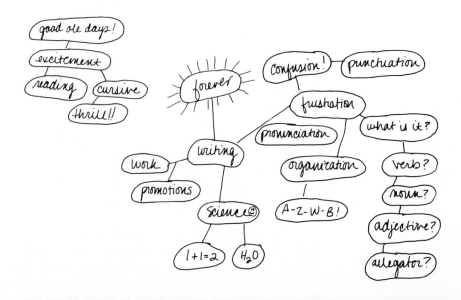

b. Just as you do with clustering, write down all ideas that occur to you. Don't worry about whether or not the ideas seem important or relevant. Be uncritical. Accept your ideas.

c. When you have exhausted your ideas, reread your list. Place in a group the ideas that seem related. Cross out ideas you do not wish to use.

d. Write the essay inspired by your brainstorming.

e. "Writing: A Secret to Success," the essay inspired by the brainstorming in Figure 1.2, appears on page 16 in the "Student Star Essays: The Polished Product" section at the end of the chapter.

FIGURE 1.2   A Brainstorming Sample

Writing

Teachers warned me:
   Goofed off in high school.
   Busy impressing classmates—having FUN.
   Learning—boooo! Boring! Who needed it?
      Not me. I knew everything.
Why am I such a lousy writer?
   Good question.
Busy having fun.
Frustration!!!
   Sloppy writing
   Spelling—The GREAT MYSTERY!
   vocabulary? what do all the words mean?
   like swimming upstream getting ideas.
Now: the BIG BLOCK
   job rejection—SHOCK!
   must improve writing
Writing can be fun for me.
   poetry for myself
   without criticism—Let my
   ideas, let me, alone!

3. Freewriting.   Write all ideas that occur to you when you examine your thoughts and feelings about writing. Do not worry about any mechanical mistakes such as run-on sentences, sentence fragments, proper spelling and punctuation, or correct grammar.

The secret of freewriting is to keep on writing. Ideas inspire ideas. Even if you have to write the word *writing* over and over, keep your pen—or keyboard—moving. Get those ideas down on paper as you think of them.

"Determined to Write," the essay inspired by the freewriting in Figure 1.3, appears on page 17 in the "Student Star Essays: The Polished Product" section at the end of the chapter.

The Next Steps

Use the following ten steps to help you make the best use of prewriting.

1. The "Aha!" message.   As you use one of the prewriting methods, an "Aha!" message may occur to you. At this point, you will realize what you want to say about writing, and you can begin your actual first draft. If you do not have the "Aha!" experience, *relax*. Reassure

---

FIGURE 1.3   **A Freewriting Sample**

I can't do it — write that is. I can think of a thousand problems that keep me from writing. My mind floods with these problems leaving the idea I want to write about submerged with my worries about mistakes. It probably all started with my high school teachers — how negative! If you don't learn it now it'll get harder and harder as you get older and older. Its been 10 yrs. & to top it off English was my very worst subject. I've go to swim upstream to overcome my negative feelings about writing — everything from lousy handwriting to worse spelling and a bad vocabulary.

Its really sad because I actually enjoy writing—poetry especially. But just for me — to feel better.

Unfortunately if I'm going to advance at work I have to learn to write for others too — the pain of confronting that! oh! Getting turned down for a job was the last straw. I will improve — I will do it!

yourself, and select another prewriting method. Remember, had they listened to their critics, Columbus would have stayed in Italy and Thomas Edison would have lit his way with a gas lamp. Allow yourself to experiment. The world you have to discover is inside you.

2. Select one major idea about writing.   Do not simply make a sentence out of each idea that popped into your mind during prewriting. Read each of the student star essays at the end of the chapter and note the way the authors selected one idea about writing to explain. After you select a central idea from your prewriting, you may need to prewrite again to generate material to help you explain that idea.

3. Put it away.   Once you have written your essay, put it away for a day or so. When you reread it after a period of time, it will be easier to make any changes you decide it needs.

4. Check the format.   Check to see that you have followed the proper essay format. Read "Manuscript Format," on page 261 of "The Final Touch: A Handbook" to check your format.

5. Reread.   Reread your paper out loud to someone, or have someone read it to you.

6. Revise.   Change any sentences that sound awkward. Add material that clarifies your point. Delete any words that are repetitious.

7. Proofread.   After you have made all necessary changes in the wording of your ideas, proofread your essay carefully to be sure your sentences are all complete sentences and not run-ons or fragments. Change any punctuation or grammar that seems incorrect.

If you have a mechanical question, look it up in "The Final Touch." For example, if you are uncertain about the use of an apostrophe, look up "The Apostrophe." We will be studying mechanics later in the course, but do the best you can with them now.

8. Proofread backwards.   Proofread your paper again, but this time begin with the last line of your paper. Put a ruler or sheet of paper under that line and circle any errors you find. Watch for spelling or typing errors. The Golden Rule for spelling is *When in Doubt, Look It Up.*

9. Name it.   Give your paper an attractive title. Read number 5 on page 263 under "Manuscript Format" in "The Final Touch" to ensure the title is correct.

10. Attach prewriting.   Staple your prewriting to the *back* of your essay, hand it in, and celebrate. (Take your cat for a walk, study math, brush your teeth—whatever you do for fun.)

STAR ESSAYS
The Polished Product

At the end of each chapter of *Practicing the Process: A Basic Text* are student essays written in response to the writing assignments for each chapter. The following essays were written in response to the writing assignment on page 11. The authors used the following steps:

1. Prewriting
2. Writing
3. Revising content
4. Proofreading and correcting mechanical errors

Study these essays carefully before you begin for hints about the way to write your own assignment.

WRITING—A SECRET TO SUCCESS?

If I had better writing skills, I could solve many problems at work. My inability to communicate with people effectively in writing is one reason why opportunities have been an inch beyond my grasp. Usually, no one seems to like my written recommendations for solutions to problems at work. For a long time I wondered why no one would buy my ideas. I finally realized that most of my ideas were presented in an unorganized fashion. Not only was my sequencing of ideas confusing, I often expressed myself in the wrong words with the wrong punctuation. My problems in expressing myself were so serious they caused a major setback in my career. But now that I am aware of my problem, I'm determined to work on some changes which I believe will offer me new hope. Encouragement from my friends and family helps inspire me, so here I am taking this course. It is my impression that if I work hard enough, think positively enough, and learn as much as I can, I can refine my writing ability so it will be an asset to me in my career.

Mario A. Alvarado

WRITING: HERE I GO AGAIN?

Ever since I can remember I have studied English in school. At first, I liked English. Learning to spell and pronounce words was exciting for me. I can still remember the thrill I felt when I began to read, and I remember my immense pride at learning cursive. But when English classes began to emphasize writing, my chronic nightmare began.

Why the abrupt change? There are several contributing factors. Unlike math, chemistry, and physics (subjects I like), writing the English language does not seem a true science. For example, one and one is always two. Two parts hydrogen to one part oxygen is always water. However, depending on how it is used, the word *swimming* can be a noun, adjective, or verb (and maybe even other parts of speech I haven't thought of).

Punctuation rules are so complicated they should be a course by themselves, and spelling! It seems every other word has its own private rule. Definitions are equally confusing. A single word can have several different definitions and almost as many pronunciations.

Another contributing factor in my attitude toward writing is my inability to organize my thoughts when I am writing. I'll start writing from "A" to "Z" and by the time I reach "W," I'll suddenly remember an important point about "B" that I want to include.

In no other activity except writing do I put forth so much effort to accomplish so little. I remember when I was in high school, I worked for weeks on research papers only to have them return to me bleeding as much red as a stuck pig.

After all my discouraging years of struggle with writing, the disheartening fact remains: I really need to write. Can you imagine how frustrating it is for me to have to do something I find so confusing and hate so much? In my job, I try to find someone who loves to write so I can assign them my writing tasks. But I know I can't advance at work unless I improve my writing skills. So here I am again, back in an English class, but this time I hope I can learn enough about writing that it won't remain a frustrating mystery.

Barry Whitehead

DETERMINED TO WRITE

When I think about writing, my mind floods with all the reasons why I am a poor writer. I realize that with each day I am growing older, and I can still hear my high school teachers saying, "If you don't learn it now, it will be twice as hard to learn when you get older." That was more than ten years ago, and to top it off English was my worst subject. So with my past bad experiences in mind, I find myself feeling very frustrated and depressed about writing. I feel like I must swim upstream.

I am very conscious of my sloppy writing, poor spelling, and inadequate vocabulary. Deep inside I really enjoy writing, but only for myself. I like writing poetry to release inward pressure, but when I write for myself, I don't have to worry whether or not to use a period or a comma. I know nobody else will ever read my poetry and criticize my errors.

I never used to think writing was important except for my own stress relief until I started pursuing a career. Recently I found myself being turned down for a job I knew I could do, but because of my weak writing skills the employer chose someone else and recommended that I take a writing improvement class. I realize now how important writing correctly is, and I know I need to improve my abilities. So here I am, determined to learn.

P. D.

2 CREATIVITY AND CRITICISM

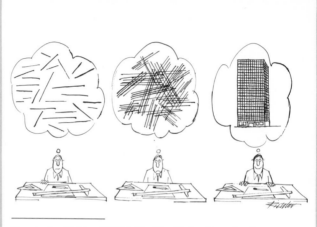

Drawing by Richter; © 1984. *The New Yorker Magazine, Inc.*

"Ideas, by their very nature, have a kind of magic—as if springing from some mysterious source."

Marjorie Holmes, from Writing the Creative Article

CONCEPTS TO LEARN

- The difference between the Left Brain Critic and the Right Brain Creator

- The difference between positive and negative criticism

- The difference between constructive and destructive criticism

---

FOR THOUGHT AND DISCUSSION

1. What is happening in the man's mind in the first frame of the cartoon which opens the chapter?
2. Does the man in the cartoon show signs of worry, or does he merely look as though he is thinking?
3. How does the cartoon apply to writing an essay?
4. Do you usually know exactly what you want to say when you sit down to write, or do your ideas become clearer as you write them on paper?

Like the cartoon, the following poem by Barriss Mills concerns an important topic: where ideas come from.

Gone Forever

Halfway through shaving, it came—
the word for a poem.
I should have scribbled it
on the mirror with a soapy finger,
or shouted it to my wife in the kitchen,
or muttered it to myself till it ran
in my head like a tune.

But now it's gone with the whiskers
down the drain. Gone forever,
like the girls I never kissed,
and the places I never visited—
like the lost lives I never lived.

Barriss Mills

FOR THOUGHT AND DISCUSSION

Why did the poem's narrator lose his good idea?

JUST THE TWO OF YOU

When creating ideas, in a sense we are two persons—a creative person and a critical person. This is a fact both scientists and writers have recognized for a very long time. In his research and writings, the famous Austrian psychiatrist Sigmund Freud increased mankind's awareness of the subconscious, a powerful part of the mind that often controls behavior. The subconscious houses our creativity and many of the memories the conscious mind thinks it has forgotten.

Science fiction writer Ray Bradbury has a sign over his typewriter that says, "Don't think." This doesn't mean Bradbury sits at his typewriter drooling and scratching his armpits. What it means is that he turns off the conscious part of his mind to use the creative resources stored in his subconscious.

Fat Cabbages and Creativity: Learning to Tap the Creative You

Like Marjorie Holmes in the quotation that introduces this chapter, Bradbury gets ideas from the mysterious subconscious, mysterious because it is not within our conscious command. Of tapping this source of creative ideas, writer Henry Miller wrote, "Some [ideas] just ooze out like fat cabbages or weeds. I write without thought . . . I take down dictation."

Ideas do have a way of popping into our minds—often at the most unexpected times—and not popping when we desperately want them to pop, just as they did for the poet of "Gone Forever." In *Practicing the Process* we will learn to control this appearance and disappearance of ideas. A key concept to learn is the conscious-subconscious or creative-critic differences which are in all of us. In prewriting for the essay in Chapter One, you turned off your critic brain so you could explore the wealth of ideas and memories stored in your subconscious.

Getting to Know You

Do you ever scold yourself for doing something wrong, or do you ever give yourself advice? Don't worry if your answer is yes. The gentlemen in white coats won't come and take you away. At times, we all talk to ourselves as if we were actually two persons. To better understand these people who live within us, that is, to better understand the different functions of the parts of our brains, read the following passage from Timothy Gallwey's *The Inner Game of Tennis.*

Vocabulary **entities:** something with a real and separate existence either actually, or in your mind. Chocolate ice cream, hamsters, people, and even ideas are entities.
monotonous: not changing, going on and on. Sometimes classes seem monotonous. This book is trying not to be monotonous.

THE INNER GAME OF TENNIS
Timothy Gallwey

Most players are talking to themselves on the court all the time. "Keep your eyes on the ball." "Bend your knees." The commands are endless. Then, after the shot is made, another thought flashes through the mind: "You clumsy ox, your grandmother could play better!" One day I was wondering who was talking to whom. Who was scolding and who being scolded. "I'm talking to myself," say most people. But just who is this "I" and who the "myself"?

Obviously, the "I" and the "myself" are separate entities or there would be no conversation. Within each player there are two "selves." One, the "I," seems to give instructions; the other, "myself," seems to perform the action. Then "I" returns with an evaluation of the action. For clarity let's call the "teller" Self 1 and the "doer" Self 2.

Now we are ready for the first major postulate of the Inner Game: . . . the key to better tennis—or better anything—lies in improving the relationship between the conscious teller, Self 1, and the unconscious [subconscious], automatic doer, Self 2. Imagine that instead of being parts of the same person, Self 1 (teller) and Self 2 (doer) are two separate persons. How would you characterize their relationship after witnessing the following conversation between them? "Okay, dammit, keep your stupid wrist firm," he orders. Then as ball after ball comes over the net Self 1 reminds Self 2, "Keep it firm. Keep it firm. Keep it firm!" Monotonous? Think how Self 2 must feel! It seems as though Self 1 doesn't think Self 2 hears well, or has a short memory, or is stupid. The truth is, of course, that Self 2, which includes the unconscious [subconscious] mind and nervous system, hears everything, never forgets anything, and is anything but stupid.

FOR THOUGHT AND DISCUSSION

1. What other types of activities inspire the kind of dialogue Timothy Gallwey cites in his book?
2. Why are New Year's resolutions so frequently broken? What does this have to do with the idea that more than one person lives within us?
3. How do you feel when you are criticized by another person the way Self 1 criticizes Self 2?
4. How does Gallwey's tennis lesson apply to the thinking needed for writing?

A TENNIS PRO CAN HELP ME WRITE BETTER?

Gallwey shows Freud is not the only one who can help us gain insights into our subconscious minds. Tennis pros, too, can give us views into our subconscious minds. San Jose State University Professor Gabriele Rico has come up with some useful methods for understanding this secret place within us that stores creativity. According to Rico in *Writing the Natural Way,* our left brain (Self 1) is in charge of details. The left brain can remind us of certain superior know-it-alls we have met. "The Final Touch: A Handbook," at the end of *Practicing the Process* is the province of the left brain.

The Left Brain Critic

The left brain is good with language, and it delights in using language to remind us when we make mistakes. The left brain likes to make lists and charts. It likes to divide experiences and objects into their basic components. It thinks diagramming sentences and memorizing spelling lists are the Purpose of Life. (After all, what could be more fun or fascinating?) Sentences become a string of adjectives, subjects,

FIGURE 2.1   **Right Hemisphere and Left Hemisphere Functions in the Brain**

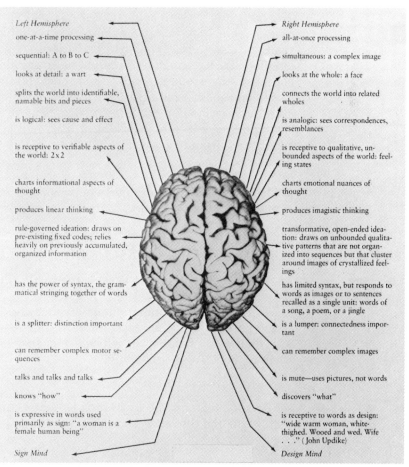

Left Hemisphere	Right Hemisphere
one-at-a-time processing	all-at-once processing
sequential: A to B to C	simultaneous: a complex image
looks at detail: a wart	looks at the whole: a face
splits the world into identifiable, namable bits and pieces	connects the world into related wholes
is logical: sees cause and effect	is analogic: sees correspondences, resemblances
is receptive to verifiable aspects of the world: 2 x 2	is receptive to qualitative, unbounded aspects of the world: feeling states
charts informational aspects of thought	charts emotional nuances of thought
produces linear thinking	produces imagistic thinking
rule-governed ideation: draws on pre-existing fixed codes; relies heavily on previously accumulated, organized information	transformative, open-ended ideation: draws on unbounded qualitative patterns that are not organized into sequences but that cluster around images of crystallized feelings
has the power of syntax, the grammatical stringing together of words	has limited syntax, but responds to words as images or to sentences recalled as a single unit: words of a song, a poem, or a jingle
is a splitter: distinction important	is a lumper: connectedness important
can remember complex motor sequences	can remember complex images
talks and talks and talks	is mute—uses pictures, not words
knows "how"	discovers "what"
is expressive in words used primarily as sign: "a woman is a female human being"	is receptive to words as design: "wide warm woman, white-thighed. Wooed and wed. Wife . . ." (John Updike)
Sign Mind	Design Mind

From *Writing the Natural Way* by Gabriele Rico. Reproduced with permission.

verbs, and adverbs instead of unified ideas. Needless to say, the left brain seldom comes up with creative ideas. It is too busy dividing, criticizing, and analyzing to create.

The Right Brain Creator

The right brain, on the other hand, is curious and creative. It likes to have fun, and, like a child, it is emotional. Instead of dividing and analyzing, the right brain sees total objects and experiences. To illustrate, think of Christmas, Hanukkah, any special holiday. The word *Christmas* gives you a mental impression—an image that includes the smell of an evergreen tree, the sight of a colorful array of presents, and the "ho, ho, ho" of a jolly, plump man. This right brain impression does not come in tiny chunks but rather as a kaleidoscope of experiences.

An Example: Two Views of an Apple

The left brain sees an apple, and it thinks, "This is a medium-sized, pippin apple. It is very green; therefore, it will have a sour taste." The right brain sees the same apple, and a series of sense impressions and emotions flash through it. The right brain recalls Grandpa sitting in a corner of the kitchen peeling such an apple for the flaky-crusted, sweet-sour pies Grandma used to make. The kitchen is warm and fragrant with cinnamon and brown sugar. Figure 2.1 on page 23, from Gabriele Rico's *Writing the Natural Way*, will help you better understand the left and right brain functions in your brain—and in your writing.

Vocabulary   **analogy:**   a particular similarity between essentially different things
syntax: sentence structure or the arrangement of words

FOR THOUGHT AND DISCUSSION

1. Which side of the brain is concerned with the number of apples a recipe calls for?
2. Which side of the brain remembers the way it feels to bite through the crunchy crust and taste the soft, smooth apple slices?
3. Which side of the brain will tell you that mixing the dough too much makes the crust tough?

The following poem by Marcia Kruchten illustrates the way the right brain and the left brain interact in the writing process.

The Hands She Wore

Looking at the hands she wore each day,
one could not say they carved words

into thorns. They looked
like farming hands. A mother's hands perhaps,
fit to pick over fruit but never words.
No grace to them. Rough and brown,
they'd not hold a peacock quill with ease.

And yet she wrote.

Her poems were the kind that came
silently from dim small spaces.
Somewhere inside they grew,
four, five at a time, and like
a clutch of warm quail eggs, would fall
upon the page
almost without the writing. Almost without
the hands doing anything.
So that she would sit, surprised sometimes,
turning her hands over in a dream,
wondering if they wrote what she saw on the page,
and wondering how.

Marcia Kruchten

FOR THOUGHT AND DISCUSSION

1. Describe the two selves of the poem. How do they differ from each other?
2. Why does the author say "they'd not hold a peacock quill"? What feelings and associations does a peacock quill create that would not occur had the line read, "They'd not hold a ballpoint pen"?
3. To which side of your brain does the peacock quill image appeal?
4. From where did the ideas for the poems come?
5. Why is the line "And yet she wrote" separated from the rest of the poem?

Aha! It All Fits!

The poet in "The Hands She Wore" is a good example of the author's point in *The Inner Game of Tennis.* Like a good tennis player, a writer must be able to turn off the self-conscious commands of the left brain. A writer—like a tennis player—needs to see good form and then imitate that form.

We all have a natural talent for imitation. After all, we learned how to talk by imitating those around us. As we read, we are giving ourselves writing models to imitate. We are planting the seeds of good writing in our fertile right brain so they can bloom later in our own compositions. This is why all good writers have done a great deal of reading. The health food advocate will tell you, "You are what you eat." So too, your writing is fed by what you read.

This does not mean there is no place in writing for the analytical skills of the left brain. We must master the mechanics of spelling, punctuation, and grammar. Just as a cook needs to know what kind of apples and flour will make a good apple pie, and a tennis player needs to know the rules of the game, we need to know the rules of the writing game. Like a cook and a tennis player, however, we also need to separate the creative activities of the right brain from the analytical and critical skills of the left brain. When we do not separate these activities, the right brain may go on strike and refuse to come up with ideas. Such a strike is the subject of the following article by John Leo.

TAKE ME OUT OF THE BALL GAME

HOW MENTAL BLOCKS CAN SHORT-CIRCUIT BASEBALL CAREERS
John Leo

© 1983 United Feature syndicate, Inc.

In the second inning of this season's All-Star game, Los Angeles Dodger Second Baseman Steve Sax fielded an easy grounder, straightened up for the lob to first, and bounced the ball past First Baseman Al Oliver, who was less than forty feet away. It was a startling error even for an All-Star game studded with bush-league mishaps. But hard-core baseball fans knew it was one more manifestation of a leading mystery of the 1983 season: Sax, twenty-three-years old, last year's National League Rookie of the Year, cannot seem to make routine throws to first base. (Of his first twenty-seven errors this season, twenty-two stem from bad throws.)

Sax is not alone. Over the years, a number of major league baseball players have developed odd mental blocks and sent psychologists scurrying for explanations. Among the most dramatic examples:

Mike Ivie, an outstanding catching prospect, was signed as a teenager by the San Diego Padres in 1970. In his first workout with the Padres, Ivie threw the ball too low to the pitcher and hit the screen used to protect pitchers during batting practice. A fellow catcher, Chris Cannizzaro, joked about it, and Ivie developed a block about throwing the ball back to the pitcher. Ivie switched to first base and, after a mediocre career with two other teams, is now a journeyman player for the Detroit Tigers.

Steve Blass, a World Series hero for the Pittsburg Pirates in 1971 and an All-Star pitcher in 1972, mysteriously could not get the ball over the plate in 1973. As a result he was out of baseball in 1974, at thirty-two. Blass could throw with near-perfect control in practice but apparently developed a phobia about facing hitters in a game.

Kevin Saucier, now twenty-seven, a flamboyant pitcher called "Hot Sauce" by his teammates, was 7-3 with the World Champion Phillies in 1980 and a brilliant Tiger reliever with a 1.65 ERA in 1981. The following year, he developed a dread of going to the ballpark, walked too many batters, and reported that when he threw a ball he didn't "have any idea where it's going to go." He retired last spring because "I thought I was going to kill somebody with an errant pitch."

Jim Eisenreich, a promising outfielder, hit .303 and .286 with the Minnesota Twins in 1982 and 1983. He quit during both seasons because of nervous twitching and hyperventilation.

Some players have coped with their problems by changing positions. As a catcher, Dale Murphy had a milder form of Ivie's phobia. In Murphy's case, it involved throwing the ball to second base. The Atlanta Braves eventually moved him to the outfield. Last year he was the league's Most Valuable Player.

Some therapists think that these physical difficulties are the result of deep-seated emotional problems. Manhattan Clinical Psychologist Donald Kaplan says that they are "conversion symptoms"—psychic troubles that express themselves as psychomotor problems. Other therapists look upon them as anxiety reactions, like cases of stage fright or writer's block, that may or may not have anything to do with deep inner turmoil. Says Los Angeles Psychologist Tom Backer: "The fear of never being able to do it again is almost universal with performers."

Pitcher Blass gamely opted for several kinds of treatment, including Transcendental Meditation, psychotherapy and hypnotism. He also tried "optome-therapy" sessions with a California optometrist who asked him to visualize himself pitching well as a form of self-psyching. Nothing worked.

The most faddish therapy in baseball is hypnotism. "What's a psychiatrist going to do?" says Hypnotist Arthur Ellen of Los Angeles. "Ask a fellow how he gets along with his mother? Who cares?" Ellen says he has treated the quirks, slumps, and other problems of a number of past and present stars, including Nolan Ryan, Don Sutton, Steve Yeager, and Orlando Cepeda. Los Angeles Dodger Pitcher Jerry Reuss visited Ellen twice in 1974 and 1975. "I had a couple bad games at Wrigley Field," recalls Reuss, "and I got to the point where I was afraid to pitch there." Reuss says that Ellen helped him conquer his fear of the Chicago Cubs' park. Says Ellen: "I give them a kind of composure. I just won't let them think they cannot do it." Ellen once hypnotized the entire California Angels team in 1977 when the manager felt that his ballplayers needed pepping up. (Despite Ellen's efforts, the team finished fifth in its division.)

Another hypnotist, Harvey Misel of St. Paul, is under contract to the Chicago White Sox; several weeks ago, he got permission from the Sox to treat Outfielder Eisenreich. Hypnotists put the players into a trancelike state and try to teach them how to relax. "I'm not saying that personal problems are not involved," says Ellen. "But extended psychotherapy is no good to the team or the player who has to snap out of it quickly."

Ellen failed with Steve Blass, but successfully treated several players for problems that went beyond slumps and bad streaks. One of them, he says, was former Los Angeles Dodger Shortstop Maury Wills, who developed a leg problem in 1962, partly because of psychological reasons, after he stole a record 104 bases that season. As Wills said at that time: "People will say the pain was all in my mind, which is true. But that's the worst place to have it."

So far the Dodgers have fended off at least ten hypnotists who want to try curing Steve Sax, says Al Campanis, vice-president of personnel. "It's just a temporary thing," Campanis insists. "The coaches are telling him, 'Don't think about a bad throw, just throw the ball.'" That, of course, usually makes matters worse. Says Sax: "It's like if somebody comes up to you and says, 'Don't think about an elephant for the next five seconds.' The first thing you're going to think about is an elephant." Or, as San Francisco Outfielder Jim Wohlford once said in a now classic comment, "Ninety percent of this game is half mental."

FOR THOUGHT AND DISCUSSION

1. Describe the common problems afflicting the athletes in the article.
2. How are the athletes' problems similar to writer's block?
3. How could a better understanding of left and right brain functions help people avoid such problems?

An Instructor Comments

The following poem by Dick Albert satirizes criticism of a student by a composition instructor—that is, the poem exaggerates the instructor's comments to show what is wrong with them.

As you read the poem, note the interplay between the left brain and right brain concerning the instructor's comments on a paper written by a refugee who escaped Southeast Asia after harrowing experiences at sea.

What I Did Last Summer

On this assignment you were required
to write a paper describing an event
of some significance to you. The essay
is unified by theme but rambles
just a bit when you describe
your guilt at having lived. Verb tenses
still are haphazard; you should have said

Thai pirates rap*ed* and kill*ed.* Tense endings
are important, and omissions cause
the reader some confusion. I know
prepositions are maddening to control,
but that Malaysian patrol boat sliced
into our boat, or *through,* not *at,*
Don't jump about so much in time;
the past perfect could have been used
to good effect, as in the sentence,
When the women were raped, we wished
we *had fought* to save them. Also,
I was a bit confused by your handling
of numbers. Were you the one survivor
of the twenty-one? Were forty on the boat
before or after the women were raped?
Or did twenty-one out of forty live?
Confusion about numbers wouldn't occur
if they were rescued from that tangle
of sentences. With these exceptions, the essay
seems just fine. Correct your errors
before going on to chapter nine.

Dick Albert

FOR THOUGHT AND DISCUSSION

1. What real-life experiences did the student write about in the essay?
2. How would the student receiving the comments in the poem feel? Would the comments help the student become a better writer?
3. Which side of the brain was used predominantly by the student writing the paper? Which side was used by the instructor?
4. Suggest comments that would clearly separate the left brain, mechanical skill problems in this imaginary student paper from the writing activities controlled by the right brain.
5. What is ironic about the title, "What I Did Last Summer"?
6. "What I Did Last Summer" brings up some important questions about the impact of criticism. How do you feel when you are criticized? If you receive a lot of criticism, does it make you want to try harder to correct your faults, or do you sometimes feel like giving up? When you are criticized, what factors determine whether you will try harder or give up?

TO CRITICIZE, OR NOT TO CRITICIZE?

Novelist Somerset Maugham wrote, "People ask you for criticism, but they want praise." Of course praise is lovely, but most of us would like to know about the piece of spinach stuck in our teeth or the smear of strawberry jam on our cheek. Yes, we hope our best friend *will* tell us.

But contrary to what many believe, the word *criticism* does not leave out the possibility of praise. Included in its definition of *criticism, The Thorndike/Barnhart Dictionary* lists "the act of making judgments or evaluations; approving or disapproving; analysis of merits."

Some Critics Bring Good Cheer

Criticism, then, does not have to emphasize the flawed. It may, in fact, point out how wonderful a performance has been. Often criticism is a combination of positive and negative comments. Certainly, the student who wrote "What I Did Last Summer" was writing about heart-rending hardships far beyond what most of us will ever experience, and comments acknowledging this would have helped the student accept the negative comments about mechanics. We need to know what we are doing right as well as what we are doing wrong.

Constructive Versus Destructive Criticism

Criticism that points out a specific error so it can be corrected is helpful or *constructive* criticism. Criticism that is too general to act upon is *destructive* criticism. Telling someone they are stupid is destructive criticism. Telling someone they have misspelled a word is constructive criticism.

Too much criticism or the wrong kind of criticism can cap our creative fountain of ideas just as Self 1 can render Self 2 unable to hit a tennis ball. We must recognize the difference between positive and negative criticism and constructive and destructive criticism to improve our writing. After all, an effective way to improve a piece of writing is to have someone read it and comment on it—in other words criticize it. This book has, in fact, undergone an extensive review process during which composition instructors, editors, and students made comments that have helped make its ideas clearer.

THE BEST THINGS IN LIFE ARE FREE

Freud helped his patients open their subconscious minds by free association, that is, by simply saying whatever came into their minds when he said a word. Free association helps us bypass the Left Brain Critic. (The clustering, brainstorming, and freewriting in Chapter One, used free association to help you get past your Critic Brain.)

The Treasure in Your Attic

Your subconscious is a treasure house of ideas for essays, but your Left Brain Critic is afraid of what frightening secrets are stored in that treasure house. After all, when you unlock your subconscious, you open yourself to emotions, which are usually easier avoided. It is safer to memorize mechanics rules. Unfortunately, you could go down in the *Guinness Book of World Records* as the all-time best memorizer of mechanics rules, but you still might not have any ideas about which to write.

We are going to sneak past the censoring Left Brain by free associating. As you do the following exercise, remember that your left brain is a very pushy sort. It will want to horn in. It may use all sorts of tricks to try to trip you up. It may say, for example, "This is dumb. This won't work. You don't have any ideas stored in your treasure house. In fact, you don't even have a treasure house."

Take a deep breath and relax. Tell yourself that of course you can do it. Ignore your Critic. When it gets especially pushy, take another deep breath, and feel yourself relax. Without your Critic blocking the door, you will be amazed at what gems you have stored in your treasure house of ideas.

WRITING ASSIGNMENT
Using What You Have Learned

Write an essay of at least two hundred words about the impact criticism has or has had on you.

The clustering method used in Chapter One is an excellent way to discover what you think and feel about criticism. Since your creative brain stores experiences in vivid detail, it can help retrieve experiences that will *show* your readers what criticism means to you.

Some students are reluctant to try new methods of writing. If we do not try new methods, however, we will never find better methods. The following exercise is an important part of your essay. You must hand it in with your essay. Explore your Creative Brain through the following seven steps:

1. Write *criticism* in the center of a sheet of paper, and circle it.
2. Around *criticism*, write and circle any words or ideas that pop into your mind when you think of criticism. Ignore your censuring left brain and relax as you do this.
3. Some of your ideas will lead to other ideas. When this happens, write the new idea near the idea that led to it, and connect related ideas with lines. Figure 2.2 on page 32 is a clustering sample for "A Being in Error," the essay which follows it.
4. After you have clustered in this way for a few minutes a lightbulb may go on in your brain. *Aha!*, you will think. *Now I know what I want to write.* At this point, you are ready to begin your theme about criticism. If the light bulb does not go on, reread "The Next Steps," on pages 14 and 15 in Chapter One.

5. The following are some helpful ideas to think about before you begin:
   a. Examples often help inspire ideas. Read the "Student Star Essays: The Polished Product" section at the end of the chapter.
   b. Include specific examples of the way you react to criticism. Does your heart pound? Is your mouth dry? Can you think of a specific experience with criticism to *show* your reader its impact on you? Once you begin your clustering process, however, do not force yourself to think of a specific reaction. Just record what pops into your mind until you have the *Aha!* message and you know what you want to say.
   c. Your essay must be more focused than your clustering. In clustering, several unrelated ideas will occur to you. When you begin to write, focus on one central point you want to make about criticism; do not simply make sentences out of your cluster-bubbles. Concentrate on and explain only one idea.
6. After you have finished your essay, put it away for several days or even several hours. When you come back to it you will be better able to read it objectively. Make any necessary changes in word order and add any examples that help clarify your ideas.
7. Now let your critical left brain take over to ensure that your spelling, punctuation, and grammar is correct. If you had stopped to

FIGURE 2.2   A Clustering Sample for "A Being in Error"

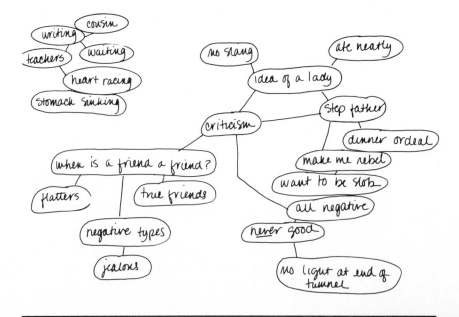

look up these rules when you were getting your ideas down, you would have gotten off the track, and you might even have forgotten what point you were making. Once you have found the right words to express your point, you must make sure mechanical errors do not muddle that point for your reader.

The following essay was written from the clustering sample in Figure 2.2.

A BEING IN ERROR

When I think of criticism I think of my stepfather sitting at the head of the table at dinner. He is always watching me out of the corner of his eye because he knows I'm going to screw up. I'm going to talk too much or too fast. Or maybe I'll talk with my mouth full. When I think back on those dinners, I'm not sure why I ever opened my mouth to talk at all. I had nothing to say that would interest him. And sometimes—horror of horrors—I used slang. Ladies do not use slang. The worst expression I ever uttered was one making the rounds among my friends at the time: "Don't get your tail in a knot." It meant don't get upset. My grandmother would have said, "Don't get all flustered."

He did—get his tail in a knot, get all flustered, turn purple with rage. I can still see him sputtering. He had just taken a mouthful of mashed potatoes, and he couldn't talk with his mouth full. I thought he might choke on his horror and indignation at what I had thought was a particularly colorful metaphor.

My stepfather's criticism was intended to turn me into a lady, and it was constructive criticism in that it was always specific. When he wasn't criticizing what I said or how I said it, he was criticizing my table manners—or how I dressed. But ultimately his criticism was destructive because it never gave way to praise. I never ate neatly, dressed attractively, or spoke cleverly enough for him to applaud my behavior. The message I got from his criticism was not a plan for improving myself, but rather the idea that I was inadequate.

Even as an adult, I am wary of criticism. I need to be convinced my critic accepts me as a person, and seeks to help me by pointing out a specific problem that needs correction. I need to know that it is not my entire being that is in error.

M. M.

STAR ESSAYS
The Polished Product

Remember: the authors of these essays used the following steps:

1. Prewriting
2. Writing
3. Revising content
4. Proofreading and correcting mechanical errors

CRITICISM—JUSTIFIED OR NOT?

When I try to formulate my ideas about criticism, my father keeps coming to mind. Although I always wanted to do my best to win his approval, I didn't know if my performance was ever good enough. Being an ex-Marine, he had high expectations of everyone. So I always felt to earn his love, I must meet or exceed the goals he had for me. I had to be the Model Daughter—a pretty, cheerful, helpful person who never spoke out of turn and always got "A's" in school.

In my present situation, as a single, recently divorced mother of two, my emotions about criticism are overwhelming—like pieces of a puzzle that I am struggling to put together although some of the pieces are missing; other pieces simply won't fit. My puzzle pieces are as jagged as glass that can slash through my skin.

Now the pain of criticism doesn't come from my father, but from my ex-husband and from myself about my failed marriage. I could never do enough to please my husband. He wanted the extra income from my job, but he complained if dinner was less than spectacular—or late. Our two youngsters were totally my responsibility, of course. He wanted to see them only when they were quiet, sweet-tempered, and clean. He always had something critical to say about my achievements. If dinner and the children were up to his standards, the house wasn't neat enough, or I should try to find a better-paying job. If he found nothing to criticize, he said nothing at all.

As long as he pushed me into a pit of unhappiness and low self-esteem with his criticism, he had the upper hand in my life. My feelings of inadequacy and stress-related physical ailments like migraine headaches flourished in this scenario.

Day by day, one step at a time, I'm discovering good things about myself that I have never acknowledged. I am a hard worker. Usually I am a kind, loving, and patient mother. I remind myself of my good points now that I'm trying to overcome the hurt and bitterness of my past, and I'm gaining self-assurance. I'm getting on with my life, knowing I will reach my goals. I will graduate from college. I will come to appreciate my good qualities. Someday I will be able to look back and see the strength and knowledge I gained by looking far beyond the unjust, destructive criticism. Then I will truly know my potential is only limited to how much I believe in myself.

Malia Christensen

TURNING DESTRUCTIVE CRITICISM INTO A CONSTRUCTIVE EXPERIENCE

When the word *criticism* is mentioned around me, it brings back memories of a ten-year-old boy experiencing life through the eyes of an alien trying to fit in.

This boy was me. When I was ten, my mother brought my brother and me from Mexico to escape poverty and to start a new life. You might ask, "How can this be relevant to criticism?" I'll tell you.

When I first started elementary school I was keenly aware of criticism and the way it made me feel. I remember my first day of school. All the kids looked at me and asked me my name. I tried to tell them. At first nothing came out of my mouth. When something finally did, the kids laughed and criticized the way

I pronounced the words. I felt so ashamed that I turned red and my whole body shook. Naturally I felt like quitting school forever.

The kids' destructive criticism might have discouraged me from learning, but instead it made me into a rebel—determined to learn so I could fit in with the rest of the kids. Ironically, thanks to this destructive criticism I learned even faster than many other kids in similar situations because every time I said something my classmates repeated it to me, and I learned the correct way to pronounce words. Through my determination, I turned destructive criticism into a constructive experience.

J. Fellipe Eniquez

FOR THOUGHT AND DISCUSSION

1. What comments do these writers make to show the left-right brain split?
2. Which comments best help you understand their feelings about writing?
3. How did these writers react to criticism?
4. Cite lines that appeal to your right brain.

HELP! FOR FURTHER WORK

In the following essay, the author needs constructive criticism to help revise problem points:

CRITICISM

I don't like criticism. Because it makes me feel really bad. When someone tells me I'm doing something wrong. I feel like not doing anything anymore. Except, of course, pulling a bag over my head and hiding from the world. Most of the time when people criticise me. I feel like they are attacking me. Some people seem to enjoy telling other people they are making lots of stupid mistakes. For example their ideas don't make any sense or are silly. Since this kind of person who is supercritical is often insecure. I guess this helps these critics feel better about themselves. Criticism sometimes however can be positive too.

FOR THOUGHT AND DISCUSSION

1. What could this author do to clarify his ideas about criticism?
2. Point out specific statements that need clarification.
3. Use your imagination to add material to statements that need clarification. Reread the "Student Star Essays" that precede it if you need help with ideas.
4. Encourage this author by pointing out what has been done well.
5. Read "Finishing the Fragment," on page 270 and "The Semicolon," beginning on page 286, through "Ellipsis Points" in "The Final Touch: A Handbook." Then, correct the sentence fragments in the essay.

3 THE JOURNAL

Your writing is trying to tell you something. Just lend an ear.

Joanne Greenburg

WHAT IS A JOURNAL?

A *journal* is a written record of an author's reaction to the world. Entries in a journal focus not so much on events as on a writer's reaction to those events. Because journals are a form of freewriting, they are an opportunity to explore the Creative Brain's treasure trove of thoughts and feelings without interference from the Critic Brain.

WHY KEEP A JOURNAL?

Unfortunately, in our busy, often confusing world, all of us, like Cathy in the cartoon—at least occasionally—feel like we could use a few more receiving and transmitting channels. By keeping a journal you will have an opportunity to monitor—and try to make sense of—the barrage of events and messages you receive each day. Journal writing will also help you become more comfortable with writing.

Journals are, in a sense, your opportunity for an analyzing-receiving channel. On your "journal channel" the news of your daily events takes a backseat to your editorial analysis of the things you discover in life. Through a journal you focus on the way you really think and feel about the events in your life.

Journals are also an excellent way to help you feel more at home with writing. If you have never kept a journal, your journal will teach you that writing down ideas is an excellent way to discover new ideas and to understand their impact on you. Because journal writing is more relaxed, you will become more at ease with your Creative Brain and its treasure chest of creativity. Writing in your journal will also give you an opportunity to experiment with the written word by turning off the receiving channel of your Critic Brain. You will stop criticizing your ideas and your expression of them.

WHAT DO YOU WRITE ABOUT IN A JOURNAL?

Journal entries respond to questions like Who am I? How do the other people in my life respond to and influence me? and What values are important to me? In "On Keeping a Notebook," author Joan Didion says a journal examines "how it felt to me." Note that the journal does not simply list the events of your life, but rather it records your reaction to those events—the "how it feels to be you" in the world.

An Idea Whose Time Came—and Stayed

Keeping a journal is not a recent idea of composition instructors. For centuries men and women have recorded and analyzed the events of their world in journals. In the following poem, Langston Hughes reflects on a writing assignment he had when he was one of the few black students at Columbia University. Typical of Hughes' poetry, his poem-journal entry, "Theme for English B," reacts to a problem central in his life—his awareness of his race and the way this awareness affects his identity both as he sees himself and as others see him.

Vocabulary

Harlem: the college is New York's Columbia University
Bessie: Bessie Smith was a famous jazz singer (1898–1937)
bop: a type of music popular from the forties through the sixties
Bach: the German composer Johann Sebastian Bach (1685–1750)

Theme for English B

The instructor said,

> Go home and write
> a page tonight.

> And let that page come out of you—
> Then, it will be true.

I wonder if it's that simple?

I am twenty-two, colored, born in Winston-Salem.
I went to school there, then Durham, then here
to this college on the hill above **Harlem.**
I am the only colored student in my class.
The steps from the hill lead down to Harlem.
through a park, then I cross St. Nicholas,
Eighth Avenue, Seventh, and I come to the Y,
the Harlem Branch Y, where I take the elevator
up to my room, sit down, and write this page:

It's not easy to know what is true for you or me
at twenty-two, my age. But I guess I'm what
I feel and see and hear. Harlem, I hear you:
hear you, hear me—we two—you, me talk on this page
(I hear New York, too.) Me—who?

Well, I like to eat, sleep, drink, and be in love.
I like to work, read, learn, and understand life.
I like a pipe for a Christmas present,
or records—**Bessie, bop,** or **Bach.**

I guess being colored doesn't make me not like
the same things other folks like who are other races.
So will my page be colored that I write?
Being me, it will not be white.
But it will be
a part of you, instructor.
You are white—
yet a part of me, as I am a part of you.
That's American.
Sometimes perhaps you don't want to be a part of me,
nor do I often want to be a part of you.
But we are, that's true!
As I learn from you,
I guess you learn from me—
although you're older—and white—
and somewhat more free.

This is my page for English B

                                                      Langston Hughes

FOR THOUGHT AND DISCUSSION

1. What details does Hughes reveal about his life?
2. Through these details, what point does Hughes make about himself?
3. How does Hughes feel about the world in which he lives?

Focus on Feelings

The racial theme of Hughes' journal entry is also an important part of a journal entry written more than a century before "Theme for English B." Charlotte Forten was the granddaugher of James Forten, a wealthy inventor, and James Forten was the son of free, black parents. A dedicated abolitionist in the early 1800s, James Forten was a powerful influence on the Philadelphia society of his day, as well as on his sensitive, intellectual granddaughter Charlotte.

The following excerpts from *The Journal of Charlotte Forten* were written when she was seventeen and the only black student in a teacher training school in Salem, Massachusetts. As you read these entries, note that Forten emphasizes the way she feels about events rather than the events themselves.

Excerpts from THE JOURNAL OF CHARLOTTE FORTEN
Charlotte Forten

FRIDAY, JANUARY 12, 1855

This evening attended a lecture by Rev. Henry Ward Beecher of Brooklyn. The subject was "Patriotism." I thought the lecture extremely interesting and many parts of it very touching and beautiful. His manner is not at all polished or elegant, but he says so many excellent things with such forcible earnestness or irresistible humor, that we quite forget it. As I had hoped he bore his testimony against the wicked and unjust laws of our land, which it is not *patriotism* to make or to obey. He also eloquently advocated the right of woman to vote; and paid a beautiful tribute to the lovely and noble-minded Lucretia Mott. In listening to Mr. Beecher one feels convinced of his *sincerity;* and we would always rather know that a person *means* what he says, even if we differ from him . . .

Although some of the punctuation in the following journal entry is unconventional, it is reproduced as Charlotte Forten wrote it. After all, in her journal she was concerned with expressing her thoughts rather than editing them.

Vocabulary   **misanthrope:**   a hater of mankind

WEDNESDAY, SEPTEMBER 12, 1855

To-day school commenced.—Most happy am I to return to the companionship of my studies,—ever my most valued friends. It is pleasant to meet the scholars again; most of them greeted me cordially, and were it not for the thought that *will* intrude, of the want of *entire sympathy* even of those I know and like best, I should greatly enjoy their society. There is one girl and only one—Miss [Sarah] B[rown] who I believe thoroughly and heartily appreciates anti-slavery,—*radical* anti-slavery, and has no prejudice against color. I wonder that every colored person is not a **misanthrope.** Surely we have everything to make us hate mankind. I have met girls in the school room[—]they have been thoroughly kind and cordial to me,—perhaps the next day met them in the street—they feared to recognize me; these I can but regard now with scorn and contempt,—once I liked them, believing them incapable of such meanness. Others give the most distant recognition possible.—I, of course, acknowledge no such recognitions, and they soon cease entirely. These are but trifles, certainly, to the great, public wrong which we as a people are obliged to endure. But to those who experienced them, these apparent trifles are most wearing and discouraging; even to the child's mind they reveal volumes of deceit and heartlessness, and early teach a lesson of suspicion and distrust. Oh! it is hard to go through life meeting contempt with contempt, hatred with hatred, fearing, with too good reason, to love and trust hardly anyone whose skin is white,—however lovable, attractive, and congenial in seeming. In the bitter, passionate feelings of my soul again and again there rises the questions "When, oh! when shall this cease? Is there no help? How long, oh! how long must we continue to suffer—to endure?" Conscience answers it is wrong, it is ignoble to despair, let us labor earnestly and faithfully to acquire knowledge, to break down the barriers of prejudice and oppression. Let us take courage; never ceasing to work,—hoping and believing that if not for us, for another generation there is a better, brighter day in store,—when slavery and prejudice shall vanish before the glorious light of Liberty and Truth; when the rights of every colored man shall everywhere be acknowledged and respected, and he shall be treated as a *man* and a *brother!*

FOR THOUGHT AND DISCUSSION

1. How do Charlotte Forten's fellow students treat her?
2. What is Forten's attitude toward her classmates?
3. Describe the kind of person Forten reveals herself to be in her journal.

The Tradition

The writing of Hughes and Forten is typical of a long tradition of oppressed people using journals to record injustices done to them and their reaction to those injustices. Guatemalan Indians are the descendants of those who built the Mayan empire and its magnificent art, architecture, and advanced understanding of astronomy. For the last four centuries, however, the Guatemalan Indians have been oppressed and persecuted in a country once owned by their proud ancestors. In the following excerpt from *I . . . Rigoberta Menchu—An Indian Woman in Guatemala,* the author uses a journal format to describe her life as an Indian woman in Guatemala. Note the way she, like Hughes and Forten, writes to an audience beyond herself.

Excerpt from I . . . RIGOBERTA MENCHU—AN INDIAN WOMAN IN GUATEMALA
Edited by Elisabeth Burgos-Debray

My life does not belong to me. I've decided to offer it to a cause. . . . The world I live in is so evil, so bloodthirsty, that it can take my life away from one moment to the next. So the only road open to me is our struggle, the just war . . . I am convinced that the people, the masses, are the only ones capable of transforming society. It's not just another theory.

That is my cause. As I've already said, it wasn't born out of something good, it was born out of wretchedness and bitterness. It has been radicalized by the malnutrition which I, as Indian, have seen and experienced. And by the exploitation and discrimination which I've felt in the flesh. And by the oppression which prevents us from performing our ceremonies, and shows no respect for our way of life, the way we are . . . Therefore, my commitment to our struggle knows no boundaries or limits. This is why I've traveled to many places, where I've had the opportunity to talk about my people. Of course, I'd need a lot of time to tell you all about my people, because it's not easy to understand just like that.

FOR THOUGHT AND DISCUSSION

1. The author addresses her ideas, not to herself, but to an audience beyond herself to whom she explains her ideas. How can the technique of explaining our ideas to an unknown audience help us better understand these ideas ourselves?
2. What does Rigoberta Menchu say motivates her to act and write as she does?

JOURNALS AND FREEWRITING

Chapter Two examined the relationship between criticism and generation of new, creative ideas. Using clustering as a prewriting technique, we explored our thoughts and feelings about criticism to help generate ideas for an essay.

In your journal you will have a chance to do *directed freewriting*. As you learned in Chapter One, freewriting is simply writing ideas that occur to you as you write. In directed freewriting, you write about a specific subject rather than recording every idea that pops into your head. In directed freewriting, you would not mention the fly buzzing around the room as you write—unless that fly were somehow related to your topic.

When you wrote about the interaction of your Critic Brain and Creative Brain, you were doing directed freewriting. For more examples of directed freewriting, read the Student Star Essays: Freewriting section on page 47 at the end of the chapter.

Freewriting and Discovering Your Ideas

The freewriting in a journal is an effective method to help you silence your Critic Brain so you will feel comfortable writing. In the following excerpt from *Writing Without Teachers*, author Peter Elbow discusses the advantages of freewriting.

Excerpt from WRITING WITHOUT TEACHERS
Peter Elbow

Freewriting may seem crazy but actually it makes simple sense. Think of the difference between speaking and writing. Writing has the advantage of permitting more editing. But that's its downfall too. Almost everybody interposes a massive and complicated series of editings between the time words start to be born into consciousness and when they finally come off the end of the pencil or typewriter onto the page. This is partly because schooling makes us obsessed with the "mistakes" we make in writing. Many people are constantly thinking about spelling and grammar as they try to write. I am always thinking about the awkwardness, wordiness, and general mushiness of my natural verbal product as I try to write down words.

But it's not just "mistakes" or "bad writing" we edit as we write. We also edit unacceptable thoughts and feelings, as we do in speaking. In writing there is more time to do it so the editing is heavier: when speaking there's someone right there waiting for a reply and he'll get bored or think we're crazy if we don't come out with something. Most of the time in speaking, we settle for the catch-as-catch-can way in which the words tumble out. In writing, however there's a chance to try to get them right. But the opportunity to get them right is a terrible burden: you can work for two hours trying to get a paragraph "right" and discover it's not right at all. And then give up.

Editing, *in itself,* is not the problem. Editing is usually necessary if we want to end up with something satisfactory. The problem is that editing goes on *at the same time* as producing. The editor is, as it were, constantly looking over the shoulder of the producer and constantly fiddling with what he's doing while he's in the middle of trying to do it. No wonder the producer gets nervous, jumpy, inhibited, and finally can't be coherent. It's an unnecessary burden to try to think of words and also worry at the same time whether they're the right words.

The main thing about freewriting is that it is *nonediting.* It is an exercise in bringing together the process of producing words and putting them down on the page. Practiced regularly, it undoes the ingrained habit of editing at the same time you are trying to produce. It will make writing less blocked because words will come more easily. You will use up more paper, but chew up fewer pencils.

Next time you write, notice how often you stop yourself from writing down something you were going to write down. Or else cross it out after it's written. "Naturally," you say, "it wasn't any good." But think for a moment about the occasions when you spoke well. Seldom was it because you first got the beginning just right. Usually it was a matter of a halting or even garbled beginning, but you kept going and your speech finally became coherent and even powerful. There is a lesson here for writing: trying to get the beginning just right is a formula for failure—and probably a secret tactic to make yourself give up writing. Make some words, whatever they are, and then grab hold of that line and reel in as hard as you can. Afterwards you can throw away lousy beginnings and make new ones. This is the quickest way to get into good writing.

FOR THOUGHT AND DISCUSSION

1. According to Elbow, what is the advantage of freewriting?
2. What effect does Elbow say criticism has on writing?
3. Spend the next ten minutes freewriting. Write whatever thoughts occur to you. As you write, notice when your Critic Brain tries to interfere.
4. When you have finished your ten minutes of freewriting, take another ten minutes to do *directed freewriting*— that is, freewriting about a particular topic. Notice the way your Critic Brain and Creative Brain interact when you write.

WRITING ASSIGNMENT
Using What You Have Learned

> Life consists in what a man is thinking of all day.
>
> Ralph Waldo Emerson

For the rest of the semester, write in your journal each week. Some entries will be long; others will be short, but they must total three hundred words each week.

The journal excerpts in this chapter examine a variety of issues and events. The lives of the authors are very different in terms of the time and place in which they lived, their age, sex, race, occupation, educational background, and social standing. After reading their journals, we can understand their thoughts and feelings. In fact, we may have had such thoughts and feelings ourselves.

In your journal, explore your thoughts and feelings; experiment with the written language and capture your ideas on paper without worrying about mechanical rules. Journals give you the freedom to experiment with language. Why not write a poem? Why not vent your frustration about a person causing problems in your life? Through your writing, you may come to understand yourself better, and you may even discover solutions to some of your problems.

More than Just the Facts, Ma'am (or Sir)

Include both concrete information and your thoughts about that information in your journal. Your journal will explain the way you feel and what you think about your world.

An example of what a journal is not. I got up this morning and brushed my teeth.

An example of what a journal is. As I brushed my teeth this morning, I glanced in the mirror. For a moment I was stunned by what I saw there. Perhaps it was because I was tired and have been under a lot of stress at work, but suddenly I looked older. The thought zoomed in on me: *Your life is running out. You're not a kid.* Suddenly, searching for grey hairs is NOT like looking for a needle in a haystack. It's more like searching for a needle in a needle-and-hay stack. And there is a permanent crease between my eyebrows. Until recently I thought my label said: "Wrinkle free. Will not fade."

This aging process is a little scary. Inside I don't feel any older than I did when I graduated from high school. The "me" in my mind is young. What will I feel like when the "me" in the mirror is seventy-five? Will the "me" I see in my mind still look young?

Your Left Brain Critic's Vacation

Because your journal will not be graded for mechanical errors, you can tell your Critic Brain to take a nap—or go to Tahiti—while you write. If you are one of the majority of people with a restless Critic Brain that keeps popping up to say, "Look up that word," "You need a comma there," or "That is a stupid, embarrassing idea," you may have to remind yourself to relax. You may have to remind your Critic Brain to get back into its cage. In fact, it may help to visualize your Critic Brain in a cage, in Tahiti, or taking a nap.

Your Critic Brain will feel more relaxed about your journal entries if you simply tell it, "Relax. The assignment is to get down my thoughts and feelings. I am not supposed to worry about mechanics. I am supposed to experience writing without you, Dear Critic, to help me out." Your Critic Brain, after all, likes to follow the rules.

WHO IS YOUR AUDIENCE?

When we write, we are not just dumping words down a black hole. We are writing to someone. Who is your audience for a journal? That is up to you. Some people think of their journal as a friend. Anne Frank, one of the most famous of all journal writers, called her journal "Kitty," and she wrote to "Kitty" as though it were an understanding friend.

Suggestions for Your Audience

The following suggestions give you a starting point from which to write. Try one of them or imagine an audience of your own.

1. Write to yourself in ten or twenty years. I still have some of my old high school diaries around, and in preparation for this chapter, I read them. Suprisingly, they were not all centered around football games, dances, and dates. I was worried about nuclear war, what college and career I should choose, and whether I would succeed in college.
2. Direct your journal entries to an imaginary friend, as Anne Frank did.
3. Imagine your journal will be placed in a time capsule. Write to someone who will read your journal in a future century. What would catch your attention if you found a journal written at the time William the Conqueror became king of England? You would want to know what the author of the journal felt and thought about the events taking place at that time. Your curiosity would not be limited to a list of historical events. You can get that in a history book. Most people are intrigued by other people and their reactions. For example, in a journal kept during Chaucer's lifetime, one entry discussed children. According to the author, children in the 1300s ate a great deal, made a lot of noise, and complained loudly when their mothers tried to wash their faces and comb their hair. It is interesting to be reminded that human nature has not changed drastically.

The Format for Your Journal

For this class, use the following guidelines as a basic format for your writing:

1. Write your journal on standard, theme-sized paper in black ink, or type your entry.
2. Keep your entries in a three-ring binder or a spiral notebook.
3. If you do not want your instructor to read an entry, simply write "Don't read" at the top of the page.
4. While your journal will not be graded for mechanical errors, do reread your entries to make sure they are legible. If they are

not, recopy the illegible entries. Instructors cannot appreciate writing they cannot read.

5. Your instructor will announce the due dates for journal entries.

WHERE DO YOU GET IDEAS FOR JOURNAL ENTRIES?

Where do you get ideas for journal entries? All around you. If you have trouble getting started, try clustering, brainstorming, or simply begin with the Peter Elbow variety of nondirected freewriting. Journals lend themselves to freewriting. The following ideas are suggestions for entries if you get stuck. Try to think of your own topic. The possibilities are endless.

- Problems—or joys—at work
- Pet peeves
- Money problems
- Hopes for the future
- Friends
- Relationships with your parents or children
- Things you hope to change about yourself or your world
- Experiences that make you happy—or sad
- Your reaction to a movie, book, or television program
- The impact a class is having on you
- Your thoughts about the interrelationship of subject matter from two or more of your classes
- Reflections on a memory from childhood—or a more recent memory

STUDENT STAR ESSAYS
Freewriting

***Remember: the authors freewrote the following essays. (For use in this text, I have corrected mechanical errors.) Because of the personal nature of some entries, some authors have asked to remain anonymous.

ENTRY ONE

I can't believe the huge problem I have to deal with at work. I am absolutely sure it was Alice who stole the money. Too bad she didn't just leave it at ripping me off. Then I would have just let her go this weekend and it would all be over. But since she ripped all that money off from Sally—well, now we have to deal with it. I don't know how. I dreamed about it all last night. What nightmares! I am *so* bad at handling this type of situation. Thank God Sally and Dorothy will be there.

I knew Alice was not right almost as soon as we hired her. Of course we don't have any proof of what she has done—which is going to make the whole thing very tricky.

What makes a person lie and steal? I think it is very complex. It must be something that she is lacking in her life. It probably goes way back. Alice is very smart and a real operator. She had a lot of people convinced of how wonderful she was. But not me. Her family is well-to-do, and she is not lacking material things. This often seems to be the case. She needs help. She needs some kind of counseling.

I wish I knew more about her personal life, her background, so I could have a little more insight into why she steals. I feel sorry for her.

And what am I going to do about references? I don't want to ruin her life. I would like to help her to get the help she needs.

Christina Price

ENTRY TWO

The final countdown! I have been going strong, nonstop in school for years. I've carried heavy loads, and I've had to commute almost an hour each way to school. I've managed (with a lot of confusion and guilt) to pull myself through. At times I've felt I couldn't keep my sanity let alone keep a normal relationship with my children. We all start with a glorified intensity, and as the pressure mounts, we begin to slip into oblivion. It's a real struggle with the papers, tests, homework, and other assignments. If things go smoothly for a while, chaos hits. The car breaks down, the kids get sick. And yet we survive. I often think I am the only one feeling so much pressure. Then I walk across campus and catch snatches of conversations and I realize everyone feels the same way.

It gives me peace of mind to think of the end to all this. It is good to sit back and remember all I've accomplished. My husband, children, jobs, finances, and countless emergencies have interfered, but in one more semester, I'll be there—my A.A. degree.

Caren Benfield

ENTRY THREE

Today you see more and more people returning to school to further their education. Many people have been out of school for ten or fifteen years. You see middle- and retirement-aged people attending classes with those just out of high school. This mixture of ages fascinates me. There are two questions I like to ask the older students: (1) Why did you wait so long before you returned to school? (2) Do you feel embarrassed or uncomfortable attending classes with people much younger than yourself?

The answers I get are interesting. Many people couldn't afford to go to college directly after high school, so they waited until they were more financially sound. Others simply weren't motivated to go to college until they saw how education could help them advance in their work. As for attending classes with younger people, most older people say it gives them a chance to understand younger people.

Another comment older students make I can really relate to is that college is such a struggle. It's like a ladder you start to climb; then you fall back down and start from the bottom rung again. With all the homework, exams, and other academic expectations coupled with having to work at a job, it's no wonder why so many people drop out of classes. But if you want something badly enough, you'll just keep trying until you finally succeed.

Johnny Austin

ENTRY FOUR

Prejudice. Pre justice. Before justice. What a stupid, barbaric animal *Homo sapiens* can be! I just finished reading *Farewell to Manzanar*. This true story is based on the experiences of a woman taking her husband and children to see the concentration-prison camp where she, her parents, and her siblings spent World War II. They were locked up in the desert of southern California under harsh, degrading conditions, along with all the other West Coast Japanese for the crime of being Japanese. The irony the book points up is they aren't Japanese at all. They were 100 percent American. Only their ancestors were Japanese. The father in the family was an old-fashioned, flag-waving-type American patriot. No matter. He lost all his possessions and was locked up because he didn't look like the ruling WASP majority.

I wonder how many of our wars are caused because we are so afraid of people who look different from us. I just saw Senator Inouye on television. He said he supported our involvement in Viet Nam until he realized we saw it as a race war. We hated the "Gooks." They were easy to hate because they looked different from us. Senator Inouye talked about coming back from World War II with all his decorations for heroism—and without the arm he lost fighting for his country even though it had locked up tens of thousands of other Japanese Americans. He walked into a barber shop where he was refused a haircut and called a "dirty Jap." Wow!

Everyone should read books like *Farewell to Manzanar* because they show the human side—the horrible pain—inflicted by the barbaric stupidity of prejudice. The word should be changed to "withoutjustice" or "withstupidity."

M. M.

ENTRY FIVE

It is 12:30 a.m. Now is the time between today and yesterday—a very special time when two days meet. What I lived yesterday enriches my life in this new day. This is a natural time to think over yesterday's events.

The Salinas flea market is alive with movement. The crowds of shoppers raise dust as they move from stand to stand. I see the happy, brown faces of Mexican vendors and shoppers. The atmosphere is definitely Latino. I feel a sense of exhilaration and belonging. I am moved almost to tears as I realize I have adopted the Mexican culture as my own.

I left my native Panama deserting my language and culture to marry a Korean. As I walk through the flea market, I realize how much I miss my culture. Now I am hearing Spanish from every direction. Perhaps I should move nearer to Salinas, where people with hair and eyes like the night pull at my heart.

As I move along loaded down with sacks of fruits and vegetables, I watch the workers selling their produce; that which they grow brings pains to their backs. How humble yet proud and friendly they are! Some are now without work thanks to the new mechanized farming methods. I am disheartened when I think of their living conditions, but I draw strength from their courageous smiles as they hand me the produce I buy from them. They smile at me even when I don't buy. How endearing, my cousins from across the border!

The bags of vegetables and fruit I buy are heavy. Yet as I walk through the crowds, I feel carefree on this—one of the happiest, sunniest days I have spent since leaving Panama. I feel at home again.

Ruth Pinnilla

HELP! FOR FURTHER WORK

You must turn off your Critic Brain during journal writing and record not just events but the way you feel about those events as well. Read the following journal entry, and then answer the Thought and Discussion questions to help you write your journal entry.

JOURNAL ENTRY

I just finished reading *The Diary of Anne Frank* then I thought about the tremendous tragedy of her senseless death. Next I went to work then I went to class however it was hard to stay awake in botany because the professor turned off all the lights to show slides. After botany I went to the library to study then I stopped at Pablo's for some tacos for dinner therefore I didn't get home until after eight.

FOR THOUGHT AND DISCUSSION

1. Where in the essay should the author focus more on his or her feelings about life?
2. Read "Remedying the Run-on," found on page 472 of "The Final Touch: A Handbook," and correct the run-on sentences. While you do not have to worry about mechanics in journal entries, revising them in this exercise will strengthen your understanding of run-ons and the way to correct them in formal essays.

4 ABSTRACT— CONCRETE

We'll be here at the center of your dial, bringing you middle-of-the-road music, with a moderate amount of talk, till a very sensible hour."

In fact, all words are abstractions. Stick is a generalization of all sticks, the crooked and the straight, the long and the short, the peeled and the shaggy. No word fits its object like a glove, because words are not things: words represent ideas of things.

Sheridan Baker, The Practical Stylist

CONCEPTS TO LEARN

- The meaning of *abstract*

- The meaning of *concrete*

- The way to write concretely

- The meaning of *fable*

- The format for writing a fable

- The use of dialogue in writing

FROM ABSTRACT TO CONCRETE

Have you ever thought about the way babies learn? When you were born, you were preprogrammed with very little information to help you survive. Within a few years, however, you amassed a tremendous wealth of knowledge. How? By using your five senses. By seeing, hearing, smelling, tasting, and feeling the world around you, you learned about the world. When you began to speak, your earliest communication involved at least one of the five senses: you were hungry or cold, you did not like the dark, or loud noises frightened you.

As you grow older, you need to communicate more complex ideas. For example, you may need to tell an auto dealer that your new car is not working properly. By the time you are old enough for a new car, however, your brain is cluttered with many facts and ideas. To communicate a complaint, the best route is still the one from child-hood: appeal to one or more of the five senses. Instead of an abstract generalization that the car does not work properly, make a concrete, specific statement. Read the following statements to see which communicates more effectively.

1. My new car is not working properly.
2. My brakes make a loud, grating noise.

As a writer, you must communicate as clearly as possible. To do this, you need to be concrete. Study the meanings of *abstract* and *concrete* in the next two sections.

Abstract

Among its definitions for *abstract* the *Thorndike/Barnhart Dictionary* lists, "thought of apart from any particular object or actual instance; not concrete"; "concerned with ideas or concepts rather than actual particulars or instances"; and not surprisingly, "hard to understand." Abstractions do not appeal to any of the five senses.

Abstractions are hard to understand. We have no specific examples of them. We cannot pin them down to examine them, yet as writers we must capture abstractions and show them to readers. To help pin down the concept *abstract* the dictionary gives examples of abstract words such as *honesty* and *truth*. These words are ideas. They do not have a physical form. They have neither fur nor feathers. They have no size, shape, color, sound, or texture. We cannot see, hear, taste, touch, or smell them—even with the help of the most sophisticated scientific instruments; therefore, they are abstract.

Concrete

According to the same dictionary, *concrete* means "existing as an actual object, not merely as an idea or as a quality; real. All actual objects are concrete." The dictionary does not only give an abstract definition of *concrete*. It also gives specific examples such as, "A *painting* is *concrete; its beauty* is *abstract.*"

Now on a roll, the dictionary continues, "The lawyer gave concrete examples of the prisoner's cruelty." Even the words *prisoner's cruelty* get your right brain to swing into action with vivid, *concrete* images. However, the judge and jury would want supporting details. They would want concrete examples of the cruelty.

WRITING EXERCISE
It's Your Turn

1. List the concrete details a jury would need to convict a burglar.
2. Make the following words more concrete: *money, tree,* an *expensive dinner,* a *good book.*
3. Now rewrite the cartoon at the beginning of the chapter. Substitute concrete phrases for the abstract phrases. In other words, give some supporting details to show what the disk jockey means.
4. Think back to Chapter One for a moment. How could the concepts of *abstract* and *concrete* help in writing a business letter about a product that did not work properly?
5. Rewrite the sentence from the following business memo. Make the statement concrete.

> The employees working in the reception area should behave more professionally.

POETRY: ABSTRACT IDEAS MADE CONCRETE

Poems communicate experience by describing concrete images that appeal to the feeling-experiencing Right Brain Creator. As you read the following poem by Marcie Hans, notice the concrete impressions—the *images*—it communicates.

Fueled

Fueled
by a million
man-made
wings of fire—
the rocket tore a tunnel
through the sky—
and everybody cheered.
Fueled
only by a thought from God—
the seedling urged its way
through the thickness of black—
and as it pierced
the heavy ceiling of the soil—
and launched itself
up into outer space—
no
one
even
clapped.

Marcie Hans, *Reflections on a Gift of Watermelon Pickle*

FOR THOUGHT AND DISCUSSION

1. List the concrete words and phrases in the poem "Fueled."
2. List the abstract words and phrases in the poem.
3. Is this a religious poem? Before answering, consider the line beginning "Fueled only by a thought from God ... " Explain in what way this poem could be meaningful to an atheist.
4. What point does the poem make about man's attitude toward nature?
5. Give other examples of spectacular natural phenomena we usually disregard because we see them so frequently.
6. By making a list of natural phenomena, you are giving concrete examples of an abstract principle. State this principle.

Choosing Concrete Words

The secret to writing concretely is finding words that *show* your reader your idea. Note that the following sentences become progressively more precise, and you receive an increasingly clearer picture of what the writer means:

1. Sally wore an unusually vivid outfit to work.
2. Sally wore a vivid, purple blouse to work.

3. Sally wore a vivid, purple blouse with her grey suit to court.
4. Sally wore a vivid, purple blouse with her grey suit the first time she appealed a case before the Supreme Court.

Note what happens in the following sentences when a more concrete phrase is substituted for "a song."

1. The woman sang a song.
2. The woman sang "You Ain't Nothin' but a Hound Dog."
3. The woman sang "Rock of Ages."
4. The woman sang "The Star Spangled Banner."

We can make the sentence even more concrete by writing the following:

5. Tina Turner sang "What's Love Got to Do with It?"

How did your mental image change as you read sentences 1–5? It is important to remember that the concrete details you include guide your readers down the mental path you want them to travel. Concrete details help ensure your reader will not misunderstand your point.

Nouns and adjectives are not the only words which must be concrete and descriptive. Notice how much more vivid the following sentence is when you substitute a more concrete verb for *walked*:
A man walked into the room.

ran	crept
stumbled	rushed
sauntered	dashed
pranced	sneaked
danced	strolled

WRITING EXERCISE
It's Your Turn

Make the following sentences more concrete:

1. I ate a big lunch.
2. I had a lot to do today.
3. My neighbor dresses strangely.
4. My dog causes me a lot of trouble.

The Abstract Made Concrete in a Story
In "Room for One More," Bennett Cerf takes an abstract concept and makes it concrete through his narrative.

Vocabulary **ominous:** of bad omen, threatening
equipage: carriage; carriage with its horses, driver, and servants
tremulous: trembling, quivering
sepulchral: having to do with a burial vault or tomb

ROOM FOR ONE MORE
Bennett Cerf

An intelligent, comely New York girl of twenty-odd summers was invited for the first time to the Carolina estate of some distant relatives. She looked forward to the visit and bought quite an extensive wardrobe with which to impress her southern cousins.

The plantation fulfilled her fondest expectations. The grounds, the manor house, the relatives themselves were perfect. She was assigned to a room in the western wing and prepared to retire for the night in a glow of satisfaction. Her room was drenched with the light of a full moon. Outside was a gravel roadway which curved up to the main entrance of the building.

Just as she was climbing into her bed, she was startled by the sound of horses' hooves on the gravel roadway. She walked to the window and saw, to her astonishment, a magnificent old coach, drawn by four coal-black horses, pull up sharply directly in front of her window. The coachman jumped from his perch, looked up, and pointed a long, bony finger at her. He was hideous. His face was chalk white. A deep scar ran the length of his left cheek. His nose was beaked. As he pointed at her, he droned in **sepulchral** tones, "There is room for one more!" Then, as she recoiled in terror, the coach, the horses, and the **ominous** coachman disappeared completely. The roadway stretched empty before her in the moonlight.

The girl slept little that night, but in the reassuring sunlight of the following morning, she was able to convince herself that the sight she had seen had been nothing more than a nightmare, or an obsession caused by a disordered stomach. She said nothing about it to her hosts.

The next night, however, provided an exact repetition of the first night's procedure. The same coach drove up the roadway. The same coachman pointed to her and croaked, "There is room for one more!" Then the entire **equipage** disappeared again.

The girl, in complete panic, could scarcely wait for morning. She trumped up some excuse to her hosts and rushed back to New York. Her doctor had an office on the eighteenth floor of a modern medical center. She taxied there from the station and told him her story in **tremulous** tones.

The doctor's matter-of-fact acceptance of her tale did much to quiet her nerves. He persuaded her that she had been the victim of a peculiar hallucination, laughed at her terror, kissed her paternally on the brow, and dismissed her in a state of infinite relief. She rang the bell for the elevator, and a door swung open before her.

The elevator was very crowded. She was about to squeeze her way inside when a familiar voice rang in her ear. "There is room for one more!" it said. The operator was the coachman who had pointed at her! She saw his chalk-white face, the livid scar, the beaked nose! She drew back and screamed, and the elevator door banged shut in her face.

A moment later the building shook with a terrific crash. The elevator that had gone on without her broke loose from its cables and plunged eighteen stories to the ground. Everybody in it, of course, was crushed to a pulp.

FOR THOUGHT AND DISCUSSION

1. What is the abstract concept that "Room for One More" makes concrete?

2. What concrete details help to make this concept concrete?
3. What abstraction does the coachman represent?

FABLES: MORE ABSTRACT IDEAS MADE CONCRETE

Stories, by their very nature, are concrete. Long before people could read and write, they told each other stories. Among the earliest of these stories were *fables*, brief, simple tales in verse or prose. Fables concretely depict an abstract idea, usually a moral, which is stated at the conclusion of the fable.

Aesop and His Fables

Probably the most famous author of fables was Aesop. Much of the written history of Greece was lost in ancient times. Tradition has it, however, that Aesop was a slave who lived about 2,600 years ago. Aesop is one of the many people who profited from learning to write well. Not only were his fables highly acclaimed, he was freed from slavery and became a hero in Athens. The following fable is typical of Aesop's work; however, the abstract principle at the end has been omitted.

THE LIONESS
Aesop

A great rivalry existed among the beasts of the forest over which could produce the largest litter. Some shamefacedly admitted having only two, while others boasted proudly of having a dozen.

At last the committee called upon the lioness.

"And to how many cubs do you give birth?" they asked the proud lioness.

"One," she replied sternly, "but that one is a lion!"

Of Mice and Lions

In the more contemporary fable that follows, observe the way concrete details appeal to your Right Brain Creator and help you better understand the principle that the fable illustrates.

THE LION AND THE MOUSE
Aesop

A lion asleep in his lair was waked up by a Mouse running over his face. Losing his temper he seized it with his paw and was about to kill it. The Mouse, terrified, piteously entreated him to spare its life. "Please let me go," it cried, "and one day I will repay you for your kindness." The idea of so insignificant a creature ever being able to do anything for him amused the Lion so much that he laughed aloud, and good-humouredly let it go. But the Mouse's chance came, after all. One day the Lion got entangled in a net which had been spread for game by some hunters, and the Mouse heard and recognised his roars of anger and ran to the spot. Without more ado it set to work to gnaw the ropes with its teeth, and succeeded before long in setting the Lion free. "There!" said the Mouse, "you laughed at me when I promised I would repay you: but now you see, even a Mouse can help a Lion."

FOR THOUGHT AND DISCUSSION

1. Write a sentence in which you state the abstract principle illustrated by "The Lioness."
2. What abstract principle does "The Lion and the Mouse" illustrate?
3. How would "The Lion and the Mouse" be changed if the dialogue were omitted and the author narrated the story? Would the fable be more abstract or concrete?

Contemporary Fables for Contemporary Ideas

Because fables have been found in Egyptian tombs dating back more than three thousand years, we know people were interested in making abstract ideas concrete long before composition teachers were discovered. (In fact the first composition instructor was discovered in an Egyptian tomb only a century ago.) The fable-writing fad did not end in ancient times. Contemporary authors like James Thurber continue to illustrate modern, abstract principles concretely.

James Thurber was an American essayist, short-story writer, and humorist whose cartoons and writing revealed the follies of modern people. In *Fables for Our Time*, from which the following excerpt is taken, Thurber shows the way an ancient fable can illustrate contemporary ideas.

THE LITTLE GIRL AND THE WOLF
James Thurber

One afternoon a big wolf waited in a dark forest for a little girl to come along carrying a basket of food to her grandmother. Finally a little girl did come along and she was carrying a basket of food. "Are you carrying that basket to your grandmother?" asked the wolf. The little girl said yes, she was. So the wolf asked her where her grandmother lived and the little girl told him and he disappeared into the wood.

When the little girl opened the door of her grandmother's house she saw that there was somebody in bed with a nightcap and nightgown on. She had approached no nearer than twenty-five feet from the bed when she saw that it was not her grandmother but the wolf, for even in a nightcap a wolf does not look any more like your grandmother than the Metro-Goldwyn lion looks like Calvin Coolidge. So the little girl took an automatic out of her basket and shot the wolf dead.

FOR THOUGHT AND DISCUSSION

1. In class, compare the sentences in which you stated your abstract principles to see how many reflected Thurber's own principle:

"Little girls are not so easy to fool nowadays as they used
to be."

2. What other morals did your classmates suggest for this fable?

PUTTING WORDS IN OTHER PEOPLE'S MOUTHS: WRITING DIALOGUE

Dialogue helps to make your writing more concrete by precisely demonstrating the action, and it makes your writing more interesting by
helping to vary the sentences. The following are tips to remember
when writing dialogue:

1. You may break the rule of writing complete sentences since
   people often speak in single words or phrases, as shown in the
   following example:

   "Where did you go?" his mother asked.
   "Out," Al replied.
   "That is a rather hostile and abstract reply to my question. As
   your mother I am naturally concerned about your welfare." His
   mother's lips drew down into a scowl as she spoke.
   "Sure, Ma," Al said.

2. Always enclose your character's exact words within quotation
   marks, as shown in the following example:

   The wolf asked, "What's in the basket?"
   "A laser gun," replied the little girl.

   If you use *that* you are not using exact words, as shown in the
   following example:

   The little girl said that she had a laser gun in her basket.

3. Begin a new paragraph with each new speaker, as shown in the
   preceding examples.

4. Quotation marks go before and after the exact words, not at the
   beginning and end of each sentence, as shown in the following
   example:

   "I don't believe you really have a laser gun in that basket. I can
   smell the chocolate chip cookies," the woodchopper said.

5. A comma, a question mark, or an exclamation mark separate
   the speaker's words from the rest of the sentence, as shown in
   the following example:

   "Get your flea-bitten paw out of my basket!" the little girl
   shouted atthe wolf.

   (See the first tip for examples of a comma and a question mark.)

6. The first word of a quotation is always capitalized.

WRITING ASSIGNMENT
Using What You Have Learned

Select one of the three methods discussed for generating ideas—clustering, freewriting, or brainstorming—and use it in your prewriting exercise for this assignment.

Write a fable of approximately two hundred words. In the fable, choose an abstract principle of your own to illustrate, or select one of the following:

1. Injuries may be forgiven but not forgotten.
2. Better beans and bacon in peace than cakes and ale in fear.
3. Do not trust flatterers.
4. Little friends may prove great friends.
5. Destroy the seed of evil, or it may grow up to ruin you.
6. It is easy to be brave from a safe distance.
7. The wicked have no gratitude.
8. Outside show is a poor substitute for inner worth.
9. Self-conceit may lead to self-destruction.
10. Better starve free than be a fat slave.
11. Example is the best teacher.
12. The gods help them who help themselves.
13. Try to please all, and you will please none.
14. Slow steady effort can yield more than an occasional flash of brilliance.
15. A small repair now can save a major repair later.

Your fable should have at least two lines of dialogue. Check your essay to make sure you followed the mechanical rules for writing dialogue. After you write your fable, add a concluding sentence explaining the principle your fable makes concrete.

STAR ESSAYS
The Polished Product

To help you see the connection between prewriting and the polished product, the first fable is preceded by its prewriting.

***Remember: The authors of these essays used the following steps:

1. Prewriting
2. Writing
3. Revising content
4. Proofreading and correcting mechanical errors

***Remember: Because the clustering method works by free association, it does not pamper the censuring left brain's fondness for structured lists. Clustering therefore, will help ideas pop into your head—and onto your paper.

THE PERILS OF PENNY PLUMP

Once there was a young lady named Penny Plump. Although Penny had indeed been plump as a child, she had grown up to be a very slender woman. At five feet and six inches, Penny Plump weighed 115 pounds.

Every morning when Penny Plump woke up she went straight to the mirror. And every morning Penny saw a frumpy, pudgy lady staring back at her. Penny Plump was very dismayed, for the image she saw in the mirror bore no resemblance to the glossy pictures she studied so enviously in *Vogue* and *Glamour*. Penny vowed not to eat until she too looked like a model.

"Penny Plump, you are far too thin," her doctor warned her. "If you do not gain some weight, you will become very sick."

"Penny Plump, I've made your favorite dinner—chicken soup with rice—but you haven't eaten a thing," her mother said night after night.

FIGURE 4.1   Clustering for "Penny Plump"

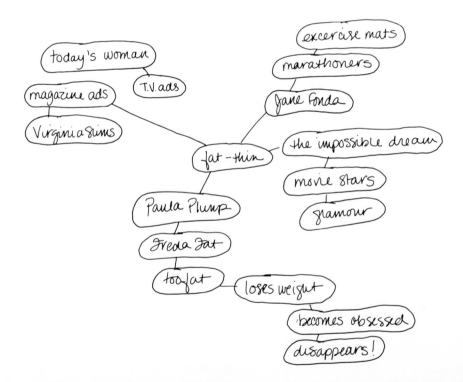

Penny Plump's weight dropped below one hundred pounds, and still she saw the same fat lady looking out from the mirror.

Then one sunny, warm morning, Penny Plump crawled out of bed, looked in the mirror—and no one looked back.

Principle: Be careful when you act on an abstract idea, for your perception may be in error.

Therese M. Markarian

Like James Thurber, the author of "The Perils of Penny Plump" chose to illustrate her fable with a cartoon:

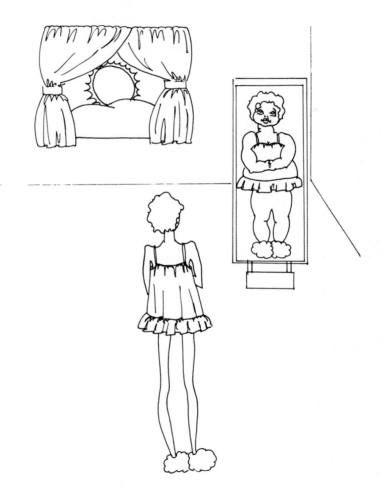

***Remember: Because you want to encourage your ideas to flow quickly, do not worry about writing complete sentences or other mechanical rules. Just capture those ideas on paper.

THE SAGA OF ANN AND FRANK

Ann and Frank had been married for six years. During those years, Ann did everything she could do to make Frank happy. After working all day, she came home and washed, cooked, and cleaned without once asking Frank for help. Instead, each night when he came home she brought him his pipe and slippers as faithfully as a cocker spaniel. When he had read the paper, she served him his favorite foods.

After awhile Frank began to think coming home to Ann each evening was boring. Instead he stayed out until the wee hours drinking beer, smoking joints, and snorting coke. When he finally got home, Ann would ask, "Where have you been, dear? I've been worried."

"Shut up, witch! You aren't my mother. It's none of your business where I've been," Frank would shout at her.

Finally Ann could no longer stand having such a bad marriage. She asked Frank for a divorce, and he agreed. Frank thought his life would be much happier if he could party every night and not have to face Ann when he got home.

Once they were divorced Ann devoted more energy to her job and earned promotion after promotion. Eventually she married a co-worker who shared household tasks with her. They had two delightful children they named Norman and Nellie.

Frank, on the other hand, snorted so much coke that he destroyed his nose. As he lay in the hospital dying of lung cancer from smoking so many cigarettes and joints, doctors discovered that his liver had been permanently damaged by his drinking. His last words were, "Ann was an angel. I wish I had been kinder to her."

Principle: Some people do not appreciate their good fortune until it is gone.

Sherrill E. Blocker

DON'T COUNT YOUR CHICKS

Once there was a student who attended El Estero Tech. Because his parents had no money, he applied for financial aid. To be sure he'd get all the necessary paperwork done on time, he applied in early September.

Although he had not yet received any money from the school, he rented an apartment, paid tuition and bought books with the last of his summer-job money. He was not worried about the bills since the clerk at the college financial window had assured him his money would arrive in two weeks.

By the end of the month, the bills were arriving and other financial obligations were storming down on his front door.

He hustled to school to confront the clerk who had misled him. "Where is the money you promised me?" he screamed.

The clerk replied, "If you haven't received it yet, it should be here in no longer than two weeks." She then shut the financial aid window in his face and locked it. On the front was a cardboard sign that read: "Gone to lunch. Be back in two hours."

Very disappointed and frightened, he reluctantly returned home. No one knows what happened after that. Some say he was lost in a black hole of bills.

Some say, just outside the financial aid window on dark starry nights, you can hear a faint voice saying, "Where is the money you promised me?"

Principle: Don't count your chicks until all of the eggs hatch.

Gary D. Hovey

HELP! FOR FURTHER WORK

Read the fables "When Enough is Enough" and "Do Unto Others," and then answer the questions which follow them.

WHEN ENOUGH IS ENOUGH

Every morning before sunrise a dog would chase every car that passed biting the tires and leaping onto the sides of the cars. "Go away stupid dog" the car owners would shout but the dog continued chasing cars and bite tires for about one year. After many near-misses bruises and broken bones the dog died of an overdose of rubber.

Principle: Learn when enough is enough. Too much of a good thing is not good for you.

DO UNTO OTHERS

On a cold foggy night at Candlestick Park in San Francisco a young man was watching the Dodgers play. He shivered as the cold damp wind whipped in from the bay and his teeth chattered uncontrollably. A man next to him saw what was going on so he asked the chilly young man "Would you like a blanket coat or sweater?"

"How very kind of you" the young man replied. "Yes I would like to borrow your coat since you are not wearing it." After a few innings the young man was warm and cozy. At the end of the game he returned the coat. "Thank you very much sir for loaning me your coat" the young man said.

The man who had been happy to help said "You are certainly welcome. I try to live by the Golden Rule."

FOR THOUGHT AND DISCUSSION

1. Add details to make "When Enough Is Enough" more concrete.
2. Include two lines of dialogue in your revision of "When Enough Is Enough."
3. The final paragraph in "Do Unto Others" does not clearly illustrate a principle. Add the necessary material to make a principle clear.
4. Add details and dialogue to make "Do Unto Others" into a fable with enough concrete details to demonstrate the principle.
5. Read "The Comma" on page 277 of "The Final Touch: A Handbook," and correct the comma errors in the two student fables.

5 DESCRIBE A PLACE

LITTLE HOUSE ON THE PRAIRIE

Drawing by C. Barsotti; © 1983. The New Yorker Magazine, Inc.

God gives all men all earth to love,
But, since our hearts are small,
Ordained to each one spot should prove
Beloved over all.

Rudyard Kipling, Sussex

CONCEPTS TO LEARN

- The meaning of *connotation*
- The meaning of *denotation*
- The meaning of *unity*
- The use of details to create a unified description of a place

FOR THOUGHT AND DISCUSSION

1. What is the central impression created by the setting in the cartoon?
2. What would the central impression be without the satellite dish?
3. Think of a spot that would meet Kipling's description in the introductory quotation. List four concrete details that make your spot "beloved over all."

UNIFIED OUR IDEAS STAND

Humans can be a stubborn lot. Among those with a special reputation for hard-headedness was President Harry Truman. His home state of Missouri bills itself as the "show me" state, and appropriately his hometown was Independence, Missouri. Before the 1948 Dewey-Truman Presidential election, pollsters were so certain Dewey would walk away with the elections that some newspapers did not bother to wait for the votes to be counted before writing their headlines. Truman—like the majority of his countrymen—was not so sure of Dewey's victory. He was not ready to concede until he saw concrete evidence of his defeat, and the gods of concrete evidence must have enjoyed a hearty laugh when Truman carried the election.

Most of us, in fact, are "show me" people. If we are told something is wonderful—or terrible—we want concrete details so we can decide the wonderfulness or terribleness for ourselves.

We will work at sharpening our "show me" skills by showing readers a particular place. We will *limit*, however, our descriptive details to those which make a central point about the place we choose to describe. In other words, our descriptions will have *unity*. Every detail in them will help to demonstrate a *unified*, central point.

Boston via San Francisco

In the introductory quotation, Rudyard Kipling said we all have a spot on earth special to us. For Robert Frost that special place was New England. He was a New England farmer for much of his life, and typical Frost poems are set in the rural, New England countryside. Surprisingly, Frost was a native of the land of surf boards and redwoods. Born in San Francisco in 1874, Robert Frost lived there for the first decade of his life.

With its watery, West Coast setting, the following poem is not typical of Frost's writing. Presumably, on the sunny day in 1523 when he named the Pacific, Balboa believed its serene mood was more typical than the mood Frost describes in the following poem.

Once by the Pacific

The shattered water made a misty din.
Great waves looked over others coming in,
And thought of doing something to the shore
That water never did to land before.
The clouds were low and hairy in the skies,
Like locks blown forward in the gleam of eyes.
You could not tell, and yet it looked as if
The shore was lucky in being backed by cliff,
The cliff in being backed by continent;
It looked as if a night of dark intent
Was coming, and not only a night, an age.
Someone had better be prepared for rage.
There would be more than ocean water broken
Before God's last *Put out the Light* was spoken.

Robert Frost

FOR THOUGHT AND DISCUSSION

1. What other central moods could Frost have selected to describe the Pacific?
2. Which words show us the Pacific storm by appealing to our senses of hearing? seeing? touching?
3. If you were filming this poem, list the scenes you would use and the order in which you would use them.
4. How would this poem change if Frost reversed the order of his descriptive details?

Zeroing in on Decisive Details

The difficulty in writing about a place you know well is just that—you know so much about it that it is hard to choose what to include in your description. In other words, it is difficult to keep your ideas *unified* to develop a central point. John Steinbeck solved this problem by limiting his description to show readers the way he felt about changes in his native region. The following excerpt is from *Travels with Charlie*, a travelogue Steinbeck wrote about his trek in a camper truck from his home on Long Island to his birthplace in California. Charlie, a standard poodle, was Steinbeck's companion on his journey.

Excerpt from TRAVELS WITH CHARLIE
John Steinbeck

I FIND IT DIFFICULT TO WRITE ABOUT MY native place, northern California. It should be the easiest, because I knew that strip angled against the Pacific better than any place in the world. But I find it not one thing but many—one printed over another until the whole thing blurs. What it is is warped with memory of what it was and that with what happened there to me, the whole bundle wracked until objectiveness is nigh impossible. This four-lane concrete highway slashed with speeding cars I remember as a narrow, twisting mountain road where the wood teams moved, drawn by steady mules. They signaled their coming with the high, sweet jangle of hame bells. This was a little town, a general store under a tree and a blacksmith shop and a bench in front on which to sit and listen to the clang of hammer on anvil. Now little houses, each one like the next, particularly since they try to be different, spread for a mile in all directions. That was a woody hill with live oaks dark green against the parched grass where the coyotes sang on moonlit nights. The top is shaved off and a television relay station lunges at the sky and feeds a nervous picture to thousands of tiny houses clustered like aphids beside the roads.

FOR THOUGHT AND DISCUSSION

1. Steinbeck created two central impressions in his paragraph—a "before" (when he was a young child in California) and an "after" (when he revisited California's central coast with Charlie). How do his "before" and "after" impressions differ?
2. Why does Steinbeck end with his description of the houses instead of ending with another detail—for example, the coyote or the concrete highway?
3. What is Steinbeck's point in the paragraph?
4. Which details appeal to our senses of seeing? hearing? feeling?
5. List the vivid verbs that help Steinbeck recreate the scene.

CONNOTATION AND DENOTATION

Part of the reason Steinbeck's descriptions are so effective is his awareness of the *connotation* (the emotional association) of the words he selects. To help readers better understand ideas, that is, to create *unity* in writing, you must select words very carefully. A good dictionary is essential for every writer. Dictionaries, however, do not always tell the whole story about a word. Dictionaries give the word's *denotation* (its literal meaning), but many words also have strong connotations.

In the selection from *Travels with Charlie*, explain the way your reactions differ with the following changes:

Original: "a four-lane highway slashed with speeding cars"
Revision: a four-lane highway traveled by speeding cars

Original: "The top is shaved off and a television relay station lunges at the sky . . . "
Revision: The top has been leveled and a television relay station rises into the sky.

Original: "tiny houses clustered like aphids beside the road."
Revision: tiny houses clustered like ladybugs beside the road.

Lassie Versus Miss Piggy

Connotative associations for words and actions are so ingrained that we often take them for granted. However, ignoring the connotation a word has for a reader can mean that the message will get lost instead of being understood, as the following excerpt from Lawrence Durrell's *Blue Thirst* illustrates:

Excerpt from BLUE THIRST
Lawrence Durrell

At the very outbreak of the war in Cairo when I arrived there, the British community, to show their patriotism, had done something so foolish that I can hardly bear to speak about it. They printed a poster of a bulldog with a British flag 'round its neck and the slogan, "Who is for liberty? Who is for Victory?" Now, at first sight it seems a very harmless thing, but the worst insult in Arabic is "dog." And this was done by people who had been residents in Egypt for half a lifetime. They should have known that *ya kelb* is the worst insult an Arab can give or take. It would be like the French being particularly sensitive to being compared to pigs—*cochon* is the worst insult in French. Can you imagine at the beginning of a war putting out a poster of a pig with the French flag around its neck and saying "Let's all be patriotic pigs together for victory?" Naturally the English couldn't understand why the Arabs were rolling about with laughter in the streets.

More Fun with Denotation and Connotation

Vocabulary **invertebrate zoologist:** a scientist who studies animals without backbones
extolling: praising
empathize: the process of entering fully into another's feelings

The turkey versus the eagle. Benjamin Franklin had a mischievous sense of humor and a lively way with words. He undoubtedly took great delight in suggesting that the United States national bird be not the eagle but rather the turkey. After all, Franklin pointed out, the turkey is a native bird, and it is a peaceful, useful creature. These three traits are, in fact, part of the bird's denotation. As he knew it would be, Franklin's suggestion was met with amusement—but not acceptance—by his fellow Founding Fathers.

The slug versus the sea lion.   Problems frequently arise because of our associations with a word or phrase. A case in point is the battle between the sea lion and the banana slug at the University of California, Santa Cruz in the spring of 1986. The student body voted overwhelmingly to change the university's mascot from the sea lion to the banana slug. Chancellor Robert Sinsheimer said, "No!" (as opposed to, "No"). He issued a press release saying that the slug is a slimy, cowardly, and sluggish creature—a spineless animal. He preferred a mascot with more "spirit and vigor"—an animal with some backbone.

Long live the slug.   Students and **invertebrate zoologists** at the university were outraged. They flooded local newspapers and the Chancellor's office with letters **extolling** the virtue of the slug. At last, Sinsheimer relented and issued a press release saying students "should have a mascot with which they can **emphathize.**"

WRITING EXERCISE
It's Your Turn

1. Describe Santa Claus's shape. Is he fat? rotund? plump?
2. Think of your favorite young woman movie star. Is she skinny? slender? bony?
3. Make a list of other words that have strong connotations.

Clustering Revisited

Your Right Brain Creator automatically registers your feelings about a place. When you cluster, your Right Brain Creator will help you conjure up words with the appropriate connotations for the mood you seek to create. Study the clustering on page 74, and then read "Volcanic Beauty" to see the way clustering helped to create a central impression in the essay.

VOLCANIC BEAUTY
Marlene Martin

It's Hawaii without the grass skirts, surf boards, and hula. Instead calderas steam in vast fields of lava punctuated by specter trees rising stark and lifeless from their brittle base. Macbeth's witches would feel right at home here in the surreal landscape that seems a long way the other side of paradise, a landscape decorated by Hawaiian goddess Madame Pele in her favorite color—basic black.

Yet not far in any direction, the lush vegetation of Hawaii blankets the earth in the verdant carpet of a tropical terrain. This is the United States' most explosive spot—Volcanoes National Park.

Those wanting to visit another small planet without the astronomical cost of a space shuttle should go to the park on the youngest and largest of the

FIGURE 5.1   A Clustering Sample for "Volcanic Beauty"

Hawaiian Islands. The rocky terrain of the mountain park is indeed an alien world. However, this is a friendly alien with temperate weather, wind orchids, and ohelo berries to welcome guests.

Hawaii's are shield volcanoes, a type that erupts in the safe manner suitable to paradise. Instead of fleeing from the lethal fiery cloud of composite and cinder cone volcanoes, thousands flock to Hawaii to watch eruptions. For visitors who miss an eruption, movies and exhibits at the Visitor's Center provide a graphic substitute for a ringside seat at the birth of a mountain.

The best place to begin a park visit is at the Visitor's Center at 4,200 feet next to Kilauea caldera. Here you can see films of a lava fountain as high as the Empire State Building. Or you can watch fat, lazy-looking lava ooze its way downhill like fiery-hot fudge.

When the lava meets the sea, it explodes in a fury of steam. According to legend, Hawaii's volcanic activity is controlled by Madame Pele, eater of trees, maker of mountains, router of war gods. The feisty goddess was briefly married to Kamapuaa, god of war. This may have been a match made in heaven, but its duration was short and violent. In a rage, Pele routed Kamapuaa from her crater of fire and chased him with streams of lava into the sea.

Madame Pele's union with the United States Park Service is a good deal more friendly. In fact, she obliged them by placing a kapu (taboo) on taking any lava from the park.

The Visitor's Center provides a capsule view of park natural and cultural history for the two million people who visit the 229,177 acre park annually.

In many parks, interpreters talk about a natural process that happened hundreds of thousands of years ago, but in this park, these processes are still happening. Sometimes molten lava gushes from Mauna Loa and Kilauea at the same time. At other times, one solos in a performance lasting from several hours to many months. In such explosive times, the park maintains a hotline (808/965-7977).

The Visitor's Center also displays the park's unique flora and fauna. Exhibits include a lesson in what happens when man meddles with Nature. The original Hawaiians brought pigs that ate the eggs of ground-nesting birds and routed out basins in trees. When mosquitoes bearing a strain of malaria fatal to many native birds arrived with Western man, rainwater collecting in the basins formed breeding areas for the mosquitoes. So fragile is the native flora and fauna, that half the species on the Endangered Species List are found only in Hawaii. Displays also give a sense of an island culture that flourished long before Captain Cook sailed into Kealakakekua Bay in 1778.

The eleven-mile Crater Rim Drive passes a spectrum of the park's attractions from tropical rain forests to forests of lava trees—eerie worlds in which lava hardened around trees before consuming them with fire. Now hollow, black chimneys stand where once a tropical forest flourished. Elsewhere a volcanic desert stretches where Nature's acid rain has left a barren landscape. Here and there steam rises from the ground in a ghostly vapor.

Kipuka Puaulu bird park is the spot for watching either native birds or bright-shirted binocular bearers. So far this gentle forest has been spared the devastation of scalding lava, so mighty koa trees still stretch their moss-covered branches and form perches for colorful birds such as the red-feathered, curved-bill i'iwi whose ancestors furnished feathers for the capes of ancient Hawaiian royalty.

At Volcano Observatory, U.S. Geological Survey, scientists track Pele's activities. From the Observatory the view across Kilauea's 3,000 foot-wide, 400 foot-deep Halemaumau firepit is spectacular. Until it blew its lid and drained in 1924, Halemaumau—the world's most active volcano—was a year-round Fourth of July and Halloween rolled into one.

The swoops and curves of the Chain of Craters Road make it one of the world's most unusual and beautiful roads. The road snakes downhill to the coast and the Wahula Visitors Center. Amidst the shiny, black, blown-glass stripes of fresh lava are older flows where ancient Hawaiians carved petroglyphs into the stone. Elsewhere lava lakes drained leaving deep craters. Other attractions include the surf at work pounding lava cliffs into black sand beaches and an ancient heiau (temple) where human sacrifices were held.

For those who stay in the park, Volcano House (run by Sheraton) is the only hotel in town. Teddy Roosevelt would have loved the ambiance of the thirty-seven room hostelry—and it looks as if it hasn't been refurbished since he charged San Juan Hill. However, it is clean and comfortable as well as funky. And where else can you watch a steaming caldera while you sip Kona coffee and munch muffins topped with ohelo berry jam? The hotel even has a volcanic steam bath.

In the hotel lobby a mountain-size lava rock fireplace warms guests as they relax in overstuffed couches and chairs. A roaring blaze on a tropical island dotted with steaming calderas might seem like coals to Newcastle, but the mountain air can be nippy—especially at night. The hotel also manages ten A-frame tent cabins.

The park service has several campgrounds. In addition, backcountry huts shelter those hiking these under-used trails. (If you plan to hike in the park, bring along sturdy shoes. Volcanic rock could hold its own against a switchblade knife.)

Because Hilo (a forty-minute drive from the park) is on the rainy side of the island, most flights now go into Kona. The drive from Kona is a pleasant three-hour jaunt through cane fields and macadamia nut plantations and past important sites like the City of Refugee Park. And that red glow on the horizon? It may well be Madame Pele's warm welcome to her explosive paradise.

FOR THOUGHT AND DISCUSSION

1. What is the central impression of the park the article creates?
2. Which words have especially effective connotations to reinforce the central impression?
3. How would the article change if it began with a poem or a description of the Visitor's Center? Why do you think it uses the current organization?
4. For what audience was this article written?
5. How would the article differ if it were written for scientists who study volcanoes (volcanologists)?

In the Mood

Every place has something special about it—even if it is especially bad or especially boring. Let's take a few minutes to examine the writing process about a place that has a special impact on me.

EXPLORING AN IDEA

As I began to write I remembered that an effective way to decide on a subject is to use clustering, brainstorming, or freewriting. Each of these techniques can help me find a location that had a strong impact on me.

I reminded myself as I did my exploratory writing that I was not trying to turn out a polished paper. Rather I was trying to discover what I thought and felt about a particular place. My initial effort would not be entirely wonderful. Instead, it would be an important step on my journey to a good essay.

FREEWRITING MY THOUGHTS

When I try to think of places that made strong central impressions on me, my initial reaction is a hodge-podge—rather like the cartoon that introduces Chapter Two. I think of the woods behind the house where I grew up in Michigan. I think of the pond in the woods where we skated in the winter and caught pollywogs in the spring. In the fall, the leaves turned orange and red and yellow. In the summer, the woods was lush and green and cool.

As I explore these ideas, yet another idea surfaces: a classroom in Fort Ord, California, where I have taught many classes. I settle on this choice. I have some resentment about classroom conditions. The students were dedicated; they deserved better. It would be fun and therapeutic to write about that room.

But I'm still not sure just how to focus my paper. When I think of the room, I think of the students I taught—and learned from—in that room. Most of them were military or family of someone in the military. These students had a lot of problems my regular on-campus students didn't have. They might be forced to miss class because they had an inspection—or they were suddenly sent to a war zone. Can I include the students and their problems in the description?

As I play with this idea, I realize that I am getting distracted from description. What I should zero in on is the room itself. Let's take a few minutes to look at my initial freewriting effort to capture that room in an essay.

WRITING EXERCISE
It's Your Turn

While the following classroom description has merit, it needs more work. More time spent in prewriting and in "after-writing" (revision) would strengthen it. Read "My Classroom," and then answer the questions following it either in class discussion or on paper, as your instructor directs.

MY CLASSROOM

In the first place I'm in a pretty grim mood before I even get there because parking is such a pain. My classroom isn't a very pleasant place to learn either. It is depressing. It is dirty and run-down. Even simple maintenance jobs like changing burned-out fluorescent bulbs and washing the floor are not done. I wonder how long it has been since it was painted. I think it is a building left over from World War II. Teachers have been writing on the chalkboard ever since then, but nobody has thought about cleaning it. How can we learn when we are not comfortable, and we are surrounded by such a gloomy environment? My classroom is a dump.

FOR THOUGHT AND DISCUSSION

1. Does this essay convince you the classroom is "a dump"?
2. What kind of details should be added to help you picture this room?
3. Can you follow the writer easily, or do you have to stop and backtrack sometimes to understand what she is writing about?
4. If you were gong to rewrite this essay, list the order in which you would present the descriptive details. Explain why you would choose that order.

Attention!

Pay special attention to your five senses, and use the information they give you to show readers a scene so they can sense it, too. For example, what details would make "My Classroom" more convincing? To help you determine this, use your imagination to answer the following questions:

1. What color is the classroom?
2. Is the paint chipped or scuffed?
3. What color is the dirty chalkboard?
4. Is there writing on the board, or has it been erased?
5. Is there chalk dust in the chalk tray?
6. Are there windows in the classroom? If so what do they look like? Are they dirty?
7. Are there curtains or shades? What color are they? What do they look like? Are they torn or stained, for example?
8. What does the floor look like? What color is it? Is it carpeted? Is it tiled?
9. Is there trash on the floor? What kind of trash—pencil shavings? paper? old potato chip bags? soft drink cans?
10. Is the floor scuffed or stained?
11. What is the central point of the paragraph?
12. Can the parking comment be made to fit with the central point?
13. Why is parking "a pain"? Is the parking lot unpaved? unlighted? too far from the classroom? Are there not enough parking spaces?
14. Is the parking discussion relevant to the essay's central point?

REVISION TO THE RESCUE

The following is a sample revision of "My Classroom." Read it and then answer the Thought and Discussion questions which follow it.

THE HIGHLIGHT OF MY WEEK

When I think of going to my Tuesday evening English composition class, I feel a dreary, grey sense of dread. It's not that I dislike the class itself. It is just that the off-campus, Fort Ord setting is so depressing. Even before I get to the room, my ordeal begins. The parking lot near the classroom has spaces for fifty cars, but the building itself holds three hundred people. If I get to class early enough to find a parking spot, I must navigate the deep ruts in the unpaved, unlighted parking lot. If I cannot squeeze my car into a parking space in the overcrowded lot, I have to park a block away and walk along a dark path bordered by tall bushes to reach the classroom building. My heart pounds as I hurry along, half-expecting a mugger to leap out at me.

Life does not improve once I arrive at the classroom. The room was probably once painted a dull, buff color—though it is possible the color is simply the result of fungus eating away on the pitted walls. The walls themselves are streaked with black scuff marks where chairs have scraped against them over the years. Heating pipes crisscross the eight-foot-high ceiling, making it seem still lower.

When I first came to class, the low ceiling seemed to close in on me, and I remembered a story I once read about a person being squashed when a ceiling slowly moved down until it met the floor. I try not to think about this story while I am in class.

Early in the semester it was still light outside when class began at 6:30 p.m. However, the windows were so mud-splattered not much light filtered through. Now our room is lighted solely by six fluorescent lights. The two in the front give very little light, and they flicker constantly. To make matters worse, they buzz with the low drone of a dentist's drill.

It is probably just as well that the classroom isn't brightly lighted. The worn beige tile floor with its long, black scuff marks looks so unsanitary in the light we have that I would rather not see it more clearly. Nor am I eager for a better view of the dust-encrusted chalkboard bordered by its tray brimming with chalk dust.

Occasionally I catch a glimpse of something moving near the baseboards. Perhaps it is a cockroach hoping to dine on the garbage piled high in the wastebasket beside the instructor's desk.

When it is time for class to begin, our teacher always says, "Good evening, class. It's good to see you here again tonight." I think she is lying.

FOR THOUGHT AND DISCUSSION

1. What is the central impression of "The Highlight of My Week"?
2. Which details does the author use to show you this impression?
3. How does the organization of this essay differ from that of "My Classroom"?

WRITING ASSIGNMENT
Using What You Have Learned

Write an essay of at least two hundred words in which you create a central mood in your description of a place. Remember the following tips to help you create a concrete and unified essay:

1. Work with your right brain to create fresh, striking images through clustering, brainstorming, or freewriting.
2. Do not include every detail of the place you are describing. Rather *limit* your details to show your readers a *unified* central point.
3. Use vivid verbs—verbs that snap, crackle, and pop.
4. Do not limit your impression to sight. Use relevant details of touch like texture and temperature. Use sounds and smells that will reinforce your central impression.

5. Avoid abstractions like *beautiful* or *ugly*. Show your reader concrete details.
6. Pay attention to the connotations of the words you use.
7. Make sure your readers do not get lost. Include words and phrases that let your readers know where you are—for example, in the back of the room, next to the sink, or near the window.

After you have completed your initial prewriting and you know what central impression you wish to create, take a few minutes to think about the most effective way to organize your material to create that impression. Think of yourself as a movie maker, and plan your essay as a series of scenes. What objects will you focus on? What order will be the most effective? Will you begin with a close-up? a panoramic shot of the entire setting that you will show to your reader through specific details?

Do not jump around aimlessly in your description. Tell your reader where you are as you move from place to place. Read through the descriptions in this chapter to see the way the authors organized their material and kept their readers from getting lost.

STUDENT STAR ESSAYS
The Polished Product

***Remember: the authors of these essays used the following steps:

1. Prewriting
2. Writing
3. Revising content
4. Proofreading and correcting mechanical errors.

OUR OLD GARAGE

Standing quietly apart from the house and ignoring the rest of the world our garage seems full of life. Sometimes at night I can hear the groans of pain as its timbers creak from old age. The ivy crawls through the weathered redwood boards that make up the sturdy, old building, but the garage accepts the invader without complaint. Cobwebs dance in the moonlight when the crisp evening breeze whistles through the cracks sending a chill along the rafters and whipping up miniature whirlwinds of dust on the floor. Field mice scamper across the floor carrying seeds to nests they have tucked into cozy corners.

When I'm lonely I visit our garage. There is always something I can do to make it feel my warmth whether it be sweeping out the dirt that has blown in from the nearby field or organizing the piles of junk—everything from old magazines and splattered paint cans to boxes of Christmas ornaments and Halloween costumes—that accumulate on its floor and shelves. When I finish my work, our garage seems to smile at me and share its quiet warmth.

Cindy McQueen

HOME, SWEET, CROWDED HOME

Our house reflects the growing pains of our family's stay here at Fort Ord. The children—Joshua (four years), Lisa (three years), and Kelly (six months)—and their cocker spaniel Duke (six years) have immeasurably contributed to its current condition by their insistence on putting their version of hieroglyphics on the walls and furniture. The walls have long since lost their luster through inordinate amounts of scrubbing with cleansers and liberal amounts of W. D. 40.

With three kids, a second bathroom is a godsend—especially now as it doubles as a holding area for clothes waiting to make the trip to the washing machine. In the living room, what used to be an overstuffed chair designed to comfort tired bodies has become a repository for clean laundry waiting to be folded. Once a great source of musical enjoyment, contemplating its days of greater use, the piano now stands at the north wall across from the laundry chair.

In the kitchen, neatly as tin soldiers, clean dishes stand in stacks near the sink awaiting their resting place in the cupboard. Nearby a half-empty jar of peanut butter stands next to a sticky strawberry jam jar.

Yes, our house is a happy yet often disorganized one. It is constantly bending to the ever changing requirements of a growing family.

Michael W. Wills

MEMORIES OF MIDDLE SCHOOL

When I rummage around in my subconscious mind, I find vivid images of the most chaotic time of my education—the years I spent in middle school. Searching through my memories, I become a time traveler, once again a fourteen-year-old amid the pandemonium of that campus.

The bell rings. A noisy crowd of laughing, shouting kids rush for the large, yellow buses waiting patiently for their rowdy cargo. After the buses leave, it grows quiet. Sea gulls swarm over the campus looking for a meal in the litter left behind by the departed kids: scraps of paper, aluminum cans, cookie foil, cardboard boxes that had housed cafeteria lunches, and bags that drift over the grass like little cellophane ghosts doomed to haunt the campus and be tossed by the breeze.

I now walk toward Room C-11. I pass the lockers where the students express themselves by writing on the doors. If I pause to open a vacant locker, I will find stickers and bits of litter that have been left by the former occupant.

I turn the door knob of C-11 carefully, so I do not touch the banana someone has squashed on the knob. Although it is often jammed by a pencil or other slender object a pupil has crammed into the lock, today it opens. I walk inside and turn on the lights. I notice a desk in the far corner that has had its top removed by a vandal during one of the classes. I look to my right and see a group of old desks in wavy lines. The desks have black scorch marks at the joints where a custodian has repaired them in the school shop. The legs and supports gleam where thousands of feet have worn off the light-blue paint. Walking to the front of the room, I notice drawings on the desk tops. One says, "I hate Mr. Wolfe." Another says, "Herr Wolfe is a Nazi."

In front of the room is Mr. Wolfe's desk covered with student work and German and English books. On the floor lies the ancient remains of a recently disemboweled grammar book. The old green carpet, slowly falling apart from the many feet that have trod upon it is dotted with dark stains. Above me the fluorescent lights hum to themselves. Above the lights is the asbestos ceiling decorated by a variety of pencils students have flung there. Over on the western wall is a bookshelf with piles of literature, grammar, and German books as well as some dictionaries and tattered magazines.

On my way out, I pass a bulletin board riddled with paper wads and covered with German posters bearing slogans such as "Visit Germany." I turn out the lights and close the door, once again careful to avoid the squashed banana.

Ian Martin

HELP! FOR FURTHER WORK

Read "Our Room" and "My Comfortable Room," and then answer the Thought and Discussion questions which follow the essays.

OUR ROOM

My room is great because we have a lot of things that make it seem like home. We have carpet on the floor. The carpet makes it look like my living room at home. We have small beds in our room that looks like mine back home. We have a twenty-four-inch television set. We have a VCR and a Beta Max, so we can watch reruns of our favorite programs like Alf and Mash. The friendship in our room is great because we share a lot of things together like books, for example. We are Sherlock Holmes fans, and our copy of Elementary My Dear Watson, a book about that fictious detective is on the coffee table. In addition, we have our current TV Guide on the television. My room is bright and sunny, and its color is light and happy too. The colorful posters and pictures on our walls are pleasant to look at. Our stereo is pleasant to listen to. We even have a plant in a corner to help make our room more homey. My room makes me feel like I am back home.

MY COMFORTABLE ROOM

My bedroom is the smallest room in the house. I chose it because a big room takes too much time to clean. When I enter it my room says Welcome home. I hate to spend time cleaning my room. Small rooms get messy quickly. My family and I moved into this house in 1984. They said, Pick out the room you want. I looked through the house and found that this room was very comfortable. The previous owner hardly even stepped into the room. He used it for storage. That's why my family members tell me that I have the best room in the house.

My room lies in the front of the house. There are very few cars on the street, making the air easy to breathe. Not much dust gets into my room when the window is open. The window is often open. Even when the window is closed the air is easy to breathe. When I close the window after having it open for a while, the air stays fresh inside the room for about four or five hours or so.

I always try to use my room for a study-only place. I do end up doing other things in there. My clarinet and my stamp collection are stored in my room. I often stop studying and play my clarinet or look at my stamp collection. Or sometimes I read a magazine like Time or Newsweek.

FOR THOUGHT AND DISCUSSION

1. How many senses does the author of "Our Room" appeal to?
2. "Our Room" does have a unified central point. Use your imagination to help the author add the necessary, concrete details to adequately develop the central point.
3. Decide on a central point for this paper. Then use one of the prewriting techniques to help the student find details to show readers the central point. Use your imagination when necessary to create details. Omit comments that do not help to create unity.
4. Using the information about transitions and sentence variety in "The Final Touch," rewrite this essay.
5. Proofread the essays with your Left Brain Critic in gear. Read "Quotation Marks" and "Italics" beginning on page 281 of "The Final Touch: A Handbook"; then correct the errors in both essays.

6 DESCRIBE A PERSON

Drawing by M. Stevens; © 1983. *The New Yorker Magazine, Inc.*

Good Lord, what is man! for as simple he looks,
Do but try to develop his hooks and his crooks,
With his depths and his shallows, his good and his evil,
All in all, he's a problem must puzzle the devil.

Robert Burns

CONCEPTS TO LEARN

- The meaning of *style*
- The meaning of *tone*

DR. JEKYLL AND MR. HYDE REVISITED

"Wonders are many, and none is more wonderful than man," Sophocles wrote more than two thousand years ago. But even a casual study of Greek history shows that Sophocles' contemporaries were not wonderful much of the time. Like those who shared the planet with Robert Burns (see introductory quotation)—and those who share it with us—most people are not one-dimensional. Although he is generally considered the greatest of Scottish poets, Burns certainly sowed his share of wild oats. Each of us can be wonderful—or unwonderful. Humans are complex creatures. On occasion, all of us aspire to be cartoon "Plan A." On occasion, even the best of us performs more like "Plan B."

To develop all of our hooks and crooks, depths and shallows, good and evil would take a hefty volume. In this chapter, however, we are going to limit our comments about people to one hook or crook. We are, in other words, going to *limit* our subject adequately so we can *show* readers one aspect of the complicated creature that each human is.

The Good, the Bad, and the Ordinary

When writing about a person we often think of someone with outstanding qualities—for instance an athlete, a politician, a movie star, or a musician. Outstanding people, however, are not the only people worthy of note. Everyone has some quality that could be developed into an interesting, unified essay. In the following poem, May Swenson shows the humanness of a person that many would scarcely notice.

Pigeon Woman

Slate, or dirty-marble-colored,
or rusty-iron-colored, the pigeons
on the flagstones in front of the
Public Library make a sharp lake

into which the pigeon woman wades
at exactly 1:30. She wears
a plastic pink raincoat with a round
collar (looking like a little

girl, so gay) and flat gym shoes,
her hair square-cut, orange.
Wide-apart feet carefully enter
the spinning, crooning waves

(as if she'd just learned how
to walk, each step conscious,
an accomplishment; blue knots in the
calves of her bare legs (uglied marble),

age in angled cords of jaw
and neck, her pimento-colored hair
hanging in thin tassles, is grey
around a balding crown.

The day-old bread drops down
from her veined hands dipping out
of a paper sack. Choppy, shadowy ripples,
the pigeons strike around her legs.

Sack empty, she squats and seems to rinse
her hands in them—the rainy greens and
oily purples of their necks. Almost
they let her wet her thirsty fingertips—

but drain away in an untouchable tide.
A make-believe trade
she has come to, in her lostness
or illness or age—to treat the motley

city pigeons at 1:30 every day, in all
weathers. It is for them she colors
her own feathers. Ruddy-footed
on the lime-stained paving.

purling to meet her when she comes,
they are a lake of love. Retreating
from her hands as soon as empty,
they are the flints of love.

May Swenson

FOR THOUGHT AND DISCUSSION

1. How well does the poet know the woman she describes? Support
   your answer.
2. To create a unified impression, the poet omits information about
   the woman. What kinds of things does she not tell us about the
   pigeon woman?

3. List the details the poem gives about the woman. Draw a sketch of the woman using the poem as a guide.
4. Is your response to this poem primarily a left brain logical response or a right brain emotional response? Explain your answer.

The Aristocrat

While May Swenson's pigeon woman seems to be someone from her current life, Maya Angelou reaches into her treasure house of childhood memories and recreates a figure from her past in the following description of Mrs. Flowers, from *I Know Why the Caged Bird Sings:*

OUR SIDE'S ANSWER
Maya Angelou

Mrs. Bertha Flowers was the aristocrat of Black Stamps. She had the grace of control to appear warm in the coldest weather, and on the Arkansas summer days it seemed she had a private breeze which swirled around, cooling her. She was thin without the taut look of wiry people, and her printed voile dresses and flowered hats were as right for her as denim overalls for a farmer. She was our side's answer to the richest white woman in town.

Her skin was a rich black that would have peeled like a plum if snagged, but then no one would have thought of getting close enough to Mrs. Flowers to ruffle her dress, let alone snag her skin. She didn't encourage familiarity. She wore gloves too.

I don't think I ever saw Mrs. Flowers laugh, but she smiled often. A slow widening of her thin black lips to show even, small white teeth, then the slow effortless closing. When she chose to smile on me, I always wanted to thank her. The action was so graceful and inclusively benign.

FOR THOUGHT AND DISCUSSION

1. Maya Angelou entitles the selection "The Aristocrat," and she limits her subject to those details that show Mrs. Flowers's aristocratic nature. How would Angelou define *aristocrat*?
2. In your own words, describe Mrs. Flowers.
3. Which details help you to see Mrs. Flowers?
4. List some important information Angelou omits about Mrs. Flowers. Why does she omit this information?

STYLE

> Style is the dress of thought.
> Reverend Samuel Wesley

Style is the way we express ourselves. Many elements such as diction, word choice, sentence length, and sentence patterns make up style.

The Sound of Style

In an article about its coverage of royal weddings, *The Times of London* poked fun at its flowery style of a century ago. As you read the following lines, notice the way the complex sentence structure and the sound of the words contributes to style:

> The fair Princess who landed on Saturday morning a stranger to the people, their habits and modes of thought is now a member of our State, the partner for life of the Heir Apparent to the Throne.

What Kind of an Attitude Is That?

Among the complex elements that make up an author's style is *tone*, that is, the author's attitude toward a subject and audience. An author can be serious and scholarly such as when he or she writes a research paper. An author can be humorous such as Mark Twain was when he said that giving up smoking was easy; he had done it hundreds of times.

Happy as an Outhouse Rat

Subject matter, audience, word choice, and even the comparisons we make help to establish tone and style. Down East, (in Maine) some people use the expression, "He is as happy as an outhouse rat." "Outhouse rat" helps create a very different tone from that created by the poet William Blake's "happy as the birds in spring."

Dressing Up—or Down—Your Language

To help create tone, an author can use formal or informal language. "Formal" language is not stuffy, tuxedo language. It is language that follows the standard grammatical rules of the English language. It is the language used in business letters or job application letters. (For more information about formal language, see "Formal and Informal Language" on page 319 of "The Final Touch: A Handbook.")

Label the degree of formality in the following expressions 1–4, with 1 being the most formal and 4 being the least formal.

1. The guy in the hot sports car was really moving out.
2. My father means well, but his jokes are cornier than Kansas in August.
3. Approximately seven of the samples had been contaminated by bacteria.
4. Peace Corps volunteers often display a quiet courage.

Reread "Pigeon Woman" and "Our Side's Answer" and answer the following questions about tone and style:

1. What was Maya Angelou's attitude toward Mrs. Flowers?
2. What was May Swenson's attitude toward the pigeon woman?

OF JOGGING SHOES AND DIAMOND NECKLACES

The important thing to remember in writing is to *make your style and tone consistent*. If you begin with an informal, conversational style and tone, stay with them. When dressing, most people strive for a harmonious style. Wall Street executives do not sport punk haircuts with their conservative business suits. Preppies do not wear diamond necklaces with their crew neck sweaters. Academy Award winners usually do not go to the ceremony wearing jogging shoes with their formal attire. Do not impetuously transpose your ideas into a formal, scholarly tone. On the other hand, do not suddenly shift to an informal tone.

Just as dress and vocabulary are not identical at a job interview and a picnic with friends, so too, writing style may vary depending on the purpose. The important thing to remember is *be consistent* within each essay.

Of Jumping Frogs and War

Like Mark Twain, Ernest Hemingway began his writing career as a journalist. Twain wrote about the colorful people and events of the Western frontier. In his articles about jumping frog contests and life in rough and tumble gold mining camps, his style was humorous, informal, and folksy. Hemingway, on the other hand, began his career writing more serious journalism for *The Kansas City Star*—a career that helped influence Hemingway's style with its flat, uncomplex sentences. As you read Hemingway's "Old Man at the Bridge," note the author's simple style.

OLD MAN AT THE BRIDGE
Ernest Hemingway

An old man with steel rimmed spectacles and very dusty clothes sat by the side of the road. There was a pontoon bridge across the river and carts, trucks, and men, women and children were crossing it. The mule-drawn carts staggered up the steep bank from the bridge with soldiers helping push against the spokes of the wheels. The trucks ground up and away heading out of it all and the peasants plodded along in the ankle deep dust. But the old man sat there without moving. He was too tired to go any farther.

It was my business to cross the bridge, explore the bridgehead beyond and find out to what point the enemy had advanced. I did this and returned over the bridge. There were not so many carts now and very few people on foot, but the old man was still there.

"Where do you come from?" I asked him.

"From San Carlos," he said, and smiled.

That was his native town and so it gave him pleasure to mention it and he smiled.

"I was taking care of animals," he explained.

"Oh," I said, not quite understanding.

"Yes," he said, "I stayed, you see, taking care of animals. I was the last one to leave the town of San Carlos."

He did not look like a shepherd nor a herdsman and I looked at his black dusty clothes and his gray dusty face and his steel rimmed spectacles and said, "What animals were they?"

"Various animals," he said, and shook his head. "I had to leave them."

I was watching the bridge and the African looking country of the Ebro Delta and wondering how long now it would be before we would see the enemy, and listening all the while for the first noises that would signal that ever mysterious event called contact, and the old man still sat there.

"What animals were they?" I asked.

"There were three animals altogether," he explained. "There were two goats and a cat and then there were four pairs of pigeons."

"And you had to leave them?" I asked.

"Yes. Because of the artillery. The captain told me to go because of the artillery."

"And you have no family?" I asked, watching the far end of the bridge where a few last carts were hurrying down the slope of the bank.

"No," he said, "only the animals I stated. The cat, of course, will be all right. A cat can look out for itself, but I cannot think what will become of the others."

"What politics have you?" I asked.

"I am without politics," he said. "I am seventy-six years old. I have come twelve kilometers now and I think now I can go no further."

"This is not a good place to stop," I said. "If you can make it, there are trucks up the road where it forks for Tortosa."

"I will wait a while," he said, "and then I will go. Where do the trucks go?"

"Towards Barcelona," I told him.

"I know no one in that direction," he said, "but thank you very much. Thank you again very much."

He looked at me very blankly and tiredly, then said, having to share his worry with someone, "The cat will be all right. I am sure. There is no need to be unquiet about the cat. But the others. Now what do you think about the others?"

"Why they'll probably come through it all right."

"You think so?"

"Why not," I said, watching the far bank where now there were no carts.

"But what will they do under the artillery when I was told to leave because of the artillery?"

"Did you leave the dove cage unlocked?" I asked.

"Yes."

"Then they'll fly."

"Yes, certainly they'll fly. But the others. It's better not to think about the others," he said.

"If you are rested I would go," I urged. "Get up and try to walk now."

"Thank you," he said and got to his feet, swayed from side to side and then sat down backwards in the dust.

"I was taking care of animals," he said dully, but no longer to me. "I was only taking care of animals."

There was nothing to do about him. It was Easter Sunday and the Fascists were advancing toward the Ebro. It was a gray overcast day with a low ceiling so their planes were not up. That and the fact that cats know how to look after themselves was all the good luck that old man would ever have.

FOR THOUGHT AND DISCUSSION

1. What is the narrator doing when he first meets the old man?
2. How does Hemingway limit his description of the old man? What does Hemingway emphasize about him?.
3. Through his description of the old man, Hemingway makes an important point about war. What is his point?
4. Does Hemingway appeal to the left brain or right brain in making his point?
5. How would the story differ if he tried to appeal primarily to the left brain? Would the story have the same impact?
6. Reread "Old Man at the Bridge" and pay special attention to Hemingway's style.
   a. Are the sentences long and complex or short and uncomplicated?
   b. Does Hemingway rely primarily on multisyllable words or short, everyday words?
7. Explain why Hemingway's style is appropriate for his subject.

Destructive as a Glacier, Soft as Warm Fudge

Jim Murray is a contemporary sports columnist. While his columns are informative, Murray seeks to entertain his reader so he uses a lively style filled with humorous, colorful phrases. In the following article, note the way exaggeration helps Murray to establish his tone.

SOFT-SPOKEN BUBBA ONCE A SYNONYM FOR STARK TERROR
Jim Murray

In the little world of football, the name Bubba invokes the same kind of terror Geronimo did in the Old West or Attila in premedieval Europe, or Capone in Prohibition Chicago.

It's a name to empty a room, increase the pulse, raise the blood pressure, promote panic in the streets. It's a name that has gone into the language to symbolize a creature so awesome that if you saw it swimming ashore in New York Harbor, you'd evacuate the city. . . .

Bubba Smith was one of the scenic wonders of North America when he first ambled out of the thickets of Beaumont, Texas to play big-time football. No one had ever seen anything this big and this fast outside of a cage before. . . .

On the football field he was as destructive as a glacier. Bullets would bounce off him. He stopped growing at just under seven feet and weighed well under four hundred pounds in his stocking feet. The rumor was, Michigan State hadn't recruited him, they had trapped him in the snows of Mount Everest.

The battle cry at home games was "Kill, Bubba, Kill!" and word was they fed him chickens live, or slid food under the door and ran. . . .

Which was all very strange. Because inside that awesome physique was the world's biggest collection of warm fudge. Without his helmet on, Bubba Smith was just a big pussycat of a man who wanted nothing more than to be loved. . . . There was no evidence that he had ever hurt anybody on purpose. Accidentally was another story.

He even put a condition on his recruitment that he be roomed with a white student, nonathlete. "I had never talked to a white person growing up in Beaumont," he recalls. "I think that's why people were scared of me. I used to get up close and stare at them.

"My roommate was like five-one and from the Upper Peninsula (of Michigan). He had never seen any black person up close. We were the original odd couple. The day he came into the room, I was in the upper bunk. I just kind of unraveled down and his eyes kept getting bigger. He later told me: 'I thought you were never going to stop.'" . . .

It's customary at this point to say, "Bubba's career was cut short by a sideline accident." It's true that his football was cut short when he tripped over the sideline chains at Miami and tore up a knee. . . .

Still Bubba's real career was more like started by that accident . . . The soft-spoken giant who made *Bubba* a synonym for stark terror now hopes to make it a word representing suave elegance. Even though it's not likely he will get any old Ronald Coleman roles, it still must be eye-opening to his old adversaries on the line of scrimmage to look at that soft-hearted lug on the screen and try to equate him with the monster they remember.

FOR THOUGHT AND DISCUSSION

1. What is the central point Jim Murray makes about Bubba Smith? Why is this ironic?
2. Describe the tone and style of the article, and support your answer by citing appropriate details. Remember to watch for the following:
   a. Types of comparisons
   b. Length and complexity of sentences
   c. Choice of words (multisyllable, unusual words, or common, short words)
3. Could Hemingway have used a similar style to accomplish his purpose in "Old Man at the Bridge"? Explain.
4. Which descriptive phrases are most effective in showing you Bubba Smith?

The Reincarnation of a Goat

Gerald Durrell is an English naturalist who spent several years of his childhood on the Greek island of Corfu, a period he describes in a series of books he wrote as an adult. Like Maya Angelou, Durrell explored the rich stores of his subconscious mind to conjure up vivid details that bring the people and events of his youth to life. In the following article from *Fauna and Family*, Durrell depicts a French count who was a friend of the author Lawrence Durrell, Gerald's sophisticated older brother.

Vocabulary   **narcissistic:**   having an excessive love or admiration of oneself
permeate: spread throughout the whole of
dogmatism: a strong assertion of opinion

Gallic: French
edibility: fitness for eating

THE FRENCHMAN
Gerald Durrell

Three days later the count appeared. He was tall and slender, with tightly curled hair as golden as a silkworm's cocoon, shining with oil, a delicately curled moustache of a similar hue, and slightly protuberant eyes of a very pale and unpleasant green. He alarmed Mother by arriving with a huge wardrobe trunk, and she was convinced that he had come to stay for the summer. But we soon found that the count found himself so attractive he felt it necessary to change his clothes about eight times a day to do justice to himself. His clothes were such elegant confections, beautifully hand-stitched and of such exquisite materials, that Margo was torn between envy at the count's wardrobe and disgust at his effeminacy. Combined with this **narcissistic** preoccupation with himself, the count had other equally objectionable characteristics. He drenched himself in a scent so thick it was almost visible and he had only to spend a second in a room to **permeate** the whole atmosphere, while the cushions he leaned against and the chairs he sat in reeked for days afterwards. His English was limited, but this did not prevent him from expounding on any subject with a sort of sneering **dogmatism** that made everyone's hackles rise. His philosophy, if any, could be summed up in the phrase "We do it better in France," which he used repeatedly about everything. He had such a thoroughly **Gallic** interest in the **edibility** of everything he came in contact with that one could have been pardoned for thinking him the reincarnation of a goat.

FOR THOUGHT AND DISCUSSION

1. What is the central impression made by the Frenchman?
2. List the details that support the central point Durrell makes about the Frenchman.
3. How would you characterize the tone of "The Frenchman"? Support your answer by citing lines from the essay.

Relax and Create

Professional writers like Maya Angelou, Jim Murray, Ernest Hemingway, and Gerald Durrell rummaged around the treasure chest of their memories to come up with vivid descriptions and recreated incidents and people for their readers. These professional writers have nothing the average English composition student does not have (except, of course, wealth and fame). They do, however, have access to concrete details and an ability to retrieve these details from their memories. Such an ability is made easier by practice.

Before you begin the following assignment, use one or two of the prewriting techniques—clustering, brainstorming, or freewriting—to help you relax and get in touch with the concrete details that will show your reader the person you wish to portray. Spend enough time in prewriting to come up with fresh, convincing details that will breathe life into your description.

WRITING ASSIGNMENT
Using What You Have Learned

Write an essay of at least two hundred words in which you capture one essential quality of a person. Do not try to tell your reader everything you know about the person. Be sure you do the following:

1. Limit your subject to a significant, central impression of the person you describe.
2. When appropriate, include quotations from the person.
3. Show the person through concrete details.

One student, for example, brought her character to life with the following vivid beginning:

> From her hat to her toes, Aunt Mattie is a riot of pinks. Emporia, Virginia, fit her like a coat too small, buttons missing, hem unraveling and torn. So at age nineteen, she fled.
>
> Eleanor Griffin

Read the clustering in Figure 6.1 on page 96, which inspired the essay, "Grandma." Note that three asterisks mark areas of uncertainty about details. Instead of looking up the information and stopping the flow of ideas from the Right Brain Creator, I jolted down the ideas. When clustering was finished, I looked up the missing details.

GRANDMA

Modern grandmothers take Geritol, play golf, and ride bikes. In television ads, they are always slim, attractive, athletic. My grandmother looked like Mrs. Santa Claus. She was short and softly round. When I picture her, she is wearing a dark, flower-print dress covered by a long, white, bib apron. I can see her standing before the black wood stove in the kitchen of her farmhouse. In my memory, her hand is extended and on it is a slice of soft, warm, homemade bread, slathered with butter and coated with cinnamon and sugar. Her plump, round face looks pleasant. I don't see her laughing, but behind her wire-rimmed glasses, her green eyes twinkle. She has been making sugar cookies. Soon the large, flat, pale cookies will be ready. I can still taste their buttery-sweet crunchiness that quickly melts into doughy smoothness in my mouth.

In my living room is an antique, oval frame containing a photograph of a proud, lively looking young lady, her head tilted slightly to one side, her wavy, dark hair piled stylishly on her head with the edge of a bow peaking out from the right side. Just above the photograph is a row of elegant, leather-bound

FIGURE 6.1 **Clustering for "Grandma"**

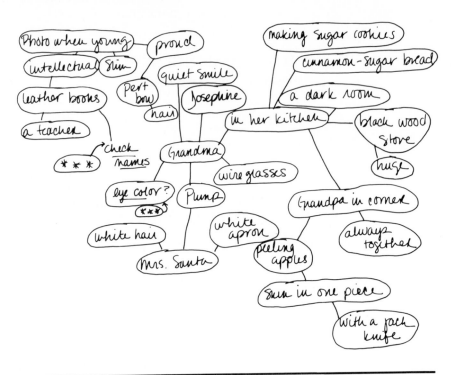

books—the works of Scott and Wordsworth and Tennyson. This photograph and these books are also my grandmother. But they are not the grandmother I remember—the gentle, warm lady with white hair who made me a rag doll named Josephine and tucked me into bed beneath a handmade calico quilt.

 STUDENT STAR ESSAYS
The Polished Product

***Remember: the authors of these essays used the following steps:

1. Prewriting
2. Writing
3. Revising content
4. Proofreading and correcting mechanical errors

THE SPIRIT OF NGA CHE

She arrives at work, ambling toward me on surprisingly tiny feet. She is dark-haired and softly plump, with rounded, generous shoulders that seem to carry an invisible weight. Her face appears almost swollen so that her eyes are nearly lost, except for their sparkle. Her name is Nga Che. She greets everyone with a cheery "Good Morning." As soon as she sees me, her eyes light up like the star on top of a Christmas tree.

Quietly she sets to work, dusting here, shining there, and sweeping up. As the crowds plow through the doors and permeate every corner of the building, Nga fades into the background, barely noticed and often rudely bumped by uncaring people. Her co-workers scarcely notice when she comes to work, or when she leaves.

No one takes the time to ask, "Who are you Nga, where did you come from, and how was life for you in Vietnam?" I realize that her English is difficult to understand, but it hurts me to see others treat her as though she were an annoyance, simply because they lack the patience to listen.

Nga's eyes are like a magnet pulling me toward her. It delights her when I stop and chat, breaking the silence of her day at work. Nga speaks the language of the heart. She could be mute and still speak clearly to me. A special aura surrounds her. Her life story is unlike any I have ever known. Her eyes show the pain she has endured, the struggle she had after losing her husband to a car accident while she carried within her their sixth child. Alone, she smuggled all her children from Vietnam to the United States, set up home, and then somehow she managed to feed each little stomach and heart.

Nga is a woman of great strength and few words. Unlike her co-workers, who complain noisily about unimportant aspects of work, Nga merely observes and gets on with things, always careful not to disturb others while she smiles often her knowing smile.

It strikes me that perhaps God puts special people like Nga in our lives for a reason. Even though she does not stand out in any conventional way, her gentle, loving manner enriches those who choose her company. When I see her during the day, my usual, hectic inner pace slows down under her calming influence. She makes me feel that the world is okay. In her presence, I sense that I have come into contact with something of beauty and stature, something that transcends the daily annoyances and trivialities of life. Nga's spirit has the same humbling effect upon me as a breathtaking sunset, a star-studded sky, or the vastness of a mother's love.

Breda Conroy

A SACK FULL OF LOVE

In one of my fondest childhood memories, I see his aged, weary figure as he made his way down the narrow path leading to our little house. He would arrive late at night with that precious sack flung over his shoulder. Wearing a dark suit, a white shirt, and a brown felt hat, he seemed a Mexican reincarnation of a Charlie Chaplin-Santa Claus cross.

Others called him "Hermano Luz," but my sister and I as children transformed this to "Mano Luz." And that is what we call him to this day. He worked in the kitchen of the local hospital where, at the end of the day, he would ask for the leftover food which he packed in his bag and carried home to us. Looking back, it occurs to me we never saw him in work clothes although his job was washing dishes. Thoughts like this don't enter the minds of children. But now I realize that he must have changed clothes after finishing work and before boarding the bus home. I'm sure people who saw him then would never have guessed this humble, proud man was a dishwasher.

To us he seemed like Santa Claus, and we greeted him gleefully, eager to learn what treats his sack contained. We never thought to ask, ''Are you tired tonight?'' or ''Did you work hard today?'' or to say, ''Thank you for thinking about us.'' No, we were children and were preoccupied with the savory delights we were about to consume.

Occasionally these foods were not adequately wrapped, so soggy ice cream coated leftover meatloaf and ham salad oozed out of sandwiches and onto chocolate chip cookies. But we didn't care; we were too busy tripping out on roast beef sandwiches and walnut brownies. Holidays brought extra special delights like hot cross buns, green shamrock cupcakes or Christmas tree cookies bedecked with red and green sprinkles.

Mother invited Mano Luz to dinner every Sunday and often during the week she sent food to his house. We would wait to see his eyes light up as he looked at the simple, nourishing Mexican meals. Hugging us, he would say in Spanish, ''Thank you, thank you. And be sure to thank your mother. She is a good woman.''

He too was a good person, our self-appointed *abuelo* (grandfather) who brought so much love into our lives. As a child I never really thanked him. But now I do and will continue to do so every time I remember him.

Socorro Gutierrez

SMITTEE

As all the college kids from back East head down to Daytona Beach, Florida, so does MTV—the music video channel—to catch all the action of Spring Break. This year, some of the action was in the form of Smittee.

A college student, he's the typical *Animal House* character: bald on top but hairy as a bear everywhere else; fat and blubbery as a beached whale; loud, obnoxious, boisterous, and often drunk.

MTV used him as a highlighted guest throughout the week at Daytona. In one scene, he was broadcasting from an oyster bar near the beach. He was wearing nothing but boxer shorts, his hairy belly hanging over the waistband. While the crowd stood around cheering, he showed them how to eat oysters on the half shell. First, he sucked five of them off the shell into his mouth. Then, after chewing on them for awhile, he decided he didn't like them very much, so he took them out of his mouth and stuck them up his nose, striking a pose for the camera before they fell out.

Smittee is definitely a man's man—or should I say a boy's boy? The next time I saw him on the air, I almost threw up. There he was again in his boxer shorts, standing behind a table he had set up with his ''props''—food. On came the music—a song called ''Eat It.'' He poured chocolate milk and cottage cheese all over himself; he then added cereal on top of that, shoving handfuls of it in his mouth. Next, he took a can of whipped cream and squirted it all over his head. I couldn't believe it when he actually bit into raw eggs and ate them, shells and all. Then other students shoved bananas into his mouth and Cheetos up his nose. Need I say more? Yes. A chicken went down his shorts next, and after he crushed a whole watermelon on his head, he pulled the chicken out of his pants and threw it out to the crowd for his Grand Finale.

What I want to know is this: did his mother see him? his father? his grand-mother? Will they let him back in the house? Or did they teach him this behavior themselves?

Hopefully MTV won't invite him back into their studio. It would cost them a fortune in food, and they would probably have to build a whole new set.

Denise Harney

REVISION TO THE RESCUE

Often a first draft—especially one written with little help from pre-writing—will be choppy and lack unity. During your prewriting, a series of details will occur to you. When you begin to write your first draft, you need to make sure your reader understands the relation-ship between your ideas.

Read the following essays, and note the way the student author created unity in the revision.

MAMA

My mother was short and very attractive. She was about five-feet-five-inches tall. The color of her skin was a dark brown like a pair of stockings. Her hair was long and black with a mole sitting in the center of her face. Her face was round with plump jaws. It seems that everything she wore fell into place.

As I see her now, she is lying in a hospital room suffering. She has tubes in her nose and arms. The doctors are coming in around the clock to check on her. The room is filled with flowers. I was only eight when Mama died, but I can still hear her last words: "Take care of my baby."

Anonymous

MAMA: THE REVISION

My mother was an attractive, high spirited lady inside and out. Even with her plump figure and round face, somehow she seemed much taller than her five-feet-five inches. Perhaps this was because every inch of her dark brown skin and black hair glowed with energy, and everything she touched—right down to the clothes she wore—fell neatly into place.

A hard-working lady, Mother was always there to give a helping hand at a church fund-raising project or a sick neighbor's house. I can still picture her sitting next to an old black iron heater working on a quilt with her quilting club or making a casserole to take to a sick friend.

But my most vivid memory of my mother is her dark skin—no longer softly plump but stretched over her bones—contrasting with the antiseptic white of her hospital bed. She has tubes in her nose and IVs in her arm. The doctors come in around the clock to check on her, and—when she is awake—she greets them with a smile and a cheery word. Even at the end, she still thought of others. Her spirit was high—just like she knew she was going to heaven. I was only eight when she died, but I still can hear her last words, "Take care of my baby."

HELP! FOR FURTHER WORK

In the following draft of an essay, the author made good use of free-writing techniques to find concrete details about the subject. Now revise it using the following steps:

1. Reorganize the details and rewrite the sentences so the details show us a central point about the neighbor.
2. Use your imagination to create any details you need in the revision.
3. Read from "The Semicolon," on page 286 through "Ellipsis Points," on page 290 of "The Final Touch: A Handbook." Then, revise the errors in punctuation in "My Neighbor."

MY NEIGHBOR

Mrs. Bullard is an elderly white lady who reminds me of my grandmother. She walks around all day wearing her white bib apron and smelling of baked sweets; which she prepares early in the morning. Mrs. Bullard is my neighbor. She is five feet three inches tall and weighs about one hundred and seventy pounds. Her eyes are grey and she is always gay.

When we moved into the neighborhood, Mrs. Bullard was the only one who welcomed us into the neighborhood! We were the only black family there. She brought over some cookies and asked if she could sit and chat. My girls were drawn to her instantly they even call her "Grandma" now. I had no idea she and I would become so close coming from different ethnic backgrounds and being such different ages. Mrs. Bullard has shown me that color is only skin deep. It is what comes from the heart that counts. Grandmothers would teach my girls the Bible and encourage me to take them to church. Mrs. Bullard does this, and I do take the girls to church now. She is a very loving and sincere person. She is also lonely because her husband died two years ago. She is always saying, "No one has time for an old lady."

I say, "Hey, what about me?" She smiles and asks if I really mean what I say.

7 NARRATION

" 'What I Did This Summer.' This summer, I went to camp. I hated it. I hated every minute of it. I hated my counsellor. I hated the food. I hated the woods. I hated the nature walks and the nature talks. I hated the outings. I hated the campfires. I hated the overnights. I hated . . ."

Drawing by H. Martin; (c) 1985. *The New Yorker Magazine, Inc.*

I am always at a loss to know how much to believe my own stories.

Washington Irving

CONCEPTS TO LEARN

- The meaning of *figurative language* or *metaphorical language*
- The meaning of *metaphor*
- The meaning of *simile*
- The meaning of *personification*
- The use of metaphors, similes, and personification
- The importance of unity in narrative essays

FOR THOUGHT AND DISCUSSION

1. Use your understanding of left and right brain functions to explain Washington Irving's statement in the opening quotation.
2. Evidently the young man in the cartoon did not enjoy camp. Use your imagination to invent four concrete details to help him convince his parents camp was truly hateful.

SHOW YOUR READER THE STORY

The poems we have read in *Practicing the Process* have made ideas and emotions concrete. Narrative poems also tell a story. In the following poem, Robinson Jeffers continues an ancient tradition in poetry by telling his readers a story.

Jeffers believed in extreme individualism. His heros were the Clint Eastwoods of their era—proud beings who could act alone and take care of themselves. As Jeffers tells his story he illustrates a point about the hawk. Watch for details that help him show us his point.

Vocabulary **talons:** the claws of an animal, especially a bird of prey
intrepid: very brave, fearless
arrogant: excessively proud and contemptuous of others

Hurt Hawks

The broken pillar of the wing jags from the clotted shoulder,
The wing trails like a banner in defeat,
No more to use the sky forever but live with famine
And pain a few days: cat nor coyote
Will shorten the week of waiting for death, there is game without
    talons.
He stands under the oak-bush and waits

The lame feet of salvation; at night he remembers freedom
And flies in a dream, the dawns ruin it.
He is strong and pain is worse to the strong, incapacity is worse.
The curs of the day come and torment him
At distance, no one but death the redeemer will humble that head,
The **intrepid** readiness, the terrible eyes.
The wild God of the world is sometimes merciful to those
That ask mercy, not often to the **arrogant.**
You do not know him, you communal people, or you have forgotten him;
Intemperate and savage, the hawk remembers him;
Beautiful and wild, the hawks, and men that are dying, remember him.

II

I'd sooner, except the penalties, kill a man than a hawk; but the great redtail
Had nothing left but unable misery
From the bone too shattered for mending, the wing that trailed under his talons when he moved.
We had fed him six weeks. I gave him freedom.
He wandered over the foreland hill and returned in the evening, asking for death,
Not like a beggar, still eyed with the old
Implacable arrogance. I gave him the lead gift in the twilight.
    What fell was relaxed.
Owl-downy, soft feminine feathers; but what
Soared: the fierce rush: the night-herons by the flooded river cried fear at its rising
Before it was quite unsheathed from reality.

Robinson Jeffers

FOR THOUGHT AND DISCUSSION

1. Describe the personality of the hawk.
2. Explain why other animals will not attack the injured hawk.
3. What is the hawk waiting for when Jeffers finds him?
4. When Jeffers finds the hawk, what does he do with him?
5. Explain what Jeffers means by the "lead gift"?
6. At the poem's end, what soared and frightened the herons?
7. Explain the abstract idea Jeffers makes concrete in this poem.

THE HAWKS, THE DOVES, AND THE MUSHROOMS

One device that will help show readers your experience concretely (instead of simply telling them about it abstractly) is *figurative* language, also known as *metaphorical language*. Your right brain naturally compares objects. For example, it "sees" a man's face on the moon and a mushroom in a nuclear explosion. We also often apply the characteristics of nonhumans to people and their attitudes. Political commentators say a congressman is a hawk or a dove, for example. The right brain helps recreate experiences for others by such comparisons. By using this natural tendency to create figurative language, we more clearly communicate our thoughts and feelings. Figurative language then is a direct transfusion of thought—with the emotions that accompany it—through images that appeal to one or more of the reader's five senses.

Poems Are More Than 3 × 2 = 6

Poems are generally filled with figurative language. If you try to read poetry using only your left brain, you have trouble understanding it. A poem does not simply communicate 3 × 2 = 6. It communicates a wealth of feelings and sense impressions. It communicates a total experience rather than a part of it, just as Robinson Jeffers communicated a great deal more about his encounter with the hawk than the actions alone.

The Wonderful World of Figurative Language

In our study of figurative language, we will focus on the following three most common types: *metaphors*, *similes*, and *personification*.

Metaphors.   A *metaphor* is a comparison between two things that are not essentially alike—for example, Shakespeare wrote "merry larks are ploughmen's clocks." These were not battery-driven birds or even wind-up birds. They were real birds, but they awoke early and let the world (including the ploughmen) know they were awake.

Similes.   A *simile* is somewhat like a metaphor. The difference is a metaphor says one thing *is* another—thereby implying a comparison—and a simile directly states the comparison by using words such as *as*, *like*, *similar to*, or *resembles*. For example, in the stage directions for *Butch Cassidy and the Sundance Kid*, Sundance's gunbelt is to "[whip] like a snake across the floor." Had the direction said the gunbelt *was* a snake it would have been a metaphor instead of a simile.

Personification.   *Personification* attributes a human characteristic to an animal, an object, or an idea. Death for example, is frequently personified as a skeleton wearing a white robe. At the end of the year we see many pictures of a bent-over, old man with long, white hair and a flowing robe; he is a personification of the old year. Meanwhile the new year is personified by a chubby baby wearing a diaper and a banner with the new year date written on it. Shakespeare personifies life in *Macbeth* when the title character says the following:

> Life's but a walking shadow, a poor player,
> That struts and frets his hour upon the stage,
> And then is heard no more; it is a tale
> Told by an idiot, full of sound and fury,
> Signifying nothing.

WRITING EXERCISES
It's Your Turn

Identify the figurative language in the following lines written by students. Notice the way each student author communicates a total experience, not just the bare-bone facts.

By the way, what type of figurative language is "bare-bone facts" in the previous statement?

1. If all the world's a stage, and so on and so forth, I'd just as soon play another part.
2. Punk Rock is the kid you slap for mouthing off while Heavy Metal is the kid you put up for adoption.
3. I build walls around myself like a fort so my critics can't hurt me.
4. I don't remember making reservations. Yet here I am transported into another dimension—like a puppet with Rod Serling holding the strings.
5. I felt like a puppy faced by an owner with a rolled-up newspaper.
6. I felt like Sprout standing next to the Jolly Green Giant.
7. The leaves are always greener on your side of the family tree.
8. I keep imagining my wife is the captain and our checkbook is the *Titanic*.
9. My brother's criticism tears me apart and makes me feel like an old cigarette butt.
10. She looked like a spring flower—in the fall.

Now, reread "Hurt Hawks" and identify the figurative language in it.

UNITY: FOCUSING YOUR LENS

In the poem "Hurt Hawks" Robinson Jeffers selects concrete details to help us understand this incident. Since the experience took place over six weeks, however, Jeffers does not list every detail of the experience. Instead he selects key details that help us to understand the way he felt about the hawk, its suffering, and finally its death. In other words, Jeffers selects details to give his poem *unity*. Further discussion of this poem will point out some principles to remember when you tell a story.

FOR THOUGHT AND DISCUSSION

1. How would "Hurt Hawks" have changed if Jeffers had included a
   detailed record of the daily care of the hawk?
2. What kinds of details did Jeffers omit?

Focusing Versus Rambling

We all know people who are guilty of rambling when they tell a story.
Because the right brain works by association, one incident naturally
reminds us of another. In fact, when we cluster, brainstorm, or freewrite, we remember details we think we have forgotten. Like a dom-
ino chain or a potato chip, one idea leads to another.

THE ACCIDENT

Two years ago, my nine-year-old son was hit by a delivery truck. When I think
about this incident, a flood of images, ideas, and emotions sweeps over me. I
think of how fast, efficient, and friendly the emergency room staff was. In fact, I
should have written a letter to them, or perhaps to the editor of our newspaper,
or perhaps to the board of directors of Community Hospital. The whole idea of
praising the emergency room staff in a letter sets off a chain of associations
about letters I could write.

LETTING THE RIGHT BRAIN RUN WITH THE STORY

When I think about what to say in the letter, that sunny August day comes vividly
back to my mind. I remember the neighbor waiting for me in my driveway. She
put her hand on my shoulder and told me not to get out of the car but instead
to go to the hospital. The more I think about this the more I remember: the thick
tangle of traffic crawling up the two-lane highway toward the hospital, the guard
in the parking lot—I abandoned my car in a restricted zone and yelled to him a
jumble of information about my son, an accident and the emergency room. He
told me not to worry about my car. More importantly, he said, "I'm sure your
son will be just fine." When he next saw me three days later, I was again entering the hospital (having legally parked my car). He remembered me and asked,
"How is your son doing?"

On the day of the accident, the lady at the emergency desk was reassuring.
She greeted me with, "Your son is in stable condition. He is with a neurosurgeon, but the doctor is optimistic." I hadn't told her my name — only about the
accident, but she had called me by name. Amazing what details you remember
when you rummage around in your subconscious.

Until I started this I had forgotten about my three worried, angry friends
waiting with my twelve-year-old son at the hospital. They surrounded him glar-
ing at a police officer trying to get an accident report. It seems the officer had
wanted my son to stay home for the interview. My son and the three friends
wanted to get to the hospital. That officer didn't have any children of her own
and didn't often have to deal with the wrath of protective Mother Hens. My
friends thought my son needed to be sheltered from questioning while he
adjusted to seeing his brother fly off his bike and lie quietly on the street, a pool
of blood haloing his head.

FOCUSING THE STORY

The neighbor, the guards, the friends, the police officer—all sorts of people and details pop into my mind when I think about this incident. And this tumble of memories is fine—when I am coming up with ideas. This is not the time for my ever-eager Critic Brain to swing into action to remind me I'm being disorganized.

Rather, slowly, feeling relaxed, I tell myself to zero in on the emergency room personnel, the doctors, nurses, and clerks. Maybe that guard could get into the story too. He was the greeter who set the tone for the hospital's mood of kindness and efficiency. Or I could change direction and focus on my friends and how quickly and efficiently they swung into action to help out. Or I could write about the police officer whose job was to get an accident report.

A Time to Focus: A Time to Unify

A story, like an office memo or a business letter, should have a central focus; it should have *unity*. Often there are side issues that are not directly related to the central issue. For instance, I did not even mention that when I learned about the accident I was returning from taking Snuzzy, a sick parakeet, to the vet. (By the way, Snuzzy has gone to that Big Aviary in the Sky. My son has recovered.)

Notice as you read the following, that I omitted side issues and zeroed in on a central point. I have given the story unity.

THE STORY IN FOCUS

The fear had long been there—looming like a storm cloud on the horizon. What if one of my children was in an accident? How efficient would my community's medical care be? I had read newspaper stories about hospitals who refused to treat children without parental consent. Even worse, I had read about hospitals refusing to treat patients who had no obvious means of paying.

Then one quiet, sunny August afternoon I got the answer to my worry-questions. When I got home from school that day, a neighbor was waiting in my driveway. She put her hand on my shoulder. "Don't get out of the car," she told me. "There has been an accident. Andrew has been taken to the hospital—about an hour ago. We tried to reach you . . . "

My heart froze as I listened to her quiet voice. Her words were a background hum as my thoughts tumbled over each other in terror. But, somehow the information registered, and I joined the thick tangle of traffic crawling up the two-lane highway toward the hospital.

By the time I reached Community Hospital, Fear had eaten away my outward calm. I abandoned my car in a spot guarded by a red "Restricted" sign. As I ran toward the emergency room doors, a uniformed guard started toward me.

"My son was hit by a delivery truck," I yelled at the guard without slowing my pace.

His glare of authority softened. "Don't worry about your car," he called. "And . . . I'm sure your son will be fine."

Panic reigned as I tried to organize my thoughts at the emergency desk. "My son was hit by a truck," I blurted.

"Oh, you must be Mrs. Martin." The receptionist smiled reassuringly. "Your son is in stable condition. Dr. Belza, a neurosurgeon, is with him. We aren't anticipating that we'll have to do surgery. The medication to keep his brain from swelling is working. I'll get someone to take you to him."

Somehow I digested this information and found it comforting. I had thought such information had to wait for a meeting with the doctor, but the receptionist had been anxious to reassure me. The IV's to keep Andrew's brain from swelling, the neurosurgeon, the rest of the medical treatment had begun long before they identified Andrew or knew who would pay for his care.

As I slept that night on a cot in a corner of Andrew's hospital room, ironically the sun had broken through one of my storm clouds of worry. In my community at least, medical care depends not on the age or financial status of the patient; it depends on the patient's need.

FOR THOUGHT AND DISCUSSION

1. In your own words, state the central point of "The Story in Focus."
2. What concrete details help you to understand both the emotional point and the intellectual point of the story?
3. How would the story have been changed if the dialogue had been omitted?

Professionals at Work

Let's examine the work of other professional writers who have stories to tell. Notice the way all the details in the stories help to communicate the central point or mood. The stories have unity.

Vocabulary   **erratic:**   not steady, irregular; having no certain course
incongruous: out of keeping; lacking in agreement or harmony

TALE OF THE RODENT
Roger Starr

The startled movement of a young woman in one corner of the bus shelter indicated that something was wrong. She moved again, a gesture of discomfort, even fear. Then I saw what troubled her: an infant rodent—perhaps a mouse, perhaps a rat—a small ball of brown cotton, with a toothpick for a tail. It had somehow crossed Seventh Avenue, climbed the curb and was moving through the shelter and across the sidewalk.

I say moving rather than running because the creature was too compact to reveal legs. Its speed was so **erratic,** and its direction so changeable, that it could have been a battery-driven toy riding on a hidden eccentric wheel. Another woman gasped at the sight of the little thing, children pointed, men went out of their way to avoid it.

To me it seemed more **incongruous** than scary, not merely outnumbered by people but intimidated by the hardness of the world into which it had suddenly emerged. From where? In what soft place on the other side of this busiest highway had its mother gnawed a nest in a fortress of brick and concrete, glass and steel?

Between the legs of pedestrians, the animal darted to the door of a candy store. Its feeding instincts were sound, although it could not poke through the slit between the bottom of the glass door and the sill. The instinct that had taken it to that store made its adult role obvious. It abandoned the candy store for the adjacent entrance to a large office building.

The superintendent, a bundle of keys hanging from his belt, was standing at the door. Rodent and superintendent vanished into the lobby, only to emerge moments later, animal first.

The superintendent kicked at it, driving the animal back to the sidewalk. Then he looked at me almost regretfully. Whatever the rodent might sometime become, the keeper of the keys knew it was not yet a fair match for the guardian of an office building.

The superintendent's kick must have hurt the animal; its movements became even more erratic than before. But to my astonishment, it crossed the curb and darted into the street, the traffic light in its favor. Unthinkingly wishing it safe passage, I saw it disappear beneath each passing car, then emerge again and move erratically onward.

The game—if game it was—was not to last. The light changed, releasing a torrent of cars across 44th Street, and when they had gone, the animal was left motionless on the pavement. No blood, no gore, just a tiny dead thing, hardly bigger than a large beetle, in the middle of the avenue, invisible to any passing motorist. Moments later my bus came and took me home to my apartment house.

I felt I had witnessed something small, but supremely serious.

FOR THOUGHT AND DISCUSSION

1. How do most people react to the word *rodent*?
2. Compare the author's reaction to the rodent to the reaction of the other people in the shelter.
3. Name other animals for which people share strong positive or negative feelings.
4. Which descriptive phrases help you to visualize the incident?
5. List the figurative language in the story.
6. Why did the author view this incident as "small, but supremely serious"?
7. What is the central point of the story?

Writing About Real Life

Notice that the narratives in the chapter are not about walking on the moon or slaying dragons. Rather their authors found significance in ordinary events, just as John Updike did when he wrote the following story about a supermarket checker.

Notice the way Updike's careful use of details and his imaginative use of figurative language make the incident at an A & P supermarket as vivid for the reader as an event sliced from real life.

A & P
John Updike

In walks these three girls in nothing but bathing suits. I'm in the third checkout slot, with my back to the door, so I don't see them until they're over by the bread. The one that caught my eye first was the one in the plaid green two-piece. She was a chunky kid, with a good tan and a sweet broad soft-looking can with those two crescents of white just under it, where the sun never seems to hit, at the top of the backs of her legs. I stood there with my hand on a box of HiHo crackers trying to remember if I rang it up or not. I ring it up again and the customer starts giving me hell. She's one of these cash-register-watchers, a witch about fifty with rouge on her cheekbones and no eyebrows, and I know it made her day to trip me up. She'd been watching cash registers for fifty years and probably never seen a mistake before.

By the time I got her feathers smoothed and her goodies into a bag—she gives me a little snort in passing, if she'd been born at the right time they would have burned her over in Salem—by the time I get her on her way the girls had circled around the bread and were coming back, without a pushcart, back my way along the counters, in the aisle between the checkouts and the Special bins. They didn't even have shoes on. There was this chunky one, with the two-piece—it was bright green and the seams on the bra were still sharp and her belly was still pretty pale so I guessed she just got it (the suit)—there was this one, with one of those chubby berry-faces, the lips all bunched together under her nose, this one, and a tall one, with black hair that hadn't quite frizzed right, and one of these sunburns right across under the eyes, and a chin that was too long—you know, the kind of girl other girls think is very "striking" and "attrac-tive" but never quite makes it, as they very well know, which is why they like her so much—and then the third one, that wasn't quite so tall. She was the queen. She kind of led them, the other two peeking around and making their shoulders round. She didn't look around, not this queen, she just walked straight on slowly, on these long white prima-donna legs. She came down a little hard on her heels, as if she didn't walk in her bare feet that much, putting down her heels and then letting the weight move along to her toes as if she was test-ing the floor with every step, putting a little deliberate extra action into it. You never know for sure how girls' minds work (do you really think it's a mind in there or just a little buzz like a bee in a glass jar?) but you got the idea she had talked the other two into coming in here with her, and now she was showing them how to do it, walk slow and hold yourself straight.

She had on a kind of dirty-pink—beige maybe, I don't know—bathing suit with a little nubble all over it and, what got me, the straps were down. They were off her shoulders looped loose around the cool tops of her arms, and I guess as a result the suit had slipped a little on her, so all around the top of the cloth there was this shining rim. If it hadn't been there you wouldn't have known there could have been anything whiter than those shoulders. With the straps pushed off, there was nothing between the top of the suit and the top of her head except just *her,* this clean bare plane of the top of her chest down from the shoulder bones like a dented sheet of metal tilted in the light. I mean, it was more than pretty.

She had sort of oaky hair that the sun and salt had bleached, done up in a bun that was unraveling, and a kind of prim face. Walking into the A & P with your straps down, I suppose it's the only kind of face you *can* have. She held her head so high her neck, coming up out of those white shoulders, looked kind of stretched, but I didn't mind. The longer her neck was, the more of her there was.

She must have felt in the corner of her eye me and over my shoulder Stokesie in the second slot watching, but she didn't tip. Not this queen. She kept her eyes moving across the racks, and stopped, and turned so slow it made my stomach rub the inside of my apron, and buzzed to the other two, who kind of huddled against her for relief, and then they all three of them went up the cat-and-dog-food-breakfast-cereal-macaroni-rice-raisins-seasonings-spreads-spaghetti-soft-drinks-crackers-and-cookies aisle. From the third slot I look straight up this aisle to the meat counter, and I watched them all the way. The fat one with the tan sort of fumbled with the cookies, but on second thought she put the package back. The sheep pushing their carts down the aisle—the girls were walking against the usual traffic (not that we have one-way signs or anything)—were pretty hilarious. You could see them, when Queenie's white shoulders dawned on them, kind of jerk, or hop, or hiccup, but their eyes snapped back to their own baskets and on they pushed. I bet you could set off dynamite in an A & P and the people would by and large keep reaching and checking oatmeal off their lists and muttering "Let me see, there was a third thing, began with A, asparagus, no ah, yes, applesauce!" or whatever it is they do mutter. But there was no doubt, this jiggled them. A few houseslaves in pin curlers even looked around after pushing their carts past to make sure what they had seen was correct.

You know, it's one thing to have a girl in a bathing suit down on the beach, where what with the glare nobody can look at each other much anyway, and another thing in the cool of the A & P, under the flourescent lights, against all those stacked packages, with her feet paddling along naked over our checkerboard green-and-cream rubber-tile floor.

"Oh Daddy," Stokesie said beside me. "I feel so faint."

"Darling," I said. "Hold me tight." Stokesie's married, with two babies chalked up on his fuselage already, but as far as I can tell that's the only difference. He's twenty-two, and I was nineteen this April.

"Is it done?" he asks, the responsible married man finding his voice. I forgot to say he thinks he's going to be manager some sunny day, maybe in 1990 when it's called the Great Alexandrov and Petrooshki Tea Company or something.

What he meant was, our town is five miles from a beach, with a big summer colony out on the Point, but we're right in the middle of town, and the women generally put on a shirt or shorts or something before they get out of the car into the street. And anyway these are usually women with six children and varicose veins mapping their legs and nobody, including them, could care less. As I say, we're right in the middle of town, and if you stand at our front doors you can see two banks and the Congregational church and the newspaper store and three real-estate offices and about twenty-seven old freeloaders tearing up Central Street because the sewer broke again. It's not as if we're on the Cape; we're north of Boston, and there's people in this town haven't seen the ocean for twenty years.

The girls had reached the meat counter and were asking McMahon something. He pointed, they pointed, and they shuffled out of sight behind a pyramid of Diet Delight peaches. All that was left for us to see was old McMahon patting his mouth and looking after them sizing up their joints. Poor kids, I began to feel sorry for them, they couldn't help it.

Now here comes the sad part of the story, at least my family says it's sad, but I don't think it's so sad myself. The store's pretty empty, it being Thursday afternoon, so there was nothing much to do except lean on the register and wait for the girls to show up again. The whole store was like a pinball machine and I didn't know which tunnel they'd come out of. After a while they come around out of the far aisle, around the light bulbs, records at discount of the Caribbean Six or Tony Martin Sings or some such gunk you wonder they waste the wax on, sixpacks of candy bars, and plastic toys done up in cellophane that fall apart when a kid looks at them anyway. Around they come, Queenie still leading the way, and holding a little gray jar in her hand. Slots Three through Seven are unmanned and I could see her wondering between Stokes and me, but Stokesie with his usual luck draws an old party in baggy gray pants who stumbles up with four giant cans of pineapple juice (what do these bums *do* with all that pineapple juice? I've often asked myself) so the girls come to me. Queenie puts down the jar and I take it into my fingers icy cold. Kingfish Fancy Herring Snacks in Pure Sour Cream: 49¢. Now her hands are empty, not a ring or a bracelet, bare as God made them, and I wonder where the money's coming from. Still with that prim look she lifts a folded dollar bill out of the hollow at the center of her nubbled pink top. The jar went heavy in my hand. Really, I thought that was so cute.

Then everybody's luck begins to run out. Lengel comes in from haggling with a truck full of cabbages on the lot and is about to scuttle into that door marked MANAGER behind which he hides all day when the girls touch his eye. Lengel's pretty dreary, teaches Sunday school and the rest, but he doesn't miss that much. He comes over and says, "Girls, this isn't the beach."

Queenie blushes, though maybe it's just a brush of sunburn I was noticing for the first time, now that she was so close. "My mother asked me to pick up a jar of herring snacks." Her voice kind of startled me, the way voices do when you see the people first, coming out so flat and dumb yet kind of tony, too, the way it ticked over "pick up" and "snacks." All of a sudden I slid right down her voice into her living room. Her father and the other men were standing around in ice-cream coats and bow ties and the women were in sandals picking up herring snacks on toothpicks off a big glass plate and they were all holding drinks the color of water with olives and sprigs of mint in them. When my parents have somebody over they get lemonade and if it's a real racy affair Schlitz in tall glasses with "They'll Do It Every Time" cartoons stenciled on.

"That's all right," Lengel said. "But this isn't the beach." His repeating this struck me as funny, as if it had just occurred to him, and he had been thinking all these years the A & P was a great big dune and he was the head lifeguard. He didn't like my smiling—as I say he doesn't miss much—but he concentrates on giving the girls that sad Sunday-school-superintendent stare.

Queenie's blush is no sunburn now, and the plump one in plaid, that I liked better from the back—a really sweet can—pipes up, "We weren't doing any shopping. We just came in for the one thing."

"That makes no difference," Lengel tells her, and I could see from the way his eyes went that he hadn't noticed she was wearing a two-piece before. "We want you decently dressed when you come in here."

"We *are* decent," Queenie says suddenly, her lower lip pushing, getting sore now that she remembers her place, a place from which the crowd that runs the A & P must look pretty crummy. Fancy Herring Snacks flashed in her very blue eyes.

"Girls, I don't want to argue with you. After this come in here with your shoulders covered. It's our policy." He turns his back. That's policy for you. Policy is what the kingpins want. What the others want is juvenile delinquency.

All this while, the customers had been showing up with their carts but, you know, sheep, seeing a scene, they had all bunched up on Stokesie, who shook open a paper bag as gently as peeling a peach, not wanting to miss a word. I could feel in the silence everybody getting nervous, most of all Lengel, who asks me, "Sammy, have you rung up their purchase?"

I thought and said "No" but it wasn't about that I was thinking. I go through the punches, 4, 9, GROC, TOT—it's more complicated than you think, and after you do it often enough, it begins to make a little song, that you hear words to, in my case "Hello *(bing)* there, you *(gung)* hap-py *pee*-pul *(splat)*!"—the *splat* being the drawer flying out. I uncrease the bill, tenderly as you may imagine, it just having come from between the two smoothest scoops of vanilla I had ever known were there, and pass a half and a penny into her narrow pink palm, and nestle the herrings in a bag and twist its neck and hand it over, all the time thinking.

The girls, and who'd blame them, are in a hurry to get out, so I say "I quit" to Lengel quick enough for them to hear, hoping they'll stop and watch me, their unsuspected hero. They keep right on going, into the electric eye; the door flies open and they flicker across the lot to their car, Queenie and Plaid and Big Tall Goony-Goony (not that as raw material she was so bad), leaving me with Lengel and a kink in his eyebrow.

"Did you say something, Sammy?"

"I said I quit."

"I thought you did."

"You didn't have to embarrass them."

"It was they who were embarrassing us."

I started to say something that came out "Fiddle-de-doo." It's a saying of my grandmother's, and I know she would have been pleased.

"I don't think you know what you're saying," Lengel said.

"I know you don't," I said. "But I do." I pull the bow at the back of my apron and start shrugging it off my shoulders. A couple customers that had been heading for my slot begin to knock against each other, like scared pigs in a chute.

Lengel sighs and begins to look very patient and old and gray. He's been a friend of my parents for years. "Sammy, you don't want to do this to your Mom and Dad," he tells me. It's true, I don't. But it seems to me that once you begin a gesture it's fatal not to go through with it. I fold the apron, "Sammy" stiched in red on the pocket, and put it on the counter, and drop the bow tie on top of it. The bow tie is theirs, if you've ever wondered. "You'll feel this for the rest of your life," Lengel says, and I know that's true, too, but remembering how he made that pretty girl blush makes me so scrunchy inside I punch the No Sale tab and the machine whirs "pee-pul" and the drawer splats out. One advantage to this scene taking place in summer, I can follow this up with a clean exit, there's no fumbling around getting your coat and galoshes, I just saunter into the electric eye in my white shirt that my mother ironed the night before, and the door heaves itself open, and outside the sunshine is skating around on the asphalt.

I look around for my girls, but they're gone, of course. There wasn't any-body but some young married screaming with her children about some candy they didn't get by the door of a powder-blue Falcon station wagon. Looking back in the big windows, over the bags of peat moss and aluminum lawn furniture stacked on the pavement, I could see Lengel in my place in the slot, checking the sheep through. His face was dark gray and his back stiff, as if he'd just had an injection of iron, and my stomach kind of fell as I felt how hard the world was going to be to me hereafter.

FOR THOUGHT AND DISCUSSION

1. Why does Sammy say, "I felt how hard the world was going to be to me hereafter"?
2. List figurative language in the story.
3. Which details show the kind of people who frequented A & P?
4. Which details show the difference between the usual customers and the three young ladies in bathing suits?
5. Should Sammy have quit his job? Why or why not?
6. What is Updike's central point in the story?

WRITING ASSIGNMENT
Using What You Have Learned

Write an essay of at least two hundred words about a unique experience you have had. First experiences are good candidates—for example, the first time you drove a car, the first time you got your driver's license, or the first time you went on a date.

In your essay remember the following:

1. If you quote people, use dialogue.
2. Use a metaphor, a simile, or personification at least once.
3. Show your reader your story through vivid concrete details.
4. Use vivid, active verbs.
5. Create unity by selecting details that show readers your central point.

STUDENT STARS ESSAYS
The Polished Product

As you read the narratives written by the following student authors, note the way they made good use of concrete details and vivid metaphorical language to show the incidents about which they write.

***Remember: the authors of these essays used the following steps:

1. Prewriting
2. Writing
3. Revising content
4. Proofreading and correcting mechanical errors

THERE'S NO PLACE LIKE HOME

Moving away from your parents can be very frightening, but when I turned twenty-one, I got a job as the head chef at East of Eden, a restaurant in Salinas, California. The job meant leaving home. My mother protested loud and long— but not as loud and long as she would have protested had she known what awaited me.

Shortly after starting the job, having spent a long day in the kitchen, I walked out of the restaurant into the misty Salinas night. Because I lived only a mile away, it was easy for me to walk. Having to transportation except my feet made it even easier. Unfortunately, my path lay through one of the sleazier parts of Salinas. On a dark stretch of road, I heard the scuffling of feet behind me. My pace quickened. I glanced over my shoulder and saw the silhouettes of two medium-sized men. Almost running, I cut through a parking lot toward the safety of a street light. Before I could reach the circle of safety, two more men blocked my path. "What's your hurry?" the larger one said. "We want to talk to you."

By this time the other two were right behind me. "What do you want?" I stammered.

"We just want to talk to you, man," the leader said. "What are you running for? Do you have something to hide?"

This was his cue to swing. I saw the motion of his arms and ducked. He hit one of his henchmen. This made him mad. "A wise ass, huh?"

The leader's knee shot into my gut. My assailants seemed to be getting taller and my breath shorter. Writhing in pain, I lay on the ground as the henchmen searched for their bounty. Tearing out the pockets of my pants and jacket, they found the money I was carrying.

"Hey, man, he only has fifty cents on him!" a henchman said. Looking down on me the leader spat on me and kicked me twice.

"Then let's go play some video games on Smart Ass here." Patting themselves on their backs like Roman warriors, they left laughing. It must have been thirty minutes before I could get up. Victimized and brutalized I went home— disgusted but still alive.

Gene Moana

ONE STRIKE AND YOU'RE OUT

My heart was thumping, not from excitement but from fear. My stepsister had set me up with one of her friends. We were going to double date. Being only fourteen, I didn't have much dating experience. In fact I had none. I was self-conscious. I was going through puberty and it didn't set well. My voice was always cracking like I had just swallowed a feather. I was tall and lanky and not at all graceful. Acne was beginning to dot my face. Worst of all, I wore big black-rimmed glasses that kept sliding down my nose. However, I agreed to go through with the date.

I spent most of Saturday morning caking on the Clearasil and washing it off my face trying to clear up those pubescent spots before the big evening. I spent hours in front of the mirror practicing my smile and what I would say: "Hello, Cathy. Hi, Cathy. Nice to meet you, Cathy." Each time making the tone of my voice go deeper. If someone were to walk by they might think I was rehearsing to be a contestant on *Dating Game.*

When I arrived at my stepsister's home I was disappointed. Not from meeting Cathy. She was terrific. I was disappointed that we would not be going to a movie. I would have felt more secure at a movie. My acne would disappear in the darkness, I wouldn't have to talk much, and I wouldn't have to wear my glasses. I would know what was happening just by listening. I had, in fact, left my glasses at home.

When we entered the bowling alley, the bright lights made my pimples glisten. I hated those lights. Everyone could see my every move. Here I was blind as a bat, tripping over my shoes and looking like Jerry Lewis in *The Nutty Professor.* I didn't even know how to bowl. I selected a ball that my puny arms could lift and waited my turn, making sure I was last so I could see how it was done. My turn came and I walked stiffly to the line. Trying to focus on those fuzzy things down that long alley, I swung the ball back ready to roll it. I fell flat on my face with that big black ball still clinging to my fingers. The last thing I remember is laughter before the memories of this date drift off into a haze.

Rick Lee

The author of the following narrative is a petite lady.

PARADISE LOST

Have you ever wondered how you would react if you found yourself in a situation where your actions would determine whether someone lived or died? I found myself in just such a situation when I was living in San Francisco several years ago.

It was my last night in the city. The next day I would be Hawaii-bound to start a new life in paradise. On top of the world and filled with positive expectations, I truly felt that there were only good things ahead for me.

I had so much energy that evening, I decided to go to Golden Gate Park for a tennis lesson. Dressing quickly in my sweats and tennis shoes, topping my outfit with a very yang headband of black,white and blood red, I felt like a samurai warrior ready to do battle. My invincible tennis racket swung over my shoulder, I took off running to the courts.

As I made my way through the park, the atmosphere created by the rolling San Francisco fog and the sunlight filtering through the trees seemed like a scene from a Fellini film. I passed several people but hardly noticed them—a man of medium stature . . . a girl with a sweater tied around her shoulders. She was obvious in her lackadaisical walk, a deadpan expression on her face—a total contrast to my present state.

Shortly after I passed the girl, something made me turn around. For a moment I could not believe what I saw. The man had grabbed the girl around the neck and was dragging her off the sidewalk onto the grass.

A series of thoughts flashed through my mind: Were they playing: Did they know each other? Should I stop them?

Suddenly I knew they were not playing. I must stop them. The man's eyes were glassy and his movements were jerky and rough. The girl looked like a rag doll in his hold, lifeless, offering no resistance. She was not making a sound. I knew her fate was up to me!

Running toward them at full gallop, wielding my samurai tennis racket over my head, I yelled at the top of my voice, "Let her go! Let her go!"

Distracted, he released her. I quickly grabbed her hand and pulled her away shouting, "Let's get out of here!"

We ran to the tennis courts, never looking back and called the police. The girl was dazed but unhurt, and I was just thankful to have gotten away.

As I walked back to my apartment, I felt like I had just been the heroine in my own television drama. And I wondered how many similar scenes were being enacted in San Francisco that night. I hope they all ended as happily as mine had.

Socorro Gutierrez

HELP! FOR FURTHER WORK

Read "My First Pair of High Heel Shoes" and answer the Thought and Discussion questions which follow it.

MY FIRST PAIR OF HIGH HEEL SHOES

I can remember this day very well. Its one of my happiest memories. I was fourteen years old. I begged and I begged, almost down on my knees' asking my mother to please buy me a pair of high heel shoes. At this time all of my friend's were wearing high heels.

My mother shouted Sally, your too tall for high heel shoes.

I was five-feet-ten-inches at fourteen—taller than all the boys' in my class. In fact, I never had a boyfriend who was taller than I was in high school.

Finally I got the shoes. Can you see me long and lean almost reaching the sky? I was very happy. Although I looked like a giant and my five-foot-eight-inch boyfriend looked like my little brother.

FOR THOUGHT AND DISCUSSION

1. Write positive criticism about this theme. Remember that positive criticism mentions strengths and makes specific suggestions for revision.
2. Rewrite the last paragraph to make it more concrete.
3. Correct the mechanical errors in "My First Pair of High Heel Shoes," which are covered in the first nineteen items of "The Final Touch: A Handbook." Read "The Apostrophe" beginning on page 291 of "The Final Touch: A Handbook," and correct the use of apostrophes in the essay.

8

THE TOPIC AND THESIS SENTENCE

The aboutness puts an argumentative edge on the subject. When you have something to say about cats, you have found your underlying idea. You have something to defend, something to fight about: not just "Cats," but "The cat is really man's best friend." Now the hackles on all dog men are rising, and you have an argument on your hands. You have something to prove. You have a thesis.

Sheridan Baker, **The Practical Stylist**

> **CONCEPTS TO LEARN**
>
> • The three components of a topic sentence
>
> • The difference between a topic sentence and a thesis sentence
>
> • The use of a topic and thesis sentence in an essay
>
> • The importance of supporting details for topic and thesis sentences
>
> • The effective use of transitions in an essay

CAN A BALLAD BY ANY OTHER NAME SOUND AS SWEET?

As you read the following Woody Guthrie poem, your Left Brain Critic may jump up and down, laughing, "Ho, ho. The stupid author doesn't know Woody Guthrie was writing a folk song, not a poem."

Shove Lefty back in his closet. Songs, in fact, are poems set to music. Long before English classes began, men and women sat around campfires and exercised their right brains by recording their experiences in song-poems. Astoundingly, these people of ancient times recited poetry, not for a letter grade or even for a credit-no credit option. They were doing something that is natural to humans; they were expressing themselves with rhyme and rhythm in vivid, concrete words, using lots of figurative language.

In fact, the first stories passed from generation to generation (like *Beowulf* of Chapter One) were ballads, that is, stories told in song. Music appeals to the Right Brain Creator, and words that have rhyme and rhythm are easier to remember than words without a regular pattern. For this reason, nursery rhymes were probably the first groups of words you memorized.

Woody Guthrie was inspired to write the following ballad when, on January 28, 1948, twenty-eight workers who were being deported to Mexico died in a fiery plane crash.

Vocabulary   **creosote:**   an oily liquid used to preserve wood
"adiós, mes amigos":   "goodbye, my friends"

Plane Wreck at Los Gatos (Deportee)*

The crops are all in and the peaches are rott'ning
The oranges piled in their **creosote** dumps;

---

* "Plane Wreck at Los Gatos (Deportee)" lyric by Woody Guthrie, music by Martin Hoffman. TRO copyright © 1961 (renewed 1963) Ludlow Music, Inc. New York, NY. Used by permission.

You're flying them back to the Mexican border
To pay all their money, to wade back again.

Refrain:
    Goodbye to my Juan, Goodbye Rosalita;
    Adiós mes amigos, Jesús y Maria,
    You won't have your names when you ride the big airplane;
    And all they will call you will be deportees.

My father's own father he waded that river;
They took all the money he made in his life:
My brothers and sisters come working the fruit trees
And they rode the truck till they took down and died.

Some of us are illegal and some are not wanted.
Our work contract's out and we have to move on;
Six hundred miles to that Mexican border,
They chase us like outlaws, like rustlers, like thieves.

We died in your hills, we died in your deserts,
We died in your valleys and died on your plains;
We died 'neath your trees and we died in your bushes,
Both sides of this river we died just the same.

The sky plane caught fire over Los Gatos Canyon,
A fireball of lightning and shook all our hills.
Who are all these friends all scattered like dry leaves?
The radio says they are just deportees.

Is this the best way we can grow our big orchards?
Is this the best way we can grow our good fruit?
To fall like dry leaves to rot on my topsoil
And be called by no name except deportees?

Woody Guthrie

FOR THOUGHT AND DISCUSSION

1. What had the workers just finished when they were deported?
2. Give an example of a metaphor in the poem.
3. State the central point of "Plane Wreck at Los Gatos" in your own words.

SO WHAT'S THE POINT?

In Chapters Five, Six and Seven, you concentrated on selecting details that showed readers a central point, just as Guthrie did in "Plane Wreck at Los Gatos." When you focus on the details relevant to a central point, you are halfway to a topic or thesis sentence.

A *topic sentence* states the central point of a paragraph or a cluster of related paragraphs. A topic sentence then works with concrete examples to prove your point to readers.

The Big Three

A topic sentence must do the following three things:

1. Introduce an idea
2. Limit the idea
3. State an opinion that can be supported by evidence

Introducing an idea alerts readers to the subject of your essay. An example of an idea is the subject of drugs.

Limiting the idea is the same as the focusing done in Chapters Five, Six, and Seven. An example of a focused idea about drugs is athletes using steroids.

Stating an opinion that can be supported by evidence is exemplified by the "argumentative edge" in the quotation which introduces this chapter. In the last three chapters, you used concrete details to make your central point. In other words, you supported your point with specific evidence. While your support for a topic sentence is concrete, the topic sentence, itself, is abstract. The topic sentence is the idea you are going to prove—or show—to your readers. The following sentence from Pete Axtheim's article in *Newsweek*, "A Star Flunks His Test," is an example of a well-constructed topic sentence:

> While the hazards of steroids are fairly well documented, the question of how and whether they should be used remains highly controversial.

WRITING EXERCISE
It's Your Turn

1. Return to the cartoon at the beginning of the chapter. What is its topic sentence? What concrete details develop that sentence?
2. Make up a topic sentence Cathy might use to sell her car. Suggest concrete details to support the topic sentence.

Topic Sentences Are Important—They Are Not Mickey Mouse.

Analyze the way the author of the following article from *Newsweek* states a topic sentence and then presents concrete details to show that point.

Since her creation, Minnie Mouse has been overshadowed by her more dynamic rodent companion Mickey. In an attempt to keep up with the changing image of women, however, Walt Disney Productions has decided that Minnie should have her own spotlight.

WHO SAID MINNIE WAS MOUSY?
from *Newsweek*

The face is familiar, but my goodness, check out the style: lime green jumper, trashy purple beads, red lace fingerless gloves. She's hot. She's now. She's an eighties kinda gal—Minnie Mouse, who has undergone a startling fashion make-over, from plain Jane to downtown fun machine. A rodent Madonna. Literally a party animal.

The idea is for Minnie to break out of Mickey's shadow, much as Tina Turner separated herself from ex-husband Ike, and spin off a batch of profitable products. Minnie, of course, has an advantage that Tina never had: the formidable marketing muscle of the Walt Disney Company. An LP, "Totally Minnie," was recently released and a video for the title tune is due out in March. Over the next year the all-new Minnie will star in her own TV special, appear at shopping malls, lead a parade at Disneyland and a stage show at Disney World, put out a line of plush toys and a collection of children's clothing. "Who knows what I'll be up to next!" she squeaks in a Disney press release.

FOR THOUGHT AND DISCUSSION

1. What is the topic sentence of "Who Said Minnie Was Mousy?"
2. What concrete details develop the topic sentence?
3. Will the new Minnie be more or less of an ideal for feminists than the original Minnie? State your answer in the form of a topic sentence and then give three concrete sentences supporting it.

Team Work with Topic and Thesis Sentences

Essays often have several topic sentences that work together to develop the overall central point, that is, the *thesis* of an essay.

A *thesis sentence* states the central point of an essay long enough to contain several topic sentences. Short essays such as the assignments for this book may have only a topic sentence.

The following essay has several topic sentences that support its larger thesis sentence. To see how topic sentences work to support a central thesis, read the following article and answer its "For Thought and Discussion" questions.

CONFESSIONS OF A NICOTINE FREAK
Jack E. White

For twenty-six years I've been a slave to cigarettes. For at least ten, I've been trying to emancipate myself. Only nicotine freaks who have tried repeatedly to kick the habit and failed can fully appreciate how difficult it is to give it up.

I started smoking at fifteen in order to feel more grownup. It wasn't long after my first drag on a cigarette—in a locked bathroom with the windows wide open so the telltale odor would dissipate—that the cough I developed suggested that smoking was a mistake. Nevertheless, I kept puffing away relentlessly until my smoke rings were picture perfect. A year later, motivated perhaps by the vivid illustrations in my father's medical textbooks, I made my first effort to quit. It fizzled out under the pressure of high school final exams.

I've tried a multitude of techniques to wrestle the nicotine monkey from my back: cold turkey (five or six times), hypnosis (once), and tapering down (more times than you could count). Switching to brands with less tar and nicotine than the ususal lung busters. Putting mayonnaise jars stuffed with butts on the desk, nightstand, and bathroom shelf as nauseating reminders of what smoking was doing to my lungs, which after some 250,000 cigarettes must be as sotty as an unswept chimney flue. Chomping on golf ball-sized wads of foul-tasting nicotine chewing gum. Toting up what a two-pack-a-day habit costs over the course of a year: more than one thousand dollars up in smoke.

Nothing has worked for more than three months. Not—in my case at least—because withdrawing from cigarettes causes excruciating physical agony. Far from it: the mild jitteriness and irritability last only a few days. Nor have I been tempted to substitute insatiable eating for smoking. In my experience, the biggest threat to the fledgling nonsmoker is the nicotine habit's subtle, sneak-thief ability to reassert itself whenever one's guard is down. Almost any of life's little anxieties can trigger an irresistible urge to light up. More vexing still, many of life's pleasures—sex, a cup of coffee, just getting up in the morning—can have the same effect.

Overconfidence can undermine even a seemingly victorious campaign to abstain. Take, as a dismaying case study, the last time I quit. A hypnotist implanted a mantra in my subconscious, to be summoned up whenever I felt the urge: "Smoking is bad for me." For this service, the hypnotist demanded two hundred dollars, which seemed a wise investment. It worked. Food tasted better. Morning bouts of coughing ceased. I felt great. So great that three months later, I decided to prove I was truly liberated by attempting to smoke *just one* without becoming hooked again. Before I knew it, I was back to two packs a day.

Medical researchers have now substantiated what failed nonsmokers discovered long ago: smoking is a powerful addiction. Unable to free themselves, nicotine addicts often seek to justify their cravenness with bombastic rationalizations that smoking is a matter of considered choice—and their constitutional rights. "I can quit whenever I want to, but I don't want to right now," the smoker tells himself and the world. It just ain't so.

Perhaps New York City's stringent new antismoking law, which went into effect last week, will finally accomplish what willpower, peer pressure, and nagging by my children have failed to do. From now on, having a smoke means slinking off, like a junkie in search of a fix, to the designated smoking area, fittingly located in the men's room. Even for a hardened nicotine freak like me, that is too much of a nuisance. Still, I'm not confident. As I write, a pack of cigarettes stares up from my desk, silently imploring me to light up just one more time.

FOR THOUGHT AND DISCUSSION

1. What is the thesis sentence of this selection?
2. List the topic sentences that support this thesis.
3. After each topic sentence, list the concrete details that support it.

4. Why does the author use a series of sentence fragments to end the second paragraph? What effect do the fragments help him make?
5. What effect was the author trying to create by using *ain't* at the end of the fifth paragraph?

The Future Predicted in Thesis and Topic Sentences

In the following essay from *Money*, author Lani Luciano dips into the future using a team of topic sentences to support her thesis, which concerns what our workplaces will be like in the year 2000.

SEEING THE FUTURE WORK AT IBM
Lani Luciano

The corporate workplace of the future will probably not differ greatly from conditions already enjoyed by the 400,000 employees of International Business Machines. By 2000 it's expected to be the biggest company on earth, and other firms are likely to adopt its successful methods.

Employees like IBM so much now that fewer than 1 percent leave by choice every year. Says Victor Heckler, a Chicago consultant, "IBM knows how to pick the people it needs, develop them, and motivate them. So they stay, grow in their jobs, and become more valuable." Some ways the IBM system works:

Corporate culture.   Nobody ever forgets whom he works for or why he's there—or that the company is a stern taskmaster. Promotions are made on merit only, and employees who consistently fail to meet objectives are fired, as are those who run afoul of the thirty-page ethics code that covers, for example, company secrets. On the other hand, no one loses his job because of an economic downturn or personal misfortune, such as an illness or marital troubles.

Recognition.   It's frequent, direct, and tangible. Each year about 25 percent of IBM's employees earn cash bonuses by, for instance, improving a sales presentation. Salaries, however, are only slightly higher than the industry average.

Equality.   In 1958 IBM blurred the distinction between white-and blue-collar work by abolishing hourly wages, and there are no highly visible perks. Among managers, about 14 percent are women and 10 percent are minorities. In 1984 36 percent of all company-wide new hires were women and 20 percent were minorities.

Education.   Managers spend at least forty hours a year in classrooms improving their management skills. Sample lesson: always finish sentences; don't make people read body language. Several thousand technicians are retrained annually.

Participation.   To monitor morale, IBM frequently surveys employee opinion on everything from cafeteria food to the performance of top managers. Executives are encouraged to challenge any business plan they think is ill advised. "Bureaucracy is our enemy," says Walton Burdick, vice-president for personnel. "It stifles initiative."

Entrepreneurship.   Since 1963 IBM has provided a few extraordinary employees called IBM Fellows with the staff and financial support to pursue their own ideas. One of its first independent business units developed IBM's highly successful personal computer. Now there are ten of the semiautonomous units.

Responsiveness.   Nine-months-a-year jobs are occasionally available in categories such as systems analyst and computer programmer. Staffers nearing retirement can take company-paid courses on such subjects as starting a second career and finding a retirement community. IBM doesn't supply day-care, but it does provide a nationwide referral service on where to find day-care centers as well as seed money to develop suitable facilities in areas that lack them. Nor does it allow employees to work at home instead of in the office.

Not surprisingly, the embrace of this beneficient uncle can prove suffocating to some people. A few former employees complain that IBM is too big and too predictable, supportive but not exciting. Since most are hired at entry level, fast trackers are identified early, but late bloomers sometimes not at all. Says ex-manager Robert McGrath, now an executive recruiter who publishes the IBM Alumni Directory, which is sold to recruiters, "I left because even though I felt good about my job, I couldn't make a real difference."

What might the IBM of the year 2000 be like? William Simmons, IBM's long-range planner from 1967 to 1972 and now a consultant, offers a hint: the computer giant will further decentralize so that divisions can act more autonomously and employees feel that they are in charge of their own destinies. Says Simmons, "If any company can achieve that elusive environment in which no one feels left behind, it'll be IBM."

FOR THOUGHT AND DISCUSSION

1. Give concrete examples of differences between your workplace and the one described in the article. If you do not work, use a workplace you know about.
2. What are the greatest advantages of working for IBM?
3. What are the greatest disadvantages of working for IBM?
4. Write a thesis sentence for the article.
5. Under the thesis, list the topic sentences.
6. Under the topic sentences, list their concrete support.

A Team of Topics Help a Thesis Score Its Point

In the following article from *Discover*, former professional baseball player and manager Steve Boros uses a team of topic sentences to develop his thesis about the importance of computers to baseball.

EXCERPTS FROM COMPUTERS IN THE DUGOUT
Steve Boros

There are many possible uses for the computer in baseball—the most obvious one administrative. Scouting information on the thousands of major and minor league players and free agents . . . throughout the world could be stored in a

The A's battled Murphy (right) in clean-up position because the computer showed he was hitting .444 against the Tiger's Petry (left); result: a grand slam.

club's computer. Whenever the club considered acquiring a player it could have all the scouting reports on that player printed out at a moment's notice. That information would include written reports by every scout who saw that player, as well as statistical data.

The computer could be used as a teaching tool as well. For example, pitching coaches and managers have been imploring pitchers, since Abner Doubleday put them out on that mound in the middle of the diamond, to get ahead in the count. Computer printouts could be used to show disbelieving pitchers how a hitter's batting decreases the more the pitcher gets ahead in the count, and how the hitter's average gets further behind. (Batting instructors could use the same printouts as a tool to teach patience to their hitters.)

Another possible use for the computer is in an area that has been largely overlooked—the evaluation of baseball tactics. I think the computer, if enough accurate information is compiled, can answer a lot of questions about the validity of certain tactical moves, such as the sacrifice bunt and the stolen base. But a tremendous amount of data would be required. . . .

Finally, we come to the use of the computer in the dugout. Allowing that present baseball rules do not permit the presence of a television monitor in the dugout, I still don't see any major obstacles to having a computer on the bench. Many clubs already use walkie-talkies in their dugouts to receive directions from a scout in the press box (''an eye in the sky'') as to how their fielders should be positioned. [Let's imagine what would have happened in a great hitter-pitcher battle of the past had a computer been in the dugout:]

Reggie Jackson, the Angels's slugger is at the plate facing Bill Caudill, the A's ace reliever. A coach assigned to the computer punches in the necessary information and the screen shows a diagram of the strike zone. The diagram shows the type and location of the pitches thrown by Caudill in the past that Reggie has missed or hit poorly. The computer has selected the three best pitches to throw Jackson to get him out. It indicates as well the type and location of pitches to be thrown out of the strike zone in order to set up the pitches used to get Jackson out. The pitching coach or manager uses a system of signs with the catcher to insure that the proper pitch sequence will be used.

The coach at the computer punches in more information, and a diagram of a baseball field appears. This display shows what happened to all the balls Jackson has hit off Caudill (hits, outs, errors, fielder's choices, and so on). The display also reveals the kind of pitch that was hit and where it was located in the strike zone. As the count changes, the display changes; most hitters will hit differently depending on what the count is. Another coach signals the infielders and outfielders, who adjust their positions accordingly.

Now the best possible choice of pitches and location is combined with the best possible alignment of the infield and outfield to give Bill Caudill of the A's the best opportunity to get Reggie Jackson out. Reggie may still air-mail one to the bleachers. . . . But in terms of preparation we have done everything we can to get Jackson out. Now it comes down to pitcher versus hitter, one of the most exciting confrontations in sports.

There are other ways the computer in the dugout can be used to help the defensive team. The coach at the computer could punch in information as the game progresses. And as certain runners get on base, certain hitters come to the plate, and the count and out situation changes, the computer could alert the manager to the possibilities of a steal, a bunt, a hit-and-run, a suicide squeeze, or whatever tendency the computer has discerned in the opposing team based on all the collected data.

The coach at the computer could call up the same sort of data when his team was hitting. The computer would then tell the manager when he had fallen into an obvious pattern that the opposing team might recognize, or when the opposing team could be surprised by a certain tactic. And of course the computer could help each hitter determine how the opposing pitcher was pitching him.

FOR THOUGHT AND DISCUSSION

1. Write a thesis sentence for "Computers in the Dugout."
2. What topic sentences does Boros use to develop his thesis?
3. How does the tone of this article differ from the style in "Who Said Minnie Was Mousy?" (Read Chapter Six to review style.)

SO FAR SO GOOD: NOW SOME WORDS OF CAUTION

Remember the following three tips when composing thesis sentences:

1. Topic and thesis sentences are complete sentences. They are not titles.
   A title: The Controversy Concerning Surrogate Mothers
   A thesis sentence: Surrogate motherhood is raising important legal and ethical questions.

2. Topic and thesis sentences are statements. They do not ask questions.

   A question: Are adjustable-rate mortgages the best choice?

   A thesis sentence: Adjustable-rate mortgages offer an attractive option to home buyers with a gambling instinct and a sound financial base.

3. Topic and thesis ideas sometimes take more than one sentence to express. If you cannot fit your idea smoothly into a single sentence, do not stuff, cram, or jump up and down on the sentence. Simply write another sentence or two.

   The following is an example of *too much stuffing for one sentence:*

   > Because it takes so much time for light from distant stars to reach Earth, astronomers who study the evolution of the cosmos can witness events that happened billions of years ago, and this ability to see into the past gives these astronomers an enviable advantage over more worldly historians.

The Team Approach to a Thesis Idea

The following excerpt from Sharon Begley's article, "A Cosmic Birth Announcement," is an example of a well-expressed thesis idea:

> Astronomers who study the evolution of the cosmos have an enviable advantage over more worldly historians: the universe's past is still gloriously present. Because it takes time for light from distant stars to reach Earth, astronomers can witness events that happened billions of years ago.

Occasionally, a writer does not actually state a thesis idea. Instead, concrete development leads the reader to understand the thesis without actually having it stated. For instance, Woody Guthrie did not state his thesis in "Plane Wreck at Los Gatos." Since poetry appeals primarily to the right brain, it is less likely to have a stated thesis sentence than an essay. Essays, on the other hand, gain more attention from the left brain once writers rummage around in their right brains to find the ideas and images needed to express and develop a central point.

***Remember: Stating your thesis pays big dividends for both you and your reader. Your thesis statement will help your reader follow your ideas. In addition, stating your thesis clarifies it for you and keeps you from getting sidetracked to issues not directly relevant to your point.

WRITING EXERCISE
It's Your Turn

1. Which of the following are good topic or thesis sentences? Which sentences should be thesis sentences because they are too complex to develop in a single paragraph?

2. Explain what is wrong with those sentences that are inadequate.
3. What type of information would you need to develop the good topic and thesis sentences?

    a. Spanish is the national language in Central American countries.
    b. Spelling in Spanish is easier than spelling in English.
    c. Guatemala has a large Indian population.
    d. Cultural and economic differences cause conflict between Guatemala's Spanish and Indian citizens.
    e. Democracy means sometimes having to accept policies with which you disagree.
    f. God disapproves of _____. (You fill in the blank.)
    g. Learning disabilities often cause serious psychological problems.
    h. The services offered by computer dealers are as important as the products they sell and the prices they charge.
    i. Careers are more attractive to women than early marriage.
    j. Basic writing skills are important today.

MORE PRACTICE

Use the following six steps to help you develop a thesis sentence and topic sentences for an essay:

1. Write a thesis sentence about a current, controversial issue. Begin by using one of the three prewriting techniques we have discussed to decide what you want to say. Then, when an idea crystallizes for you, write a thesis sentence. Hint: current controversial issues are as common as fleas, and they come in as many different sizes, shapes, and personalities as dogs do. Examples include nuclear power, the death penalty, abortion, arms limitation, defense spending, taxes, Central America, the Middle East, mercy killing (euthanasia)—all have controversial issues attached to them.
2. Check your sentence.
    a. Do you adequately limit your subject? Most current controversial issues have enough aspects for a whole book, not just one paper.
    b. Do you state a complete sentence and not just a title?
    c. Do you make a statement and not ask a question?
    d. Do you make a statement you could develop with facts?
3. When you have finished writing, share your sentence with your classmates.
4 As you share the sentences, help each other by pointing out revisions that would improve the statements.
5. If your sentence needs revision, remember the principles of positive criticism from Chapter Two. Do not be too hard on yourself. If everyone was going to do this perfectly, we would skip the exer-

cise. Often we learn most by revising our mistakes. Hank Aaron did not hit the first ball he swung at out of the park. He missed a few—and he learned from his mistakes.

6. Once you have a good thesis sentence, list three topic sentences you could use with it. Then repeat Steps 4–6.

SMOOTHING THE WAY WITH TRANSITIONS

Transitions are bridges between your ideas. Transitions help bridge gaps in your ideas so readers can cross from one idea to the next. Although the concept of *transition* in writing may be new to you, you are already accustomed to responding to them, as shown in the following examples.

Examples of Transitions

To increase your incentive to write a good topic sentence, I thought about giving each student writing a good topic sentence a reward of twenty-five dollars. *However . . .*

When you see the transition word *however*, you know what is coming next—a reason not to give you twenty-five dollars. However, if we substitute a transition word like *and, or, moreover,* or *furthermore,* for the word *however,* the message would be far different. Other examples of transitions include the following: *and, adjacent to, after, after a few days, although, as if, because, before, besides, but, even if, ever since, finally, first, for, for example, for this reason, furthermore, hence, here, if, in addition, in contrast, indeed, in fact, likewise, next, opposite to, or, second, similarly, since, so, unless, until, whatever, when, where, whereas, whether, while, why,* and *yet.* Of course, there are many others.

WRITING EXERCISE
It's Your Turn

The most common transitions fit into the following categories:

1. Addition (words like *furthermore*)
2. Comparison (words like *similarly*)
3. Place (words like *opposite to*)
4. Purpose (words like *for this purpose*)
5. Result (words like *therefore*)
6. Summary (words like *in brief*)
7. Exemplification and emphasis (words like *for example* and *indeed*)
8. Time (words like *meanwhile*)

Put the transitions listed under "Examples of Transitions" into their correct categories.

More About Transitions

Any word or phrase that forces your reader to move back and forth making connections between your ideas serves as a transition. Pronouns like *he, she, it,* and *who* help link your ideas. Sometimes the repetition of a key word or phrase serves as a transition, as do *nicotine and cigarettes* in "Confessions of a Nicotine Freak."

FOR THOUGHT AND DISCUSSION

1. List the transitions in "Seeing the Future Work at IBM."
2. List the transitions in "Computers in the Dugout."

WRITING ASSIGNMENT
Using What You Have Learned

For the following assignment, *you do not need to believe in horoscopes.* In fact, you can agree with one student who wrote, "What Christmas was to Ebenezer Scrooge, horoscopes are to me: Bah Humbug!" However, you need to write an essay that convinces your reader of your viewpoint by using concrete examples of why your horoscope for a particular day—or part of your horoscope—was or was not accurate.

Why limit yourself to just one day? A good question. Review the principles of writing topic and thesis sentences at the beginning of the chapter. What your thesis sentence says you are going to prove, you must prove with supporting details. Since many horoscopes are very complex, limit your subject to a point you can develop concretely.

Usually you do not begin an essay by formulating a thesis sentence. First you use right brain exercises like clustering, brainstorming, or freewriting to discover what you want to say.

In this paper, be sure you do the following:

1. If your horoscope is complex, it will not be possible to prove or disprove all of it in a paper of two hundred words. Limit your subject so you can support your point convincingly.
2. To help you choose a central point, use a prewriting technique (clustering, brainstorming, or freewriting).
3. Once you choose your central point, use a prewriting technique to help you find concrete details to develop your point.
4. Interest your reader by using dialogue or figurative language when appropriate. (Hint: clustering is an effective technique to inspire figurative language.)
5. Once you have prewritten your essay, and then written a draft, check to be sure you have included adequate transitions.

6. Revise any sentences that do not flow smoothly, and add concrete material where it is lacking.
7. Make sure your style is consistent.
8. Proofread to eliminate mechanical errors.

STUDENT STAR ESSAYS
The Polished Product

***Remember: the authors of these essays used the following steps:

1. Prewriting
2. Writing
3. Revising content
4. Proofreading and correcting mechanical errors

FALSE POPULARITY, TRUE HOROSCOPE

Yesterday my horoscope stated: "relationship under fire." Such a statement is always accurate in my family because the parent-child relationship is always being tested.

Take last Friday, for example. I discovered a fifth of Jim Beam in the gym bag of Cathy, my fourteen-year-old daughter. With this discovery, my blood began to boil. I had trusted her not to get involved with liquor, and, in fact, she had convinced me she hated all alcohol.

As I thought about the Jim Beam, it began to dawn on me: the liquor wasn't for her. Lately she had been having problems making friends. She was using liquor to give her popularity a boost. She had taken something to school no one else had the guts to bring. Such status! Gradually my blood stopped boiling. Cathy must be truly desperate to have done such a thing. So what was I going to do about it? I certainly couldn't ignore it, but would punishing her really solve the problem?

What I did was to give her back the liquor to show her I trusted her to leave it home—and leave it alone. Then we talked about why she had taken it to school. We both cried. Had I punished her, she would have probably continued to rebel. By showing her I understood her and trusted her not to repeat her mistake, I built a stronger relationship. In the relationship my horoscope said was being tested, I think I passed the test.

Sandra Nandy

MY LITTLE SCRAP OF PAPER

Although I have no belief in astrology, I am amused by scanning the horoscope. Love, money, travel, popularity: my horoscope promises me all these with great regularity. And why shouldn't it? Would you read a horoscope that was constantly filled with gloom and doom?

My horoscope recently promised me I would be traveling in the near future—a pretty safe prediction as the majority of Americans do some traveling every day. But this particular horoscope said I would focus on travel. That didn't sound like a trip to school. The horoscope added that I would be coming into some money. This last part was hard to believe because the commercial salmon season in Alaska had opened a week earlier, and my dad hadn't called me to join him yet. He obviously wasn't swamped with fish. For some reason, though, I ripped out the horoscope and stuck it in my pocket.

Something made me keep reading it during the next several days which I spent entwined in cobwebs sitting next to the phone hoping for my dad's call. Finally I asked my mother to bring me the garden shears so I could cut the cobwebs chaining me to the chair. I decided to get some sleep.

I walked down the hall, small pieces of cobweb trailing behind me. As I crawled into bed, even before I could turn out the light, the phone rang. It was Dad. The fish were in. I grabbed my bag and headed for the car. When Mom slid into the driver's seat to take me to the airport she asked, "Do you have everything, dear?" I raced back to the house, grabbed the tattered horoscope and shoved it into my pocket.

The fishing was fantastic. We were the top boat for five days straight. Each night before bedding down, I took out my mangled horoscope and reread it. By the time Dad and I came home, we had made a hefty profit. Finally I showed Dad my little scrap of paper. He read it with great interest, and then shook his head. "I don't know what that has to do with fishing. You know I'm not superstitous." With that, he left the room.

I stared at my little piece of paper, and reread it a last time before tossing it into the trash. Off to bed I went to catch up on my sleep. At first I couldn't sleep knowing my horoscope was with the broken egg shells, coffee grounds, and empty dog food cans. Finally, however, sleep won.

When I awoke, I stumbed into the kitchen. Dad was sitting at the table reading the morning paper. I sat down with my coffee, and there on my placemat was my little "good luck" charm.

"I don't know if it helped, but it sure didn't hurt," Dad said rising from the table. He got as far as the doorway then turned and winked. I had to agree. I didn't know if it had helped, but my trusty good luck horoscope sure hadn't hurt.

Christopher Anthony Lonero

DESTRUCTIVE HOROSCOPES

How many times have you met someone for the first time and had them ask you, "What is your zodiac sign?" This question is a popular springboard for relationships. As a handy ice-breaker, conversations about zodiac signs are harmless. On the other hand, many people feel that if their signs are compatible a relationship has a better chance of being successful, and this search for compatibility in horoscope signs can be disastrous. For example, one night, I met an attractive, intelligent lady. We talked about our goals in life and what we were doing to reach them. We quickly learned we were both interested in baseball, classic movies, and computers. We both attended church regularly. We both voted straight Democratic. Obviously, this was a relationship destined to flourish.

Suddenly she asked me, "What is your zodiac sign?"

"Aries," I replied. "Does it really matter?"

"Well, our signs are not compatible," she responded. "The last person I dated was an Aries, and I ended up hating him. I have a basic conflict with Aries people."

From that moment on, the conversation became less worthwhile. She had built in her mind a negative attitude toward all Aries people (unfortunately, including me) that made me feel defective.

Believing in horoscopes can be very destructive when you are trying to build relationships. People who believe in horoscopes see a predetermined set of personality traits that may have nothing to do with reality. Human beings are too complex to be summed up by something as abstract and general as a horoscope sign. After all, isn't this kind of generalizing about people the same attitude that leads to the evils of racial prejudice? Such prejudice does not serve people; instead, it stymies their growth.

Kenyatta M. Patton

HELP! FOR FURTHER WORK

Read "Horoscope Hogwash" and "Future Forecast." Then answer the Thought and Discussion questions which follow them.

HOROSCOPE HOGWASH

Horoscopes is hogwash. Being able to predict one's future day by day is totally ridiculous. To a certain point, the horoscope is true, but it is also very vague. Looking at my horoscope, I find out that my day was going to be a good day. It states that my financial status will change, my love relationship grows, and a major wish would come true. Well, my day goes on like usual. I got paid today at work, and I met an attractive lady later on that evening, but I did not receive a fifty dollar bonus that I had wished for from my boss. Well, it was not bad. Two out of three isn't bad, but the things wasn't exactly stated in my horoscope. Knowing exactly what is going to happen and when it will happen is a true horoscope.

A popular horoscope can be found in *Monterey Peninsula Herald* by Sydney Omar. He supposedly have a talent that enables him to predict people's daily events according to their birthdays, but the statements he make can pertain to anyone and everyone in general. As I begin to think about it more and more, I realized that there will be thousands of people who were born on the same day and who will have the same horoscope. It isn't impossible to believe that all of these people will have the same experiences in one form or another, but when a person writes a horoscope that predicts a person's future, wouldn't it make sense to give more specific details?

FUTURE FORECAST

After reading my horoscope yesterday I was startled. I usually don't read horoscopes. This may soon change. First of all let me explain what happened last week. I get a car. I am very excited about it I want to start working on it right away. I was concerned with its appearance. I totally neglect the engine. Sure enough my car breaks down. My horoscope told me to focus on variety. I obviously didn't. It also said to keep my mind open without being gullible. Well, after reading this I was depressed, but I read on. The concluding line says that I was due to recoup a loss, and to locate missing articles. Like a baby bird receiving a worm from its mother, my spirits were lifted.

FOR THOUGHT AND DISCUSSION

1. What is the topic sentence in each essay?
2. Are the topics adequately limited to develop a theme of each essay's length? If not, suggest a means of limiting the topic.
3. Do the topic sentences state an opinion that can be developed concretely?
4. Which concrete details help to develop the topic sentences?
5. Point out any details irrelevant to the topic sentences.
6. Read from "Making Subjects, Verbs, and Pronouns Agree," beginning on p. 295 through "Shifts in Tense" in "The Final Touch: A Handbook." Then correct subject-verb agreement and shift in tense errors in the essays.

9 BEGINNINGS AND ENDINGS

As the King of Hearts said to the White Rabbit, "Begin at the beginning, and go on till you come to the end: then stop."

Lewis Carroll, Alice in Wonderland

CONCEPTS TO LEARN

- The meaning of *paradox*
- The way writing changes to suit an audience
- The meaning of *irony,* *satire,* and *sarcasm*
- The use of effective beginnings and endings in essays
- The proper format for crediting sources

FOR THOUGHT AND DISCUSSION

1. Why is the King of Hearts' advice sometimes difficult to follow when you are writing an essay?
2. In what sense does the Gary Larson cartoon illustrate both a beginning and an ending?

PARADOX

One of the tricks writers can use to interest and attract readers is a *paradox,* that is, a statement that seems self-contradictory. Paradoxes are, in a sense, mini-mysteries that inspire readers to solve them.

Some old sayings are paradoxes: For example, "more haste makes less speed" is a paradox.

Notice the way Robert Francis uses a paradox to catch his reader's attention in the beginning of the following poem.

Vocabulary   **eccentricity:**   not following a normal or established pattern
aberration: a change from the usual or expected

Pitcher

His art is eccentricity, his aim
How not to hit the mark he seems to aim at,

His passion how to avoid the obvious,
His technique how to vary the avoidance.

The others throw to be comprehended. He
Throws to be a moment misunderstood.

Yet not too much. Not errant, arrant, wild,
But every seeming aberration willed.

Not to, yet still, still to communicate
Making the batter understand too late.

Robert Francis

FOR THOUGHT AND DISCUSSION

1. What statement in "Pitcher" is a paradox?
2. According to the poem what is a pitcher's goal?
3. Read the poem aloud. Note the unevenness—the eccentricity—of the rhythm. How does the eccentric rhythm of the poem reflect the art of the pitcher?
4. To what kind of reader, that is, to what *audience* would this poem most appeal?
5. What is paradoxical about the cartoon introducing the chapter?

AUDIENCE

As writers, we are in a very real sense salespersons of our ideas. Like other salespersons, we must gain the attention of an *audience* before we can make a sale. Your *audience* is the readers of your writing. As writers we must always remember them, their knowledge, their beliefs, and their interests.

In real life we almost unconsciously make adjustments in vocabulary and subject matter to suit an audience. We do not talk to our bosses, children, co-workers, friends, parents, or dogs in the same way.

To better understand the way writing changes to suit an audience, look through the following list of magazines before your next class. (This is a suggested list. Your instructors may add others.)

1. *Ms.*
2. *Sports Illustrated*
3. *Scientific American*
4. *Business Week*
5. *Ladies Home Journal*

An efficient way to do this assignment is to work in groups. Check magazines out of the library (or photocopy material that illustrates your point) and bring them to class so you can give your classmates specific examples of the vocabulary, subject matter, and advertising that are directed to the magazine's audience. Explain to the class for what audience each magazine is designed.

Selling Our Ideas

Once we have examined effective techniques for beginning essays, we will examine techniques for ending them. After all, we do not want to leave readers searching—either literally or figuratively—for the missing paragraph once they have finished reading a paper. Like an effective salesperson, we must package our ideas neatly so we can make a sale.

In this chapter, we will adopt the King of Hearts' advice from the introductory quotation; we will start with beginnings and work our way to endings.

How Ironic!

One way of capturing our readers' interest is by using an ironic tone. (To review *tone* see Chapter Six.)

"The most perfect humor and irony," wrote Samuel Butler in *Life and Habit,* "is generally quite unconscious."

"Aha," you say. "What ever it is, *irony* must be in the province of the right brain if it is unconscious."

True. But what is irony? *Irony* is a type of tone that is used every day. Irony involves a difference between what we say and what we mean, or a difference between the way we expect something to be and the way it really turns out to be. For example, Martin Luther King spent his life working for justice. He was a man of peace who insisted on justice through nonviolent methods. He earned the Nobel Peace Prize for his work toward peaceful integration. Ironically, he was murdered.

Satire.   Irony used in a literary work to show the ridiculousness of a situation is called *satire.* Mark Twain, a master satirist, was being satiric when he said, "Man is the only animal that blushes—or needs to."

Sarcasm.   While *satire* uses wit to point out folly, *sarcasm* is a mocking, ironic statement intended merely to wound another person. Examples of sarcasm include saying, "You're a real prince," or "You're certainly a beauty" and meaning the opposite.

WRITING EXERCISE
It's Your Turn

Mad Magazine is satiric. Often satire requires thinking, but like a joke, readers love "getting it."

Study the cartoon from *Mad* in Figure 9.1, and then explain what it is satirizing.

BEGINNINGS

Now let's begin with beginnings. Regardless of the technique you use to capture your readers' attention, remember to consider their knowledge and interest in your lead ("Lead" is another term for "begin-

FIGURE 9.1   A Satiric Cartoon from *Mad Magazine*

ning.'') A group of avid football fans might be attracted to a lead concerning the Superbowl while the same lead would leave an audience of opera buffs cold. The following excerpts are examples of different techniques you can use to open your essay.

Beginning Technique Number One: Use Irony.

We use various forms of irony in conversations. Ironically, despite our successful use of it in conversation, many of us haven't used irony in writing, and it is an excellent way to capture reader interest. The following beginning from Dave Barry's article, "Filling a Bottle with Integrity," effectively uses irony:

> As we approach that time of year when you young people go forth, clutching your diplomas, to try to get the kind of job where you don't have to wear a comical grease-spattered fast-food outfit and have unintelligible conversations about "nuggets" over the drive-thru intercom, I'd like to offer you three words of advice—three words that, in today's competitive job market mean the difference between success and failure; three words that can mark you as the kind of young person most likely to get on the "fast track" to the top. Those three words, young graduates, are: "clean urine sample."
>
> Dave Barry, "Filling a Bottle with Integrity"

Beginning Technique Number Two: Ask a Question.

When you read something and the author suddenly asks you a question, how do you respond? Does the question wake you up? Does it make you think about what you are reading?

The following introduction from Wayne Scheer's "How I Decided to Stop Worrying and Love My Gradebook" was intended for an audience of college teachers:

> Most of us give grades for the same reason we go to the dentist—
> we fear repercussions if we don't. Grades have become a form of
> self-protection. We use them to hide behind if an irate student storms
> into our office or if a curious administrator wonders what we're doing
> here. But can grades play a constructive role in the thinking/learning
> process?
>
> Wayne Scheer, "How I Decided to Stop Worrying and Love My
> Gradebook," from *Innovation Abstracts*

Beginning Technique Number Three: Catch Your Reader's Attention by Creating Suspense.

Do you ever get hooked by your curiosity into reading a mystery or watching a drama on television? There is a part in all of us that is fascinated by mystery or drama. The following beginning of Mary Tesoro's "Women Learn to Fight Back" uses suspense to spark readers' attention:

> The room is dark and still. Except for the soft, rhythmic movement of
> her chest, she lies motionless. She neither sees nor hears her
> assailant's approach. It isn't until his massive frame is entirely upon
> her that she has any indications of the attack.
>
> An eerie, unfamiliar voice whispers, "Your husband's dead in the
> other room. Don't resist if you want to live . . . "
>
> Her heart pounds wildly, every nerve in her body screams and a
> wave of nausea overwhelms her as she realizes she is pinned. She
> offers no resistance as he moves down her body. Just as he reaches
> her feet she turns slightly, draws one leg up and kicks him in the
> face.
>
> "I'm gonna kill you!" he screams.
>
> Again she thrust-kicks. As her heel strikes his head, he falls off
> to one side. Somehow, he manages to get back on top of her. She
> jams her fingers into his left eye, sending both into spasms. He reels
> back, clutching his face. She kicks one more time—and something
> within her knows it was the knockout blow—the blow which will
> incapacitate him for at least twelve minutes (long enough for her to
> escape and get help).
>
> Simultaneous with his collapse is the sound of a shrill whistle
> and wild cheering. The scenario takes place not in the woman's
> home but in a special training room. The "victim," Maureen McEvoy

of Pacific Grove, is graduating from twenty hours of what experts believe to be the most effective self-defense training available: Model Mugging.

Mary Tesoro, "Women Learn to Fight Back"

Beginning Technique Number Four: Get Your Reader Involved Through Concrete Description.

When we help readers see a setting, we put them in our own shoes and get them involved in our writing. Note the way Cliff Jahr's description gains readers' interest in "Marie Osmond on Her Own at Last":

> High noon, Youngstown, Ohio. In the sun's harsh glare, it's apparent that Marie is wearing heavy make-up. Her hair is punk-styled into a big spiky puff and slicked back along the sides. Her red lips shine with gloss, and there is enough black liner and shadow around her eyes to turn on a raccoon. Near the suburban theater where she is performing with brother Donny in a road tour of the old *Donny and Marie* show, we enter a restaurant, and her hip appearance draws open-mouthed stares.
>
> Cliff Jahr, "Marie Osmond on Her Own at Last," from *Ladies Home Journal*

Beginning Technique Number Five: Disagree with a Common Opinion.

A little disagreement between friends can break up monotony and add spice to life. Correctly used it does not alienate the friends. Disagreement can serve the same purpose in writing. Most readers do not want to read the same old idea or information; new information or a new point of view functions in much the same way as the paradox, that is, readers want to read on to find out about the unfamiliar. Gloria Steinem makes an uncommon statement in the following introduction from "Dolly Parton:"

> People who haven't listened to Dolly Parton or to feminism may be surprised to learn that they go together. In fact, she has crossed musical class lines to bring work, real life, and strong women into a world of pop music usually dominated by unreal romance. She has used her business sense to bring other women and poor people along with her. And her flamboyant style has turned all the devalued symbols of womanliness to her own ends.
>
> Gloria Steinem, "Dolly Parton," from *Ms.*

Beginning Technique Number Six: Tell a Story to Attract Your Reader.

We all enjoy a good story—so why not use our natural affinity for stories to attract readers? Mike Royko uses this technique in one of his columns entitled, "Stop Nagging Him, He's Trying to Quit:"

> Among the people I dislike most in the world are those who nod at the cigarette I'm smoking and say something they think is profound. Something like, "You know, those things are bad for you."
>
> When they say that to me, I think, "Does this schnook think that I don't know the difference between a Pall Mall and a carrot stick?"
>
> Of course I know smokes are bad for me.
>
> Mike Royko, "Stop Nagging Him, He's Trying to Quit"

Beginning Technique Number Seven: Use the Facts, Ma'am (or Sir).

Facts get readers' attention by showing them that the writer knows what he or she is writing about. John Lee, Miriam Horn, and Andrea Gabor wrote the following excerpt from "Fortunes in Missing Masterpieces." Note the way they use facts as a springboard to more detailed discussion of lost art:

> London art authority Peter Watson leafs through his records and recites just a few names and a few numbers—"Titian, 62; Velasquez, 67; Frans Hals, 20; Mantegna, 35; Veronese, 82; Kandinsky, 103"—a short but revealing fragment of a long list of masterpieces that have been lost for years. With paintings and sculptures commanding record prices in auction houses, bounty hunters are stepping up a worldwide search of attics, basements, and even back yards for the missing treasures. "Art," Watson explains, "is about the only area in which you can get something for nearly nothing and have it become worth a fortune overnight."
>
> John Lee, Miriam Horn, and Andrea Gabor, "Fortunes in Missing Masterpieces," from *U.S. News and World Report*

Beginning Technique Number Eight: Borrow Someone Else's Good Ideas and Words by Using a Quotation.

Vocabulary   **proclivity:**   tendency, inclination

An effective quotation adds spice and authority to writing. Ralph Waldo Emerson captured the essence of using quotations in writing when he said, "By necessity, by **proclivity**—and by delight, we all quote." Barbara Grizzuti Harrison also makes use of an opening quotation in the following essay from *McCalls*, "The Stubborn Courage of Mother Teresa":

> *Blessed are you poor, for yours is the kingdom of God* is not an idea that has caught on like wildfire; its revolutionary implications that the poor are of no less value than you or I doesn't, in a world where what is deemed *good* is what is deemed *bankable,* appear to reward contemplation.
>
> Barbara Grizzuti Harrison, "The Stubborn Courage of Mother Teresa," from *McCalls*.

Beginning Technique Number Nine: Puzzle and Unpuzzle Your Reader by Beginning with a Paradox Which You Then Explain.

While readers like to understand quickly, paradoxically, they also delight in the challenge of a puzzle. Paradoxes are, after all, thought-puzzles and most people love puzzles. The following excerpt from "Anglers All" begins with a paradoxical statement.

> There's something fishy about the California Academy of Science at Golden Gate Park in San Francisco, and the fishiness has nothing to do with the residents of Steinhart Aquarium. *Anglers All* is an exhibition designed to make a big splash with the growing legions of those devoted to the art of fly fishing.
>
> Marlene Martin, "Anglers All," from *American Way*

Beginning Technique Number Ten: Use Figurative Language.

Vocabulary   **paramo:**   high, bleak plain; cold region (a Spanish word)

You became familiar with figurative language in Chapter 7. Why not use it to open your essay as Nancy Shute does in "After a Turbulent Youth, the Peace Corps Comes of Age"?

> John F. Kennedy had a dream. Twenty-five years later, in the village of Cumbijin high in the Ecuadorian Andes, that dream makes house calls.
>   Paula Enyeart, a twenty-six-year-old registered nurse from North Dakota, hikes up the green, treeless paramo that coats the ridgetops at 13,000 feet, en route to check up on one of her 550-odd patients. As a Peace Corp volunteer, Enyeart is a mobile twenty-four-hour-a-day health-care system . . .
>
> Nancy Shute, "After a Turbulent Youth, the Peace Corps Comes of Age," from *Smithsonian*

We could continue analyzing methods of beginning essays. The point is there are many techniques to catch readers' attention. Sometimes a combination of techniques works best. Spend time playing with your beginning. Use prewriting techniques to inspire your Right Brain Creator to help you capture your audience's attention.

An important point to remember is do not imitate the supermarket "news" papers that begin with misleading, high-interest leads. If your lead states that a colony of six-eyed extraterrestrials is living near Des Moines, your reader will be insulted and turned off if your essay, in fact, does not verify or explain your lead.

ENDINGS

When composing your ending, be sure you do the following to avoid common pitfalls:

1. Do not introduce a new idea in your conclusion! Remember, your conclusion wraps up the ideas you are trying to sell.
2. Do not shock your readers so much they lose track of your point. While you want to express your ideas in a fresh way, make sure your conclusion harmonizes with the rest of your essay.

What *can* you do in a conclusion? The following are some of the ending techniques you can use. Perhaps you can suggest others.

Ending Technique Number One: Present a Solution to the Problem Developed in the Paper.

For years women have been instructed not to fight back. But knowing when and how to fight back can mean the difference between life and death.

As instructor Danielle Evans says, "No one can attack you without leaving an opening. In Model Mugging, we teach women what to do with that opening."

Mary Tesoro, "Women Learn to Fight Back"
(Note the way this ending works with its beginning on pages 142–143).

Ending Technique Number Two: Ask a Thought-Provoking Question.

And the better you eat, the longer you can expect to be around to do so. People who take a nutritive approach to disease prevention, the evidence strongly suggests, can actually add years to their lives. Now doesn't that sound like a medical miracle?

Stuart M. Berger, "How What You Eat Can Add Years to Your Life"

Ending Technique Number Three: Answer a Question Posed Earlier.

Vocabulary   **Nemesis:**   a just punishment; (from the Greek god of vengeance)

Of course, the **Nemesis** hypothesis has not yet been proved. [But if] the sun does have a companion star, we should be able to find it [and confirm its orbit in the near future.] It is probably a red star [about twenty trillion miles away, barely bright enough to be seen with powerful binoculars. A team of physicists and astronomers at Berkeley is examining five thousand candidates. If they find the real Death Star, there will be little room left for controversy. This latest adventure is just under way.

Richard A. Muller, "Did Comets Kill the Dinosaurs?" from *New York Times Magazine*

Ending Technique Number Four: Use Irony.

There's no way to pack for an airport bombing. But you can keep your pockets stuffed with tourniquets, plasma, gauze bandages, and blood packets, and stay away from the baggage areas. Before leaving home, make sure your blood type is tattooed on four separate parts of your body, and give your dental records to your executor. Bon voyage!

Emily Prager, "Traveler's Update," from *Penthouse*

Ending Technique Number Five: Summarize the Main Points of the Article.

Americans know too little of Japan, the Japanese, and in particular their educational system, one that in many respects deserves study and possible experimental adoption in our own and in other nations. Although nearly all Japanese school children learn to read English and a few learn one or two other languages as well, very few foreigners have learned the Japanese language, a great handicap to the rest of the world. But mastery of their language is unnecessary to know that their steady and large educational, family, and personal investments in education have brought them great dividends in national and individual accomplishment that enrich the rest of the world.

Diane Profita Schiller and Herbert J. Walberg, "Japan: The Learning Society," from *Educational Leadership*

Ending Technique Number Six: Use a Relevant Quotation.

To sell records, though, the video must get wide exposure, and that means MTV must play it. MTV has written guidelines on sex and violence, but they are the kind of civic-minded pieties that permit unlimited flexibility. "Videos containing gratuitous violence are unacceptable. . . . Exceptional care must be taken in instances where women and children are victims of, or are threatened by, acts of violence."

Eric Gelman and Mark Starr, "MTV's Message," from *Newsweek*

Ending Technique Number Seven: Conclude with an Argument Based on the Evidence in Your Paper.

The several tons of toxic waste collected by grassroots programs demonstrate that hazardous chemicals are everywhere—in old and new products precariously shelved in almost every household in America. But there are no rules and regulations controlling what happens to these wastes. The responsibility for disposing of them safely lies in the hands of every consumer.

Dave Galvin, "Toxics on the Home Front," from *Sierra*

Ending Technique Number Eight: Use a "Story Description" That Puts Your Reader in the Picture.

For weeks, the villagers have been organizing daily *mingas,* volunteer work parties in a tradition that traces back to the Inca empire's highly organized public works program, to dig trenches for the tubing that will carry fresh water down from the spring to their homes. As many as four hundred workers have come in a single day, swathed in magenta and blue shawls and more somber ponchos, babies tied on the women's backs. Laughing and chattering as they toss shovelfuls of black volcanic mud over their heads, they make a bright line snaking through the green meadow below Chimborazo peak. On a good day, they've dug a mile.

At the site, O'Connor helps organize the work parties and interprets blueprints. When a worker approaches to ask the deaf man a question, he does it with gestures. O'Connor "talks" back just as easily, not in American Sign Language but with universally articulate motions illustrated by occasional points at the blueprints. Information conveyed, the two men smile and the work continues.

The spirit that drew O'Connor to the Peace Corps explains, more than anything else, why the agency endures. Like everyone else, when asked why he had joined he wrote that he sought experience and then adventure. Then he continued; "My primary reason is . . . I was sent to a residential school for the deaf which was supported by the state. Went through college with the help of vocational rehabilitation and the Social Security people. Made it through classes with the help of support services, such as interpreters, note takers, and tutors. . . . I felt like somebody has been giving me the help all my life. Now the Peace Corps is there, where I can contribute my engineering skills. That's something I am able to give, for a change."

Nancy Shute, "After a Turbulent Youth, the Peace Corps Comes of Age," from *Smithsonian*

(Notice that this nicely ties in with its beginning on page 145.)

WRITING EXERCISE
It's Your Turn

One of the advantages in working with right-brained thinking is that the right side of your brain sees whole images. When you use this thinking, a conclusion will often suddenly, without your conscious effort, tie the paper together by referring back to the beginning.

1. Analyze and explain the way the following beginnings and endings work together.
2. Explain which beginning and ending techniques the authors use.
3. Note the form used to cite sources for each selection. Complete notation usually appears in a "Works Cited" at the end of an essay, but it is provided in the following exercise to familiarize you with the proper form.

Beginning

Not so long ago, a thirty-eight-year-old accountant came to me saying she had a problem with her nose. Indeed she did. There was a hole in the partition separating the nostrils—a hole so big that you could look in one side and see daylight out the other.

Ending

Given these facts, why do people still insist on messing with coke? As with anything else that's dangerous, they don't believe bad things will happen to them. They don't understand that by the time the chronic user is driven to seek help, she probably can't work, socialize, or run her own life. It may sound corny, but that's a high price for a little fun.

Mirkin, Gabe, M.D. "Cocaine Con." *Health Magazine* January 1985: 8.

Beginning

Almost everyone has a relative or two who can't recall having had breakfast an hour before or hasn't mastered a new idea or skill since turning forty. Others look with pride on their middle-aged and older family members who strut into their forties, fifties, and sixties in the tradition of Picasso, Pauling, former First Mother Lillian Carter, and the indomitable Charlie Chaplin, creating, matriculating, ever-learning, and clearly in charge of their minds and the monthly math puzzles in *Scientific American.*

Ending

The relationship between learning and aging needs more investigation. But with what is already known, it's a good bet that today's forty, fifty, and sixty-year-olds will have as much to learn in the future as they have to teach.

Rodgers, Joann Ellison. "Our Insatiable Brain." *Annual Editions: Psychology* 1985/1986: 102.

Beginning

In my first year of teaching freshman composition I had a little act I performed whenever a student asked, "Will spelling count?" I pretended to be surprised by the silliness of the question. By frowning, taking my pipe out of my mouth, and hesitating a moment, I tried to look like a man coming down from some higher mental plane. Then I said in a voice I hoped sounded like a mix of confidence and disdain, "No. Of course, it won't."

Ending

Now in my fifth year of teaching freshman composition I have a little act I perform whenever a student asks, "Will spelling count?" I pretend to be surprised by the silliness of the question. By frowning, taking my pipe out of my mouth, and hesitating a moment, I try to look like a man coming down from some higher mental plane. Then I say, in a voice I hope sounds like a mix of confidence and disdain, "Yes. Of course, it will."

Jack Connor. "Will Spelling Count?" *The Chronicle of Higher Education* 1980: 211 and 214.

FORMAT FOR CREDITING SOURCES

All quality writing includes documentation of ideas and quotations taken from other writers. The following is the proper format for documenting sources:

1. Author's Name—last name first (followed by a period). If no author's name is listed, begin with the article title.
2. "Article Title" (in quotation marks, followed by a period).
3. *Magazine or Book Name* (underlined, followed by no punctuation).
4. Date of publication (followed by a colon).
5. Page number (followed by a period).
6. Indent the second line of your source credit.

Note the punctuation marks in the following example and do likewise:

Weiner, Daniel P., Joseph P. Shapiro, and Esther B. Fein. "Of Mice and Men: Harvard Patents a New Life Form." *U.S. News & World Report* 25 April 1988: 49.

Lufkin, Liz. "My Breakfast with the Baroness." *San Francisco Focus*
    November 1985: 94.

WRITING EXERCISE
It's Your Turn

1. Find and copy an effective beginning and an effective ending from
   nonfiction.
2. Using proper punctuation, capitalization, and order, write a source
   credit for the beginning and ending you have selected.

WRITING ASSIGNMENT
USING WHAT YOU HAVE LEARNED

Because our right brain thinks in a unified fashion, when we relax
and trust it, it will help us create unity in our writing. For your next
assignment you will have a golden opportunity to use your creative
brain power to *rewrite* one of the essays you have previously handed
in this semester. This time around, however, you will use one of the
beginning and ending techniques in this chapter to begin and end
your essay.

Many professional authors do not write an introduction until *after*
they finish writing their essay, so the method of adding an interesting
beginning is not as odd as it sounds at first thought. Use the following
steps to help you write a reader-catching introduction:

1. Reread the essays you have written thus far this semester, and
   select the essay you want to rewrite.
2. Let your Creative Brain play with ideas for a compelling beginning.
   Try clustering, brainstorming, or freewriting to help inspire ideas.
   (Staple the prewriting method you use to the back of your essay
   when you hand it in.)
3. The length of an introduction must be in proportion to the length
   of the essay it introduces. You would not want a three-paragraph
   introduction for a two-paragraph essay. Because this assignment
   seeks to get you to use one of the methods you have just studied,
   make your introduction at least forty words long.
4. Once you have created an introduction that will inspire others to
   read your essay, you should reread the whole essay. At this point,
   a conclusion may simply pop into your mind from its storage place
   in your right brain. If no concluding ideas pop, once again try a
   prewriting technique to encourage your Creative Brain to come up
   with an idea for a conclusion that is at least forty words long.
   ***Remember: never introduce a new idea in your conclusion.*
5. Before you begin, go back through this chapter and review the
   beginning and ending techniques it demonstrates.

6. Your introduction and conclusion must do the following:
   a. Harmonize in tone and subject with the rest of your essay
   b. Take into account the interests of your audience
7. From now on—for the rest of the writing assignments in this book and for the rest of your life—think about the principles of beginning and ending effectively when you write.

STAR STAR ESSAYS
The Polished Product

***Remember: the authors of the essays used the following steps:

1. Prewriting
2. Writing
3. Revising content
4. Proofreading and correcting mechanical errors

BIRTH BLUES

Beginning

Have you ever thought about the changes in relationship a husband and wife go through when they are expecting their first baby? Having a baby before the importance of the team approach became popular was the mother's responsibility. The father was either in the hospital waiting room or at a bar already celebrating. However, the modern approach is for fathers to get involved throughout the pregnancy, and I certainly wanted to use the modern approach when my wife Jackie and I were expecting our first child.

Middle

I accompanied Jackie to the doctor, and listened to the baby's heartbeat. Together we read everything we could find about what to eat, and what vitamins to take. We wanted to learn everything we could to insure ours would be a healthy baby. When we signed up for a childbirth class at the hospital, I became even more excited as I realized I was going to be a partner in our baby's delivery. Faithfully, we attended the classes and practiced relaxation and breathing techniques. By the time our baby was due, Jackie had great faith in me as a coach and partner.

Of course, I was on duty at the fire station when Jackie phoned to say she was in labor. Quickly I notified my captain, and I was on my way home. At home, I monitored Jackie's contractions and decided it was time to head for the hospital.

Once in the labor room, we settled in practicing the techniques we had learned. Our doctor and various nurses checked in from time to time. Everything seemed to be going well. It was an exhilarating experience!

Then came the announcement: the doctor was worried about how slowly Jackie was dilating. He took an x-ray, and then the sky fell in. "The baby is too big to risk delivering naturally, Sal," the doctor told me. "We'll have to do a Caesarean."

"Whatever you think, Doc," I said, "Will I be able to be with my wife?"

"Sorry, Sal, you have to take a special class if you are to accompany your wife during a Caesarean section."

"Ok," I said, trying to swallow my immense disappointment. Of course, I wanted what was best for Jackie and the baby, but I never felt so alone or disappointed in my life as I felt when they wheeled Jackie out. We had worked so long and so hard together. I felt so cheated.

Ending

Certainly having their first baby is one of the most exciting experiences a couple can have, and modern medicine has done a great deal to recognize the importance of a couple acting as a team to share both the responsibilities of pregnancy and the process of birth. However, childbirth classes should incorporate information about Caesarean sections, so the important teamwork does not fall apart should a Caesarean delivery prove necessary. The joy of birth shouldn't be marred by loneliness and disappointment.

Sal Sardina

THE INFAMOUS GAMBLING GAMBIT

Beginning

Like countless millions of others, I had seen gambling casinos filled with glamorous people winning piles of money on television. So naturally I was very excited when my husband Rod, my friend Stefanie, and I arrived for a weekend at Lake Tahoe.

Middle

After a quick stop at our room, we headed for the casino where we were engulfed by slot machines. Lights glared from the ceiling of the huge, noisy room making its brilliant red, orange, and yellow decor vibrate with energy. The jingling of change and the shouts and laughter of winners filled the air. Cocktail waitresses in fanny-length, skin-tight, gold sequined dresses circled the room distributing drinks to the gamblers who were in their own little worlds so absorbed were they in the machine in front of them. As we walked to the back of the casino we could hear the klink, klink, klink of the balls on roulette wheels and the screams from blackjack tables with people crowded around trying to beat the dealer.

Rod bought his chips for blackjack, but Stefanie and I decided to "play it safe" and stick to the slot machines. At first, the repetition of dropping coins into the machine and pulling the arm was boring, but after I won a few dollars, I became almost hypnotized by the process. I began to imagine myself winning a million-dollar jackpot. I was so engrossed in pulling that arm that it became almost a part of me. I lost track of how much I drank; a cocktail waitress appeared magically when I finished a drink. Soon I had no idea how much I had won—or lost.

Eventually Stefanie arrived to break my trance. We found Rod at the blackjack table flashing a victorious grin. Despite his winning, however, he had not become absorbed in the gambling. He was ready to head next door to see a show, so we made our way back through the throngs of slot machine players and left the casino.

Ending

As I took a deep breath of the cool, fresh air outside, I began to shiver—a response caused in part by the cold mountain air and in part by the fear I felt at having been sucked so totally into gambling. It was frightening how easy it had been to fall victim to the glitz and hype of the casino.

P. C.

HELP! FOR FURTHER WORK

Read "The Ruin of Rudolph" and answer the Thought and Discussion questions which follow it.

THE RUIN OF RUDOLPH

Rudolph the Red-nosed reindeer was recently found in a meat locker near Des Moines, Iowa. His owner admitted he had been shot on public land posted: "No hunting." He was of a rare species of reindeer. He had been shot and then drawn and quartered. His carcass hung from the ceiling, his hind legs attached to a large, metal hook.

"God wouldn't have made reindeer if He hadn't wanted us to hunt them," he said when interviewed from his jail cell.

This tragic discovery does much to highlight a problem far too common today: a total disregard for the balance of nature. Certainly the Bible admonishes us:

> Be fruitful, and multiply, and replenish the earth, and subdue it: and have dominion over the fish of the sea, and over the fowl of the air, and over every living thing that moveth upon the earth.

Between you and I, "subdue" and "have dominion" imply a responsibility to nature that far exceeds a mere exploitation of it. . . .

FOR THOUGHT AND DISCUSSION

1. The thesis of the essay argues that society has its priorities wrong, that is, we do not consider seriously enough the impact of actions like developing land, hunting, and dumping toxic wastes. Is the

introduction of the essay appropriate? Suggest an alternative beginning.

2. Suggest an introduction more appropriate for a short essay.
3. Read from "Possessive Case Pronouns," beginning on p. 302, through "Shifts in Pronouns" in "The Final Touch: A Handbook," and then correct pronoun errors in "The Ruin of Rudolph."

10 DEFINING AN ABSTRACT TERM

"Do you think it's possible to love someone you don't like?"

Drawing by Frascino; (c) 1985. *The New Yorker Magazine, Inc.*

Love does not consist in gazing at each other, but in looking together in the same direction

Antoine de Saint-Exupery

CONCEPT TO LEARN

- The way to define an abstract term to make it more concrete

FOR THOUGHT AND DISCUSSION

What kind of relationship does the introductory quotation describe? Give a concrete example of what "looking in the same direction" means.

BY DEFINITION

When we write, we often use abstract words whose meanings are clear in our own minds, but we cannot assume our readers necessarily share our definitions. The cartoon at the beginning of the chapter plays on the uncertainty we have about many common abstract words. Is it, in fact, possible to love someone you do not like? To clarify your answer, you need to explain what you mean by *like* and *love*. They are, of course, abstract words.

In this chapter we will further explore the very important concepts of *abstract* and *concrete*. By defining abstract terms, you come to understand your thoughts and feelings about them better. Only then can you clearly communicate your thoughts and feelings, which involve both the denotation and the connotation of the words. (See Chapter Five to review *connotation*.)

Love?

In expressing love we belong among the undeveloped countries.

Saul Bellow

As the introductory cartoon and quotation affirm, *love* is one of those abstract words with a variety of definitions. As children, few of us really think about what *love* means. As we grow up, our definition of *love* and the way we express it becomes clearer and more mature. In the following poem Robert Hayden describes a kind of love it took him many years to understand.

Vocabulary **banked** (fires):   to make a fire burn more slowly
austere: stern in manner or appearance

Those Winter Sundays

Sundays too my father got up early
and put his clothes on in the blueblack cold,

then with cracked hands that ached
from labor in the weekday weather made
banked fires blaze. No one ever thanked him.

I'd wake and hear the cold splintering, breaking.
When the rooms were warm, he'd call,
and slowly I would rise and dress,
fearing the chronic angers of that house,

Speaking indifferently to him,
who had driven out the cold
and polished my good shoes as well.
What did I know, what did I know
of love's **austere** and lonely offices?

Robert Hayden, *Selected Poems*

FOR THOUGHT AND DISCUSSION

1. What type of work did the poet's father do for a living?
2. Which details show us how uncomfortable the father's tasks were?
3. How did the father make life more pleasant for his family?
4. Give concrete examples of what the poem might have meant by "the chronic angers of that house."
5. For the poet's father what did *love* mean?
6. Give an example of an act of love from your own life.

A Penny Saved Is Boring

Vocabulary   **cliché**: a timeworn expression such as "white as snow." (See "Clichés" in "The Final Touch," on p. 316.
frugality: the quality of being thrifty

Woody Allen's humor is a good example of using right-brain thinking to generate ideas. In the following excerpt from *Without Feathers*, Woody Allen purports to define ***frugality***. In doing so, he alludes to several **clichés**—among them: "Money isn't everything" and "Money can't buy happiness."

In addition, Allen alludes to the fable of the grasshopper and the ant—a fable in which the ant worked all summer and was rewarded for its effort while the grasshopper played and was punished by winter's harshness. Like most of us, Allen is bored by clichés, and he is even more bored by preachy clichés like those about being frugal and sensible. In "Frugality," Allen gives his Right Brain Creator free rein to poke fun at the clichéd preachiness of many definitions of *frugality*.

FRUGALITY
Woody Allen

As one goes through life, it is extremely important to conserve funds, and one should never spend money on anything foolish, like pear nectar or a solid-gold hat. Money is not everything, but it is better than having one's health. After all, one cannot go into a butcher shop and tell the butcher, "Look at my great suntan, and besides I never catch colds," and expect him to hand over any merchandise. (Unless, of course, the butcher is an idiot.) Money is better than poverty, if only for financial reasons. Not that it can buy happiness. Take the case of the ant and the grasshopper: The grasshopper played all summer, while the ant worked and saved. When winter came, the grasshopper had nothing, but the ant complained of chest pains. Life is hard for insects. And don't think mice are having any fun, either. The point is, we all need a nest egg to fall back on, but not while wearing a good suit.

Finally, let us bear in mind that it is easier to spend two dollars than to save one. And for God's sake don't invest money in any brokerage firm in which one of the partners is named Frenchy.

FOR THOUGHT AND DISCUSSION

1. Woody Allen begins with two abstract ideas about *frugality*. What are they?
2. Give some concrete examples of Allen's abstract ideas.
3. Why does Allen change the fable of the grasshopper and the ant? Would the actual fable work in his essay? Why?
4. How would you react had Allen's paragraph urged you to work hard and save money?

Success? What's That?

"She's the kind of girl who climbed the ladder of success wrong by wrong," Mae West once quipped. While Ms. West's pun is indeed witty (and very right-brained), it points out a contradiction in our definition of *success*: How can people be successful if they have done many things society considers wrong?

People disagree about the definition of *success*. Before reading the following essay, discuss your definition of *success* with your classmates; be as concrete as possible. Then make a list of the points about which class members agree and disagree in their definitions.

Michael Korda is the author of several books that explain his formula for achieving success. As you read the following excerpt from his book, *Success! How Every Man and Woman Can Achieve It*, watch for points that resemble or differ from your definition of *success*.

Vocabulary   **conglomerate:** made up of various parts (in the essay a giant company)

grandiose: magnificent, grand in a showy or pompous way

superseded: displaced
unethical: not ethical—that is, not following standards of right and wrong

DEFINING SUCCESS
Michael Korda

Success is relative; not everybody wants to put together a four-billion-dollar **conglomerate,** or become President of the United States, or win the Nobel Peace Prize. It is usually a mistake to begin with such **grandiose** ambitions, which tend to degenerate into lazy daydreams. The best way to succeed is to begin with a reasonably realistic goal and attain it, rather than aiming at something so far beyond your reach that you are bound to fail. It's also important to make a habit of succeeding, and the easiest way to start is to succeed at something, however small, every day, gradually increasing the level of your ambitions and achievements like a runner in training, who begins with short distances and works up to Olympic levels.

Try to think of success as a journey, an adventure, not a specific destination. Your goals may change during the course of that journey, and your original ambitions may be **superseded** by different, larger ones. Success will certainly bring you the material things you want, and a good, healthy appetite for the comforts and luxuries of life is an excellent road to success, but basically you'll know you have reached your goal when you have gone that one step further, in wealth, fame, or achievement, than you ever dreamed was possible.

How you become a success is, of course, your business. Morality has very little to do with success. I do not personally think it is necessary to be dishonest, brutal or **unethical** in order to succeed, but a great many dishonest, brutal and unethical people in fact do succeed. You'd better be prepared for the fact that success is seldom won without some tough infighting along the way. A lot depends on your profession, of course. There is a great deal of difference between setting out to become a success in a Mafia family and trying to become vice-president of a bank, but the differences simply consist of contrasting social customs and of what is the appropriate way to get ahead in a given profession or business. Whether you're hoping to take over a numbers game or an executive desk, you have to make the right moves for your circumstances. In the former example, you might have to kill someone; in the latter, you might only have to find ways of making your rivals look foolish or inefficient. In either case, you have to accept the rules of the game and play to win, or find some other game. This is a book about success, after all, not morality. The field you go into is your choice, but whatever it is, you're better off at the top of it than at the bottom.

FOR THOUGHT AND DISCUSSION

1. What words in the essay have strong connotations?
2. How does Michael Korda define *success?*
3. According to Korda what is the difference between setting out to become a success in the Mafia and trying to become vice-president of a bank?

4. Do you agree with Korda? Defend your answer.
5. Are the issues of right and wrong (ethics) relevant to success?
6. On television or in a magazine, find an ad that defines *success* and bring it or a description of it to class for discussion.
7. Compare and contrast Korda's definition of *success* with that of Albert Einstein in the following quotation:

> A successful man is he who receives a great deal from his fellow men, usually incomparably more than corresponds to his service to them. The value of a man, however, should be seen in what he gives and not in what he is able to receive.

Albert Einstein

FINDING OUT WHAT YOU THINK
Writing to the Rescue

One problem with using—and defining—abstract words is deciding what you mean by them. This problem is, of course, the central problem in the introductory cartoon. In the olden days when I was a student, students were taught to write *after* they figured out what they wanted to say. This method is certainly putting the chicken before the egg and the horse before the cart.

As Chapters One and Two pointed out, the process of writing, in fact, is an important method for figuring out what you think.

Let's just take almost everyone's favorite abstract word—the word that makes the world go 'round: Love. So far in this chapter we have examined three different aspects of *love's* definition.

1. The introductory Saint-Exupery quotation suggests that love consists in shared efforts, experiences, and goals.
2. The cartoon explores the relationship between affection and the mystical, chemical attraction of love.
3. "Those Winter Sundays" eloquently and concretely demonstrates love nurturing love in action.

Let's look at how one student decided what she meant by *perfection*. Her clustering is shown in Figure 10.1.

As this student clustered, her ideas about perfection became clearer to her. She then wrote the following first draft:

PERFECTION IS A GREMLIN: ROUGH DRAFT

Perfection. The dictionary says "freedom from fault or perfect: flawlessness." Ha! That is a fixed, permanent definition. But where is fixed, permanent perfec-

FIGURE 10.1   Clustering for *Perfection* Essay

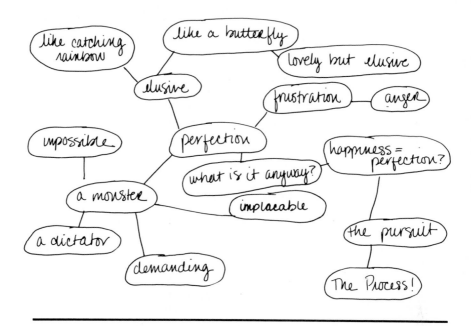

tion? Just when you think you have Perfection, zap, it's gone. Perfection is like a gremlin or other magic creature—a monster really—that can never be trapped no matter how hard you try.

I know. Sometimes in the past, I've been sure I had Him captured. He was nice. But after a short celebration and congratulation period, I've glanced at my hand to see that all I had was a little of his fur. He was no where in sight. This is, of course, very frustrating! It makes me angry and discouraged. Certainly if I could latch onto Perfection, I would be forever happy and fulfilled.

Or would I? As I think about it, I realize that over time I've learned that I can befriend Perfection instead of being ruled by this tyrannical master that is also an elusive gremlin. He can be like a coach who tries to get from me the highest—the best I can produce.

Anyway, what would happen if I did capture Perfection forever? I now realize I am most happy when I can come close and grasp him for a moment. If everything I did turned out perfectly, there would be no point for me to strive for, no higher goal to achieve, and no joy from conquering a difficult task or fear.

Maybe, in fact, the ticket to contentment is the Process—the sweat and determination—and not in the final product. maybe Perfection is a carrot in front of my nose to tantalize me while it inspires me to try harder.

Now that I realize this, I don't see Perfection as an enemy, but as a friend—though I can still get angry and frustrated. Now he also adds Zip and interest and challenge to my life as I try for those goals I set for myself to achieve—perfectly.

FOR THOUGHT AND DISCUSSION

1. How does the author's attitude toward perfection change from the beginning of this draft to its conclusion? In other words, what does the author discover through the writing process?
2. What does the author need to do to turn this draft into a unified, polished essay?
3. Suggest a thesis sentence that would give this essay unity.
4. Now read the revised, polished essay that follows. Then list the changes the author made in organization and content.
5. Explain why you think the author made these changes.

PERFECTION: FRIEND OR FOE?

Perfection, according to the *Merriam-Webster New Collegiate Dictionary* means "freedom from fault or defect: flawlessness." However, I know Perfection to be a sly and cunning beast who teases and cajoles me into trying to catch and keep him forever more. Then I and all the world would be able to look upon him and marvel at my accomplishment and good fortune. Yet, when I have him just within my grasp, he usually scurries off in the other direction laughing to himself at the folly of someone trying to claim him for her own.

Perfection cannot be caught and locked up. He is not static but always running forward, always changing directions. Sometimes, after much work and determination, I believe I have finally captured Perfection. However, after a short time of elation and self-satisfaction over my success, I glance down only to see a handful of his fur clutched between my fingers. On these occasions, I used to become frustrated, discouraged, and angry. I thought that if only I could find Perfection and hold onto him for good, I would be happy and fulfilled.

Through the years I have learned that Perfection can become a good friend—not a tyrannical master or an elusive rogue, but an encouraging coach who calls from me the highest quality of work and effort I can produce.

I am more comfortable with myself when I am content with my relationship with Perfection. I can come close and grasp him for a moment, but to capture him for good would make my life unexciting and unchallenging. For instance, if I was assured that everything I touched would turn out perfectly, there would be nothing significant for me to strive for, no higher standards of excellence to achieve, and no joy from accomplishing a task I fear or find difficult.

The ticket to contentment is in the process—in the sweat and determination it takes to reach for a goal, not in the flawless end product. Perfection, for me, is like a carrot in front of a horse's nose. The carrot tantalizes me while it inspires me to try harder. Perfection used to be my enemy. At times he can still irritate and frustrate me, but now he also adds an interesting and challenging aspect to all those goals I set for myself to achieve—perfectly!

Michelle Brinsmead

WRITING ASSIGNMENT
Using What You Have Learned

Select an abstract term and define it. In writing the definition, use your left brain skills to look up the word in a dictionary. Use the dictionary definition as a part of your essay, and be sure to give the name of the dictionary from which you took your definition. (Remember to underline the name of the dictionary or put it in italics. Also remember to enclose the exact words you quote from the dictionary in quotation marks.)

Once you have copied the dictionary's definition, put your right brain in gear by doing the following:

1. Write and circle the word you plan to define on the top third of a blank page.
2. Now relax and turn off your censuring left brain. Do not criticize the ideas that occur to you when you think about the abstract word you have circled. Simply write down the words and phrases that pop into your mind. Continue to cluster about the word you have selected until you know what you want to say about it.
3. When the lightbulb turns on in your brain (when you say *Aha! This is it*) you are ready to begin to write concretely about your word.
4. Write a definition from the ideas your clustering inspired.
5. Now reread the definition of the abstract word you copied from the dictionary, and work this definition into your essay.

   A few words of warning: use the dictionary's definition as a springboard for your own definition, not as the sole defining device. Remember to include the connotation of the word as well as its denotation in your definition—as the student star essays do.
6. Pay special attention to tying your beginning and ending together. Reread the student essays in the chapter, and note the smooth way the students tied their ideas together.
7. When you have finished writing, proofread your writing aloud and make any necessary revisions in content. Pay special attention to the connotation of the words you have chosen.
8. Note that when a word is referred to as a word and not for its meaning, it must be italicized. See "Italics," beginning on page 283 in "The Final Touch: A Handbook."
9. Proofread your essay for mechanical errors.

STUDENT STAR ESSAYS
The Polished Product

***Remember: the authors of these essays used the following steps:

1. Prewriting

2. Writing
3. Revising content
4. Proofreading and correcting of mechanical errors

FOOD FOR THOUGHT

Mature, according to *The American Heritage Dictionary* means "fully grown or developed, fully aged or ripened, worked out fully by the mind; perfected." In the physical sense, it is not difficult to understand what is meant by maturity. When a delicious apple is streaked with vivid red it is mature. When money has been invested in a United States Savings Bond for the required time, the bond has matured.

While maturity in the physical sense is obvious, maturity as a personality trait is an elusive concept. You do not receive maturity gift wrapped on your eighteenth birthday. Nor do you receive maturity in a lump sum. Instead maturity arrives in increments. You may be more mature at twenty-one than at eighteen, but even more mature at thirty-one. Maturity is something that grows in you slowly if it is nurtured. It requires food such as honesty, responsibility, acceptance, and concern.

The first time—at age seven—you admit you fed your broccoli to the dog you have shown the maturity growing within you. When you let the slowest kid on the block on your team so his feelings won't be hurt, it grows. It grows still more when you have to drive home so you refuse the pressure of your friends to drink.

According to *The American Heritage Dictionary* you have reached maturity when you are "fully developed" and "perfected." That definition is fine for an apple or a United States Savings Bond. For a human being, however, maturity is not static. As we grow older we continue to face new challenges. Hopefully we will continue to find the new resources to meet those challenges in an honest, responsible, thoughtful manner. Hopefully we will continue to mature.

Therese M. Markarian

A SELF-MADE MAN

Hero, according to *The American Heritage Dictionary,* means "a man celebrated for his strength and bold exploits; a man noted for his special achievements."

As children growing up I'm sure each of us had our own idea of what a hero was. Personally my heroes changed as my moods changed. I wanted to be like Buck Jones while reading a Western comic book and like Buck Rogers while watching an action-packed space adventure.

As an adult, I have a more realistic idea of what a hero is. Unlike the central figures of my childhood sagas, a hero is now someone I can relate to personally. He has achieved his goals by having undergone pain. He set his goal and pursued it with intensity.

Lee Trevino is a man who qualifies as a hero by my adult standards. He is a self-made man who has earned his status as a top golfer. Although he is now a respected professional, Trevino came from a poor family and hustled to make a living at golf. For years, he practiced long and hard and played in many tour-naments, but his efforts were't rewarded until he defeated Jack Nicklaus in the U.S. Open in 1972 in an eighteen-hole playoff.

For the next six years, Trevino continued to be very successful winning many golf tournaments. However during a tournament in 1978 he was struck by lightning and had to be hospitalized for a series of back surgeries. Nevertheless he still kept on competing even though the press and his fellow golf profession-als thought his winning days were over.

The American Heritage Dictionary says a hero is "a man celebrated for his strength and bold exploits" and "noted for his special achievements." Lee Trevino is such a man. In August of 1984 at age forty-three, he came back to show the world what a hero is. He came back to win the U.S. Professional Golf Association Championship.

John Nandy

HELP! ESSAY FOR FURTHER WORK

Read "What is Success," and then answer the Thought and Discussion questions which follow it.

WHAT IS SUCCESS?

To be successful is the wish of every red-blooded American. But if you were to ask ten people on the street their definition of success you would get at least ten different answers. What then is this thing called success? The only thing I can tell you for sure is that success means different things to everyone. Defining success, in other than the mundane manner in which Webster's does, is very difficult as it varies greatly from person to person. By-products of sucess may be intangible things as simple as self-satisfaction, gratification, or increased self-esteem. Also much more material considerations such as power, money, or elevated position, an individual's idea of success must include. Influenced by his morals and his established goals, the measure of success that is important to him is determined by each person. Whatever the motivation, achievement of some form of sucess is crucial for an individual to reach his fullest potential or simply lead a happy life. Sitting here writing about it, success is a complex concept.

FOR THOUGHT AND DISCUSSION

1. This student does not tell us which dictionary he or she used nor in what way that dictionary defined success. Revise this flawed portion of the essay.
2. List the abstract concepts the author fails to make concrete.
3. Add concrete examples to develop the essay's abstract idea.
4. Read "Misplaced Modifiers" and "Dangling Modifiers," beginning on page 307 of "The Final Touch: A Handbook" and then correct the misplaced and dangling modifiers in the essay.

11 DESCRIBING A PROCESS

Drawing by Levin; (c) 1982. *The New Yorker Magazine, Inc.*

He has gained every vote who has mingled profit with pleasure by delighting the reader at once and instructing him.

Horace

CONCEPTS TO LEARN

- The way to describe a process
- The meaning of *imagery*
- The importance of imagery in writing

FOR THOUGHT AND DISCUSSION

1. Why do you think so many people avoid reading the directions that come with products?
2. List two possible reasons the writer in the cartoon has thrown the typewriters into the corner.

GIVING DIRECTIONS

An important task required of many people in their personal, professional, and academic lives is giving directions. You can probably think of several things you would rather read—or write—than directions. In fact, many of us avoid reading directions because they are often confusing and boring.

Fortunately, this does not have to be so. More than two thousand years ago, the Roman poet Horace discovered the way to readers' hearts was by delighting them as he instructed them. When writing directions, that is, when describing a process, we are most apt to delight if we are organized, clear, concise, and concrete. You will be delighted to hear that the techniques studied and practiced in the first ten chapters of *Practicing the Process* will help us in delighting readers and instructing them clearly enough to keep their attention. Keeping their attention is important because if readers are bored or confused, their attention drifts off. In this chapter we will investigate making process writing clear, efficient, and interesting.

Vocabulary   **imagery:**   the impression created by appealing to one of the reader's five senses
chased: metal decorated by embossing or engraving it

In Chapter Six, we discussed Sophocles' idea that nothing is more wonderful than man. Ironically, while people have not been remarkably wonderful at eliminating world hunger or in settling disputes between nations peacefully, they *have* been wonderfully clever at finding ways to eliminate each other.

In the following poem, Edwin Brock alludes to a different historical period in each stanza. Note the way he arranges his **imagery** to drive home his point about mankind.

Five Ways to Kill a Man

There are many cumbersome ways to kill a man:
you can make him carry a plank of wood
to the top of a hill and nail him to it. To do this
properly you require a crowd of people
wearing sandals, a cock that crows, a cloak
to dissect, a sponge, some vinegar and one
man to hammer the nails home.

Or you can take a length of steel,
shaped and **chased** in a traditional way,
and attempt to pierce the metal cage he wears.
But for this you need white horses,
English trees, men with bows and arrows,
at least two flags, a prince and a
castle to hold your banquet in.

Dispensing with nobility, you may, if the wind
allows, blow gas at him. But then you need
a mile of mud sliced through with ditches,
not to mention black boots, bomb craters,
more mud, a plague of rats, a dozen songs
and some round hats made of steel.

In an age of aeroplanes, you may fly
miles above your victim and dispose of him by
pressing one small switch. All you then
require is an ocean to separate you, two
systems of government, a nation's scientists,
several factories, a psychopath and
land that no one needs for several years.

These are, as I began, cumbersome ways
to kill a man. Simpler, direct, and much more neat
is to see that he is living somewhere in the middle
of the twentieth century and leave him there.

Edwin Brock

FOR THOUGHT AND DISCUSSION

1. Reread each of the stanzas. What image in each stanza helps you know to what period it alludes?

2. List concrete examples of factors that make the twentieth century a difficult time in which to live.
3. Do you agree with Edwin Brock's assessment of the twentieth century? Support your answer with concrete examples.

PROCESS ESSAYS

While "Five Ways to Kill a Man" dealt with a major philosophical problem, most of the writing we have to do concerns less profound subjects. For example when you type the letter "e," it sometimes smudges: "*e*" and sometimes your typewriter may skip " " entirely.

I would like to save my trusty typewriter from the fate of those in the cartoon introducing the chapter. Of course, I could call a repairman, but I suspect the problem might be something I could fix myself. Unfortunately, my typewriter instruction manual was written by a blender—or someone with a sick sense of humor (or to be kinder, someone who hasn't mastered the principles of good writing). Certainly it was not written by someone who was successful at delighting or instructing me.

Fortunately, however, author Wayne Gash has written a clear process essay that explains ten common problems I can check before I resort to paying a repair person. Notice as you read the following essay how Gash explains technical material in terms that appeal to an audience of ordinary people.

TEN TYPEWRITER PROBLEMS YOU CAN CORRECT YOURSELF
Wayne Gash

The typewriter repairman gestures to your electric typewriter, now humming pleasantly.

"That was fast," you say. "What was wrong with it?"

"Wasn't plugged in."

No one is so mechanically inept or absent-minded that they would call a repairman before checking to see if the typewriter was plugged in, you say? Want to bet? I manage an office-machine repair shop, and I've seen such "simple" problems happen all the time. In the typewriter repair trade, these unnecessary calls are termed *nuisance calls* or, more politely (and especially if the customer is nearby), *operator errors.*

Such errors are embarrassing, certainly. But they are also expensive. Call a "customer engineer" (that's a repairman with a tie) to fix your faithful typewriter and he will charge you about seventy dollars an hour plus mileage to either fix it or plug it in. It makes no difference to him.

Operator errors can be avoided. In fact, in Washington State, where I work, some repairmen I know of estimate that they have cut nuisance calls in half simply by giving operators a ten-point troubleshooting checklist to use *before* calling for repairs. Using that checklist can save you time and money. *And* embarrassment.

Most of the suggestions on the list apply to troubleshooting problems on electric typewriters—including self-correcting typewriters and those that have "golf ball" typing elements and cassette ribbons, as do the IBM Selectrics. But some of the suggestions will work when troubles arise on manual typewriters.

Keep the following checklist near your typewriter:

1. Typewriter will not run.   Check the off/on switch. Check that both ends of the electrical cord—and any extension cords—are plugged in. Plug a lamp or clock into the outlet used by the typewriter. You may have lost electricity to that particular outlet.

2. Typewriter does not print.   Check the stencil control lever. Is it off? Check the ribbon. Have you used it up? Does it have a fold in it? Is it stuck to the correcting lift-off tape? Strike the keys and watch the ribbon. Does it move up and down with each stroke? In short, make sure you have installed the ribbon correctly. Most nuisance calls result from ribbon problems.

3. Incomplete or random inking.   Again, check the ribbon or ribbon cassette. Is it installed correctly? Remove the cassette and snap it back in again. Make sure it snaps in snugly. Is the ribbon folded? It has been installed incorrectly. Are you down to the last two or three feet of ribbon? Many carbon ribbons crack and chip near the portion that has been wound tightly at the end of the spool.

Check the correcting lift-off tape. Is it stuck to the ribbon? On most correcting typewriters, a fine wire peg separates the lift-off tape and ribbon. The tape should be on one side, the ribbon the other.

If punctuation marks or the bottom halves of the letters are not printing, check the copy control lever, which is usually on the top of the typewriter, toward the back of the machine. It will be labeled with a scale from A to E or with a series of marks. At one time, this lever served the useful purpose of reducing the pressure on the platen so you could type up to six carbon copies. No one types six copies anymore, and now repairpeople consider the device a nuisance in itself. If the lever is pushed back when only one or two sheets are in the machine, the keys don't strike squarely. Most new typewriters don't have a copy control lever. If yours does, pull it all the way forward and leave it there.

If the type is light, check the impression control lever, located next to the element on element machines and on the front of others. This lever is used to increase pressure of the keys on the platen when cutting stencils. The normal setting is three. One is too light. If your typewriter is older, you may need to crank it up to five.

Check for scratches or folds in the ribbon. Check your paper. Many carbon ribbons won't stick to erasable bond or photocopy paper.

4. Excessive inking and smudges.   Again, check the copy control lever. If it is set loose for multiple copies, the keys may slip and strike off-center.

Check that the ribbon is installed properly, and that it is moving freely and isn't bunching up. Check your paper. Erasable, photocopy, and coated papers smudge, too.

5. Incomplete correction lift-off.   Check the nuisance lever if you haven't already taped it down. The copy control lever can foul operation of the lift-off tape as easily as it fouls operation of the ribbon.

The most common cause of poor lift-off is an improperly installed lift-off tape, ribbon or ribbon cassette. Are the tape and ribbon separated by the wire peg? If not, tape and ribbon will stick together and neither will work correctly.

6. No print on top/bottom of every third letter.   This is easy to troubleshoot and correct. The ribbon cassette is not snapped in properly, which causes the ribbon to fold, and every third keystroke misses the tape. Push the cassette down until it snaps firmly in place.

7. Carrier skips spaces.   Check if the dual pitch lever (which adjusts for elements with different type sizes) is set between 10 and 12 pitch. Set it on one or the other. If the typewriter stops skipping, you're in luck. If it doesn't, you could have serious problems. Call the repair shop.

8. Paper is loose.   This one is in the same category as remembering to plug in your typewriter. If the paper is slipping in your typewriter, make sure that the feed roll release lever—which releases tension on the platen—is in the *back* position before you reach for the phone.

9. Typewriter misprints.   The *t* that is missing from all your words is also probably missing from your typing element—if you have a "golf ball" element. Check the element for chips and cracks. If the print is garbled, occasionally or all the time, remove the element and check the teeth around the bottom of the "golf ball." Missing, cracked, or worn teeth will let the element slip out of alignment. The result is gibberish.

Before you buy a new element, call local repair shops to see if one will repair elements. Many shops now make such repairs and a cracked or chipped element can often be repaired for about half the cost of a new one.

10. Typewriter rattles.   If it's a new rattle, make sure the typewriter is level. Check the cover plate and make sure that it is snapped down properly.

If it's an old rattle, don't worry about it. The typewriter is working. Don't make things worse by poking around inside it.

FOR THOUGHT AND DISCUSSION

1. Give an example of an explanation from the essay that would be helpful to a general audience, but would be too simple for an audience of typewriter repair persons.
2. Which of the beginning techniques from Chapter Nine does the article use?
3. Why is the introduction especially appropriate for the intended audience?
4. How does the organizational technique of numbering the errors help to make the instructions easier to understand?

WHEN TIME EQUALS MONEY

Professional writers are perhaps even more motivated than other people to write quickly and efficiently. For them the cliché "time is money" rings true. The Flannery O'Connor quotation that introduces this textbook is, "One thing that is always with the writer—no matter how long he has written or how good he is—is the continuous process of learning how to write." In the following essay, Alan Blackburn describes the process he used to learn to save time. Interestingly, in his research, Blackburn discovered a good deal about using his right brain to increase his efficiency.

HOW TO WRITE FAST
Alan R. Blackburn

I guessed the secret of creative writing lay deep in some fold of my brain that I was not aware of. I hied to the public library and signed out all the books on brain research I could lay my hands on.

Since then I've kept up to date on the powerful new techniques being brought to light by those probing into the unknown universe inside our skulls. I have been granted a vision of what brain power, residing below the level of awareness, can do to create for, and speed up, a writer.

The brain is no simple-minded organ to be passed by with a paternal sniff. It commands a labor force of over one hundred billion neurons (brain cells) and over one hundred trillion synapses (links between cells). These fabulous, interlocking networks are cocked, ready to work for you to select, combine, compare, alter or reject whatever you feed them. They're the quickest bunch of servants you'll ever meet.

But you don't need to put aside your writing and bone up for a Ph.D. in brain science. For writers, the point is that the brain provides a powerhouse that can set your creativity going at a full gallop if you know how to stoke it and stroke it.

There are just two ways to write. Most experts agree that right and left halves of the brain work as a team in two different modes: a fast, *natural* mode, and a slow, *logical* mode. I don't worry about *how* my brain works; I'm satisfied that it works.

It's creative, spontaneous, relaxed, timeless, and intuitive. It performs its tasks secretly, a mile away from your self-awareness.

The logical mode is critical, rational, tense, and guiltily *self*-conscious.

Make friends with *both* modes. You need them. Natural mode gives birth. Logical mode cleans up baby. Natural is effortless; logical is labored. Natural *writes;* logical *edits.*

Most of us were taught in school to write in the logical mode—artificially, ill at ease. Many (not all) English teachers did us wrong. Think back. Can't you hear a schoolmarm gasp if you misspelled a word or garbled grammar? Weren't you taught to make an outline first?

This school thinking that most of us were brought up on is rigid. Let's not kid ourselves. Left to its own devices, the brain does not proceed in an orderly fashion. Witness your crazy dreams.

The brain starts with chaos. It ends with order. It does not make an outline first and then fit content to it. It juggles the teeming data and lets them shape their own patterns. Like a Labrador retriever, the brain delights to chase after birds. It will nuzzle around in the underbrush of your neurons to startle you with distant and near-term memories which it dumps, tail wagging, at the feet of your consciousness.

The payoff to these antics is that your brain, performing in its natural mode, thinks in the same playful, zesty way your *reader* does. The brain laps up interesting things. It spurns anything that bores. It sniffs for the sequined, the dangerous, the horrible, the sensual.

THE FIVE MAGIC STEPS

But this is not a treatise on wonders of the brain. Nor an essay on how to write. I assume you know how. It's about how to write *fast.*

May I present the five steps of Fast-Write?

1. *Preset*
2. *Stuff*
3. *Buzz Off*
4. *Printout*
5. *Feedback*

Step One: Preset.   Ever watch an organist as she gets set to play? She first pulls out the stops to preset the frame for the piece she's going to play. Likewise the writer. He pulls out the stops in his brain to set it up to follow the pitch he wants.

Then pull out the stop for *efficiency.* Make sure your workroom is neat, your typewriter works, files are in order, all reference sources lie at hand. My work table looks like the cockpit of a Concorde.

These are details. The really important stop to pull is the stop that instructs the brain what to search for when it gathers material for your piece. You save a mountain of time when you know what needles to look for in what haystacks.

You see, in its raw state the brain is wild. Like a hungry lion, it prowls at random over the park. You must train it to jump through a hoop before people will pay to watch it perform. So you give your brain a hoop.

The hoop I give my brain is shown in the accompanying illustration. It's a priority-spotter for your brain to select the right items as it rummages through your research material.

Size of the rectangles in the diagram is in scale to the proportionate stopping power of the various parts of your article—their ability to seize and hold a reader's eye. All writing is directed to that supreme moment when your potential reader flips through a publication. Will it be your piece he or she picks to read?

Now, given this restrictive form, the brain knows what to fetch and its relative attention-getting value. The brain doesn't race down unrewarding and time-losing rabbit trails.

Step Two: Stuff.   With the diagram firmly in mind, stuff the brain with every scrap of information that relates to the content of your article. Overstuff: *you* will tire before your brain does—it's built to absorb a million bits of information a second around the clock.

Remember that a lifetime of living and reading also lies in your brain. When you write, that knowledge, too, becomes available to enrich your copy. Events and facts that you never knew your brain filed bob to the surface—taste of warm milk, racket of disco, Picasso's two-faced portraits. Knowledge of the world will do you more good than literary knowledge.

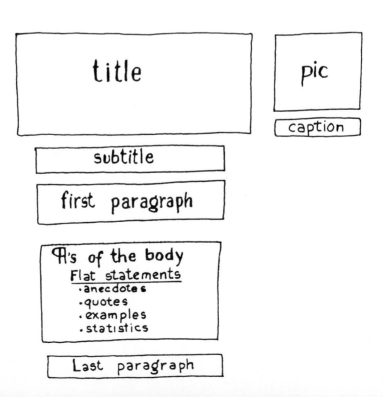

If I'm doing a piece with an unusual number of facts, I go mechanical. I write down each fact, anecdote, quote and stray thought on its own 3×5 card. I then stack them by topic.

You eye these cards and flip them over and over until your brain soaks up their messages. Don't force the brain to "memorize" or you will put the whole natural, imaginative process on ice. The brain is mulish. Lead it gently to the trough. It will know what to do *naturally.*

Finally, you run out of stuff to stuff. Facts repeat. Concepts go stale. You're overloaded and overlearned. Stop.

Step Three: Buzz Off!   Do that. Your brain must be alone to pull together what you have crammed into it.

Play tennis, watch TV, jog, visit a museum—just be sure what you do is a continent away from the subject of your immediate piece.

Your brain and only your brain, separated from you, its watchbird, can quickly, efficiently and inventively boil down this conglomeration of input—if left in solitary. Don't open the door on the man in the darkroom.

Unaware is the open sesame to brain power. Awareness paralyzes free play. Back in college I experienced this chill factor writing an honors thesis. I became aware of my act of writing. I froze. In my journal I noted, "My pen is executioner of my thoughts."

Crusade against your rational self-consciousness. I recall how a fellow writer assigned to create a fundraising brochure drew the ire of his client, who caught him sitting on the sill of an office window basking in spring sunshine—doing nothing. Actually he was allowing his brain to ferment the facts. Days later he developed brilliant copy that brought smiles back to his client's face and justified his fee.

Step Four: Printout.   It's write time. Consider again the organist. Before she can play, she must sit herself down on the bench before those banks of keys. In like fashion the writer sits himself in front of those typewriter keys with intent to make his fingers go.

That's the *most important step he'll ever take* to get himself off dead center. The longest or shortest article begins with but a single word.

But the secret above all secrets for creative writing, *and* for fast writing, is the *draft.* The draft shifts the brain into the mode of natural production.

A draft gets you over the fear of looking silly about what you put on paper. No one sees the draft but you. It's not the draft the editor buys nor the printer prints nor the reader reads. You won't be shot if you fluff. You don't have to own up to the draft on Judgment Day. Relieved of anxiety, you're free to let go.

HELPFUL TRANSITIONS

Before we go to the next step, one trick to help speed you up: Stock phrases like the following samples will move your writing along at a swifter pace. These are not trite expressions, but introductory phrases that pros use again and again to alert the reader to what's coming next. They fit *any* idea or announce *any* fact. They are like the interchangeable parts in mass production. You can find thousands of them and it's fun to pick them out from your reading.

These observations imply . . .
Soon after discovery of . . .

By the mid-1960s . . .
These facts support this view . . .
The real answer came when . . .
Four elements of a typical . . .
The record is not at all clear . . .
Consider this puzzling question . . .
The best way to describe . . .
One of the delights of . . .

Step Five: Feedback.   To this point we have operated in the natural thinking mode. Now we change to the mode of rational, conscious thinking. We are ready to edit (feed back to our brain what it has poured forth).

You now *consciously* cast your critical eye over your copy to see if it measures up to your tenets of good writing. You sit in judgment on the throne of accuracy of facts, words, correct grammar, and spelling.

IN CONCLUSION

Fast-Write is brain write—the easy way to go.

I witnessed a beautiful example of brain power one evening as I returned from a day of writing in the city. I lived then in a new suburb still semi-rural. On my walk from the bus I flushed a pheasant, which flew up from the grass and took off through a stand of trees. It never hesitated; it never brushed a twig. It took turns and twists that would stump IBM's smartest computer, instantly solving aerodynamic problems. This pheasant didn't make an outline first; it didn't submit a flight plan. It simply took off. It let its intuition work for it. This bird was thinking naturally.

A pheasant's brain weighs less than an ounce. If a featherweight birdbrain can do that well, what are the possibilities for you and me with a brain that weighs in at three pounds?

FOR THOUGHT AND DISCUSSION

1. How does the method described in "How to Write Fast" make use of left and right brain differences?
2. One of the advantages of right-brain writing is that the right brain sees the total picture instead of individual pieces, so it helps tie your ideas together in your conclusion. Explain in what way its conclusion ties the essay together.
3. What images help you understand abstract concepts in the essay?
4. List five vivid verbs used in "How to Write Fast."

TO COMPLAIN

To complain of the age we live in, to murmur at the present possessors of power, to lament the past, to conceive extravagant hopes of the future, are the common dispositions of the greatest part of mankind.

Edmund Burke, *Thoughts on the Cause of the Present Discontent*

While a great deal about life has changed in the two hundred years since Burke wrote about people's tendency to complain, most of us sooner or later have something to complain about. Sometimes we complain about lofty world problems. Most of the time, however, we complain about ordinary problems, such as sending a watch in for repair twice and paying a repair charge each time, only to find its hands still do not advance more than an hour without getting stuck.

I have more expensive complaints as well. For example, my car dealer told me it was my fault when something in the rear of my new station wagon began to shake, rattle and roar. It turned out a defective axle had worn out the bearings. (While *axle* and *bearings* may be rather technical for this textbook's audience—or for me, at least—"shake, rattle, and roar" should insure everyone adequately understands the problem.)

To fix the shake, rattle, and roar, my car dealer said, would cost me $500. Angry at my inability to get a response from my dealer or from his company's area service representative, I had the car repaired elsewhere for $300. Two years later all stations wagons of my model were recalled because they had defective axles.

I could, of course, go on and on complaining (and you will get a chance to do just that in Chapter Twelve). Before we launch our complaining attacks, however, the author of the following article from *Ms.* has some advice to help us with our battles.

HOW TO COMPLAIN

WHEN YOUR TOASTER, YOUR VCR, OR YOUR BANKER DOESN'T DO THE JOB
Emily Card

If you find yourself in the position of having to complain about products or services you are paying for, there are certain tried-and-true techniques that will increase the likelihood of your getting what you want in the end. Hear are eight pointers for systematically achieving the best results:

1. A preventive measure: Establish yourself as a preferred customer.   Can you imagine a rich or famous person having to complain to get results? Such people don't usually have to complain, because other people work hard to please them in the first place. Even though you may be neither rich nor famous, you too can receive preferential treatment if you become a regular and familiar customer. Thus, it makes sense to do business with the same establishments again and again, and to develop positive working relationships with key individuals with whom you deal exclusively as much as possible.

You can become a "card-carrying" preferred customer by establishing a charge account. After all, if you have an account at a store, presumably you trade there often. In fact, this assumption is built into consumer credit law. The Fair Credit Billing Act provides that credit customers can withhold payment on any damaged or defective goods or poor quality services if they have first made

an attempt to resolve their dispute with the creditor honoring the card. However, this right is limited if you have charged the goods or services on a bank card (MasterCard or Visa), or on a travel and entertainment card (American Express, Diners Club), rather than on a card issued by the store: your purchase must be for more than fifty dollars, and must have taken place in your home state or within one hundred miles of your home address.

Note: If you ever decide to exercise the "billing error" right also provided by this act, you must notify the creditor who misbilled you within sixty days, or you will lose your rights. Check your credit report afterward to ensure that the creditor has not incorrectly (and illegally) reported your delayed payment to the credit bureau as a late payment. (See "How to Find and 'Deep Clean' Your Credit File," *Ms.,* June, 1983.)

2. Before you complain, outline the problem for yourself and clarify how you would like it resolved. Put down on paper exactly what is wrong, as far as you can figure it out, including when the "symptoms" began and what they are, and what the "diagnosis" is.

Once you can state the problem precisely, decide whether you want your money back, or a replacement item, or a repair made (or made again) with no cost to you. Be aware, however, that in some instances the stated or implied guarantee offers only repair service and not replacement.

Furthermore, many durable consumer items such as televisions, stereos, VCRs, and kitchen appliances come with guarantees that require factory servicing. You may be able to avoid later inconvenience by reading the warranty of the product *before* you buy it; if you have a choice between two similar products and one offers the option of local servicing, that's the one to pick.

3. Be organized: As a routine habit, keep all receipts, contracts, warranties, and copies of relevant correspondence. If you have ever had your baggage lost by an airline, you may have discovered that in order to be sure you are fully reimbursed for your losses, it is helpful to present receipts for misplaced or damaged items. (The same is true for hotels with valet services and regular cleaning establishments, some of which may use your receipts to collect from their own insurance companies.) Not many people can lay their hands on a receipt for a suitcase bought three years ago, not to mention each item in the bag. If you travel often, you might want to keep a standard packing list, and mark it off as you actually pack for the trip. (Such a list obviously increases your efficiency in packing, too.) Also, keep a big file full of receipts for clothes, makeup, and personal care items purchased. Keep another file of receipts of major household purchases—it will save you time and effort in filing insurance claims should your home or apartment be burglarized, or your car and/or its contents stolen.

To ensure good mail-order service, always retain a photocopy of your order and the original catalog.

As you prepare a complaint, open a file in which you gather all supporting materials such as canceled checks, charge slips, receipts, and letters. Roger Goldblatt, former associate director of the United States Office of Consumer Affairs, and author of *Making it Work: The User's Guide to Government* (Resource Press), suggests that you "keep a log of all phone conversations, noting the date, name, and phone number and title of those you contact." Remember that if you have to go to court to resolve your problem, all these written materials will become the evidence you'll need.

It's also up to you to keep the ball rolling: "A lot of places count on your forgetting the problem and your anger subsiding," says Goldblatt. "Most people don't pursue their complaints." Thus, how the situation is resolved will depend on your persistence, and your contacting the same people at regular intervals to remind them of the passage of time and your specific efforts to resolve the problem.

4. Decide on the best person to complain to and the best means of reaching her or him, whether by letter, telephone, or personal visit. The magnitude of the problem and how you want it addressed will determine whom you should contact.

Here are some rules of thumb:

- Minor merchandise exchange problem—go back to the original counter and clerk. Approach her or him in person or by phone on a friendly equal-to-equal basis for quick results.
- Substantial problem involving a large amount of money or policy variation or waiver—start at the top.
- Consumer law or civil rights violation, fraud, or suit for damages—seek outside help. In some cases, a government agency, the Better Business Bureau, or the media can help. Sometimes you will have to solve the problem with the assistance of an attorney. You may even have to file a lawsuit, which will be time-consuming and a drain on your personal and financial resources. (See Tip Number Seven.)

5. Keep your cool at all costs. Remember that angry accusations will very likely elicit an angry and defensive response, and give the person with whom you are dealing the excuse to decide that the problem is your personality and not a legitimate complaint. In legal circles, the professional complainer is known as a "litigious" person, and being tagged with this label is the kiss of death.

Do start out with a strong, clear statement of your case: "This is what happened, and this is what I want done." Don't be tentative as in, "This is what happened . . . I think . . . but I don't know if you can do anything or if you are the right person to help." You are risking not engaging the full attention and real effort from the individual you are approaching. Whatever you do, don't begin with the threat of legal action, as in: "If my car isn't repaired by 5:00 P.M. today, I'll see you in court." Court is the appeal of last resort, *not* the first option in a complaint process.

6. If you don't achieve satisfaction at the first level you try, don't hesitate to contact the next one.   Know that *there is always someone higher up:* a manager, a vice-president, a president, a board of directors, an outside agency. A long-time IBM executive related to me an unforgettable example of this principle. When Thomas Watson, Jr., was chairman of IBM, he once called a meeting at the company headquarters in Armonk, New York. Once assembled, this group of high-powered executives were told of a problem which Mr. Watson wanted corrected immediately. The source of the complaint? An employee had written to Watson's mother.

7. If you can't get a satisfactory response dealing directly with the company in question, it's time to turn to a government agency.   If the agency doesn't respond to your satisfaction, your next recourse is to the agency's overseers—first, the legislature, and then, the courts.

It's a fact that not all government agencies are equally responsive to consumer complaints. Those such as the Veterans Administration, the Department of Health and Human Services, and the Social Security Administration, which were set up to provide benefits and services to the public, are structured to handle consumer complaints; nonetheless, because they are also overburdened, they may take a long time.

Bank regulatory agencies—from the board of governors of the Federal Reserve System to the state agencies that regulate thrift institutions—frequently come to the aid of an individual consumer's interests. The agency that oversees a particular financial institution is always listed on the front door of the institution and on all its literature.

The United States Postal Service and the Department of Transportation (DOT) can be of assistance to some consumers. The post office, for example, will trace lost mail. Under the DOT, the National Highway Traffic Safety Administration provides a consumer information hot line on automobiles, including auto recalls. The Consumer Product Safety Commission also has a consumer information hot line through which you can obtain advice about a range of products, especially those that might be unsafe for children, or report safety or fire hazards of products in and around the home. (See resource list at the end of the article for hot line numbers and addresses.)

Some agencies have special powers that allow them to intervene in a consumer's affairs, but without it necessarily being in the consumer's interest. The Internal Revenue Service has the broadest powers of any agency. The IRS, for example, can seize a taxpayer's assets without first obtaining a court order. Therefore, when you get ready to make a complaint involving the IRS, be prepared for a strenuous battle.

Since Congress holds the purse strings to the agency budgets, all federal agencies have special Congressional liaison offices that service member inquiries; in turn, every Congressmember has one or more staff persons working full-time on constituent casework. Specifically request your representative's help in writing, enclosing all relevant supporting documentation, including your case or file number if your dealings with an agency have gotten that far. The cover letter is important: if you just send your representative your file without it, it will be assumed that the agency is handling the issue to your satisfaction. (The same procedure directed to state assembly representatives and city council members works to some extent with state and local agencies as well.)

The Federal Trade Commission is another agency that has broad oversight powers, but there are limits on what it will do for the individual consumer. The staff of the FTC works on *patterns* of complaints, so while they want to hear from you if you have a problem, they will usually not pursue your issue unless it has received the same complaint about a particular company or industry from many other consumers. Sometimes, however, if you call your local FTC office, if there is one in your area, they will provide you with information about key legal guidelines relating to a particular problem. The FTC also puts out helpful consumer publications that summarize the law in problem areas about which they are most frequently queried.

8. Figure out the "opportunity costs" of making and resolving your complaint before you pursue it to the fullest extent. Spending one hundred and fifty dollars in time and money to correct a fifteen-dollar problem doesn't make sense, unless the personal satisfaction of being acknowledged "in the right" is really worth that much to you. Remember that powerful people choose their battles carefully. You may be better off if you take a walk or treat yourself to an ice cream cone, and forget a problem that's caused only minor annoyance.

RESOURCES FOR CONSUMER COMPLAINTS

The Federal Trade Commission. The FTC is supposed to achieve broad remedies for identified violations that will benefit the public in general, rather than particular individuals. The major areas that the FTC policies include: warranties, care labels; funeral costs; business opportunities, ventures and franchises: credit, used-car dealers; marketing/advertising practices; and door-to-door sales. State or local consumer agencies enforce many of the FTC's statutes and are better equipped to resolve individual complaints, so contact them first, but inform the FTC about any complaints you are pursuing locally since the FTC looks for trends it needs to act upon. Direct your inquiries or complaints in writing to: Public Reference Branch, Room 130, Federal Trade Commission, 6th and Pennsylvania Avenue, N.W., Washington, D.C. 20580.

Consumer Product Safety Commission. CPSC maintains a hot line to collect information about injuries from consumer products and to advise on those that are hazardous: (800) 638-2772.

National Highway Traffic Safety Administration, U.S. Department of Transportation. The NHTSA operates a hot line for complaints and inquiries about automotive safety: (800) 424-9393.

FOR THOUGHT AND DISCUSSION

1. Which techniques for effective complaining are the easiest to use? Which are the most difficult? Why?
2. How many of the complaining techniques involve writing skills?
3. Explain which complaining techniques rely on left brain skills and which involve right brain skills.
4. Using the article suggestions, formulate a plan to help me recover my three hundred dollars in car repairs. In your plan, consider whether I should first approach my local dealer or the company headquarters. Explain what documents will help me in my battle.

WRITING ASSIGNMENT
Using What You Have Learned

Write an essay of at least three hundred words in which you describe a process. In your essay be sure to do the following steps:

1. Before you begin, you must be thoroughly familiar with the process you describe. If necessary, read about the process or interview someone who is an expert.
2. Reread "How to Write Fast." Use the author's suggestions to help you write your theme quickly, clearly, and efficiently.
3. Once you have adequate knowledge of your subject, use one of the prewriting techniques of clustering, brainstorming, or freewriting to plan your paper. This step is especially important because process themes naturally lend themselves to left-brain thinking. Using one of the prewriting techniques will help you avoid being dominated by your left brain in this assignment.
4. Consider the knowledge level of your audience (your classmates). Define any terms not familiar to the audience, but do not insult them with the obvious.
5. Remember you are selling your ideas. Go beyond the obvious thinking. Try to interest you reader. Use vivid, concrete details to show your reader your point. Use metaphors, similes, personification, other imagery, and quotations when appropriate. Try clustering to help you create imagery.
6. Once you have completed your prewriting and writing, proofread for content.
7. Proofread once again for mechanical errors.

The following is a list of suggested topics for your process theme:

1. How to conquer the monster in your nightmares
2. How to study for an exam
3. How to fall asleep
4. How to make friends with a doberman pinscher

5. How to get into your house or your car when you have locked
   yourself out
6. How to survive with a snorer
7. How to unmash your closet

STUDENT STAR ESSAYS
The Polished Product

***Remember: the authors of these essays used the following steps:

1. Prewriting
2. Writing
3. Revising content
4. Proofreading and correcting mechanical errors

REST EASY

It's been a hard night. You're exhausted. Rest is the answer, but school takes precedence. You need Dr. Donna Dream's rule book *Falling Asleep in Class Without Being Noticed.* For those too tired to read the entire book, I have summarized the instructions as follows:

1. Put a smile on your face. Get to class on time and brightly mention to the teacher what a beautiful day it is. Looking refreshed is essential, so wear bright, happy colors like red, yellow, or orange.
2. If at all possible, sit in the back row so that your head will have a wall to hold it up. Posture is extremely important. Sit erect and let your neck fall back slightly, resting on the wall. Your chin should be raised as if you are very self-assured. If this is out of the question, sit directly behind another student. Put both elbows on the table and rest your chin on your palms.
3. Start your meditation trance. Keeping a steady motion, rock your head slowly as if in agreement. This will convince the teacher you are in concurrence. If you practice at home and become very good at this process, even closing your eyes makes it look as if you are deep in thought.
4. At the end of class other students will begin chattering, slamming books into backpacks, and zipping up tote bags. Use this noise as your alarm clock.
5. Mention to the teacher as you stroll out of class what an interesting lecture it was today. With renewed energy, jog to your next class.

Lizbeth Gieseler

HOW TO SURVIVE A DIVORCE

Those who are still hopelessly in love with the cad, will say, "It can't be done!" This is known as Phase I.

Phase II, however, uses an entirely different approach: "Shoot the son(or daughter)ofabitch!"

Alas, to your dismay, you will find this is frowned upon in most circles and can result in a long term engagement at your local penitentiary. Unless, of course (and I must warn you the following sentence is sex-specific material for women only), you have a woman judge and an all-woman jury. Then the court would find the cad was at fault, received his just reward, and you would be nominated for President of your local Women's Club.

All kidding aside, divorce is a problem facing both men and women today. Although there are no exact answers about how to survive the tragedy of divorce, here are a few survival pointers I have learned the hard way—through experience.

STEP I

All of us could learn something from the members of Alcoholics Anonymous. To start their healing process they begin with the traditional Serenity Prayer:

> God, grant me the serenity
> To accept the things I cannot change,
> The courage to change the things I can,
> And the wisdom to know the difference.
>
> Anonymous

If your mate is gone for good, accept the inevitable, and begin to reassemble the shattered pieces of your life.

STEP II

Find a good psychologist. Now before you stamp your foot and go screaming out of the room saying, "I'm not sick. I'm hurt!" you must realize that the basis for much of our society's poor mental health is the lack of knowledge about dealing with unresolved pain. We are all subjected to emotional traumas during the course of our lives. Psychologists can help us discuss this pain; they can walk and talk through it with us and explain how dealing with the trauma in the correct manner will promote healing. This will help you create a fresh new page to write on—a healthy new start.

STEP III

Take charge of your life. You've heard that cliché before? It sounds easy, doesn't it? Wrong. First you have to get to know yourself. With a lot of hard work and honesty, you may one day look into the mirror and find your best friend there—yourself.

Women especially are used to being Second in Command in Life. Many of us are accustomed to functioning in a supporting role. When we find ourselves not only cooking the bacon, but having to bring it home as well, we may be overcome.

Look at this step in a different light: Getting to know yourself can be an adventure. And searching for a glimmer of light at the end of the Divorce Tunnel will help you exercise your right brain. Think about what is in it for you. You have stopped fixing what *he* liked for dinner, or watching what *she* liked on television. Now you have the opportunity to try new foods or new television programs or new whatevers. Guess what, Cookie: You don't have to eat spaghetti or watch the Superbowl or *Dallas.* Get out of the house and have some fun! Take a composition class at a local college.

Men, I know I have slanted this toward women, but don't think I have forgotten you. You fellas can go through just as much hell as we do. One of your problems may be in finding that society has sold you a bill of goods about being Mr. Macho. Roy Rogers didn't cry. You must keep a stiff upper lip. To this I say "Garbage!"

Go sit in the sun, read a book, cry. It's good for you. Then go see a Woody Allen movie. See if you still remember how to laugh.

STEP IV

Exercise. Everyone from six days to one-hundred-and-six needs some form of exercise. It makes us feel better. It firms muscle tissue. It releases hormones that are Nature's pain killers. It promotes better physical and mental health.

Certainly when it comes to something as traumatic as a divorce, no one has all of the answers. But one thing is for sure: If you can follow the steps I've given you, your wounds will begin to heal. The future will gradually look brighter; you *will* survive. And eventually you will be glad you did.

KC King

HOW TO BECOME AN ALCOHOLIC

To become an alcoholic it is helpful, but not necessary, to be born into a family that has a history of alcoholism. Scientists tell us this will give you a head start. But do not despair if there are no alcoholics in the family closet. The heredity step—like any of the following steps—can be skipped. In fact some people have so much natural talent that during their first drinking episode they exhibit alcoholic behavior.

Most people seem to prefer becoming an alcoholic in three stages. In Stage One, most submit to either peer or societal pressure and start drinking to be cool. ("Everyone else does, why not me?") Soon after starting you need to increase your tolerance for alcohol by drinking just a little more each time. Like anything else, practice makes perfect, so practice a little more often as time goes on. Once you notice a change in your tolerance level, you are well into Stage One.

The next step in this stage is to keep on drinking even after others have stopped. With your tolerance high, this is fairly easy, so it's a good idea to move right on to the next step which is to drink before you go to a drinking function. This way you won't look out of place when everyone else stops, and you will also be ready to stop thanks to your head start.

To graduate to Stage Two you need to drink enough now and then to do things like forget where you left your car or your keys—or what you did the previous night. In addition you must get irritated when people start to talk about your drinking. You need to make sure you get defensive about it, but don't let anyone know just how much it really bothers you.

If you thought Stage One was fun, you are in for a real treat here in Stage Two. One of the best ways to begin is to start lying about your drinking. You can start with anyone. Some good people to begin with are your parents, friends, or fellow workers. You may want to follow this up by keeping a stash of your favorite brand hidden. You can try the usuals like a pint in your desk or sock drawer, a six-pack in the trunk, or a bottle by the garbage so you can have a drink when you are emptying the trash. However, since these places are old hat, try something more original. You'll become quite ingenious at this.

Remember to keep in mind this is Fun. Most people aren't ready for any heavy soul-searching yet, so enjoy your drinking. Or at least act like you enjoy it. There is plenty of time to be miserable later.

Next it's time to improve your excuse-making ability. The run-of-the-mill excuses are these:

1. All my friends drink as much as I do.
2. All I drink is beer.
3. I don't drink that much.
4. I work hard all day and deserve to drink.

With a little practice, you will develop quite a repertoire of excuses.

Here in mid-Stage Two things start to get a little more difficult. You need to be almost completely dishonest. Start with little things and build your way if necessary. With a little practice, you can lie about almost anything, so put the old nose to the grindstone. It also doesn't hurt your image to start breaking a lot of promises at this time.

Now if you just throw in a little grandiose and aggressive behavior you will be well on your way to creating family, work, and money trouble. You may even have to avoid friends and family. However you must kid yourself into thinking you're still normal; those nights you don't remember aren't really happening more often.

The final obstacle before Stage Three is to start eating less so you can drink more. And be sure to drink heavily when you're alone.

Stage Three is when most of the physical deterioration occurs, so you must really tighten your belt here—both because you should be losing weight and because you're going to work harder. Both your body and your morals must become more dilapidated. Remember, when the tough get going, they usually get nasty as well.

If you wish, you can try to quit for a while to prove you're all right. You can do this anywhere in Stage Two or Three, but by Stage Three you must fail miserably. In mid-Stage Three, you are entitled to a vacation after a few lengthy drunks. Sanitariums or hospitals are current favorites. Just make sure you forget your toothbrush.

Finally, discard all you have left—all hope, will power, self-respect, and relatives who haven't already told you to f--k off. Now all that's left is to die. That's right, die. It doesn't matter how just so long as it's drinking-related. You can get plastered and hit by a truck, have a tree jump out in front of you, get liver cancer—just about anything as long as it is attributable to alcohol.

Fun is fun, but on the serious side, if you think any of the above sound a little too familiar, even in Stage One and Two, maybe it's time to take a long, hard look at what is going on with yourself. You might need to do something about where you're headed. You don't have to follow the aforementioned program to the end. There are a lot of places you can go for help or just to talk to someone to find out if you have a problem. For example, the A.A. service center. Don't let the next truck have your name on it.

Greg M. Wright

12 WRITING THE BUSINESS LETTER

Sept. 2, 1930
Paris

Dear Sears & Roebuck:
   The hiking boots you sent are good. They are durable and warm. I would like them better if they also fit. They do not. My feet are still the size previously reported. Did you think I was wrong? Does someone on your mail-order desk suppose I have retractable toes? They bend. They do not retract. I cannot wear the boots unless I cut the ends off with the axe you sent me. I had planned to cut some wood when I went camping in Spain. But my boots do not fit. Is your mail-order desk made of wood? I can return to New York and cut your mail-order desk into firewood. I like new adventures. Or you can immediately send me a pair of boots that fit my feet, not yours.
   Please do as I ask. It is fair. Or I will splinter your mail-order desk with your splendid axe.

Truly yours,
Ernest Hemingway

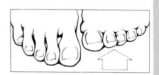

Sept. 17, 1930
New York

Dear Mr. Hemingway:
   Our mail-order desk is, in fact, made of wood. I would personally invite you to come here and chop it into kindling, as the presence of a personage of your enviable reputation would doubtless increase our sales, even if it destroyed our mail-order desk.
   I apologize for sending you the wrong boots. We have shipped a new pair that I hope satifies the extraordinary demands of your bendable but not retractable toes. Perhaps you could offer the other pair to a writer with smaller feet. F. Scott Fitzgerald comes to mind.

Very sincerely,
Leonard Danzig
Sears & Roebuck

From John Welter, "More Letters from Papa," *Saturday Review,* January–February 1984.

All letters, methinks, should be as free and easy as one's discourse, not studied as an oration, not made up of hard words like a charm.

Dorothy Osborne (Lady Temple)

CONCEPTS TO LEARN

- The meaning of *parody*
- The proper business letter format
- The importance of a résumé in job interviews
- The way to write job application letters and letters of complaint

---

FOR THOUGHT AND DISCUSSION

1. After reading the letter-parody, how would you describe Hemingway's style? (For example, were his sentences long and complicated, or short and simple?)
2. What do you learn about Hemingway's interests from the subject matter of the letters?
3. How would you react if you received a letter like Hemingway's (from someone who was not famous), and you were in charge of the complaint department?
4. Would Dorothy Osborne, who wrote the introductory quotation, have liked this letter? Why or why not?

PARODY

Comedian Rich Little has earned fame and fortune by satirizing the styles of others who have already earned fame and fortune. Since Rich Little is a performer, in his satire, he imitates and exaggerates such elements of style as gestures, facial expressions, pet sayings, and speech patterns.

Parody is a literary form in which a writer imitates the style of another writer in order to satirize that writer. (See Chapter Six to review the elements that make up a writer's style.)

THE BUSINESS OF WRITING LETTERS

In Chapter One you read a Sylvia Porter column that said "more than one-third of business letters do nothing more than seek clarification of earlier correspondence." This is a waste of the time most of us find too scarce. It is also an enormous waste of effort.

"The business of America is business," Calvin Coolidge said. Certainly knowing how to write a well-organized and clearly stated letter in the standard business style is good business whether you are trying to get a job, buy boots that fit, or get a car repaired properly. You are more likely to achieve what you want if your letter is clear, correct, concrete, and concise.

When you use the standard format, you communicate more efficiently. Just as appropriate dress for an interview helps you to make the right impression, so too does the proper dress for your ideas. The correct business letter format is not difficult to learn.

We will use the easiest of the business letter formats—the block format. All parts of the letter begin at the left margin. We will learn to write letters of job application and letters of complaint. Both are letters almost everyone needs to write sooner or later.

SELLING YOUR TALENTS

When you apply for a job, you are selling your talents, so it is important to examine those talents carefully. First, read the job description *very carefully*. Then list the qualities the job requires. Next decide which of your talents and experiences show you are a good candidate. Your Critic Brain works hard to remind you of your lack of talent but, in fact, most people have talents they might overlook. Résumé writing is an ideal time to get your right brain out of its box and put it to work. Try brainstorming or clustering about your strengths. What hobbies do you have that might be useful to an employer? For example, being a club officer would indicate management and leadership skills that might be helpful in many jobs. If you were on a debate team, you had training in logical reasoning, public speaking, and thinking on your feet. Rummage around in your treasure house of memories for any experience that might help you get the job. A good rule of thumb is to make your résumé a single page long. Begin with your most recent experience and work back from there. If you have little experience, double space your letter. If your qualifications are legion, single space it.

Remember, your letter and résumé constitute the first impression of you. Figure 12.1 on page 194 is a sample letter to a prospective employer and Figure 12.2 on page 195 is a résumé to accompany the letter.

LETTERS OF COMPLAINT

Have you ever been mailed a pink blouse instead of the blue one you ordered? Does Tab A refuse to go into Slot B? Were you charged twice for the same restaurant meal? The telephone does not work for many situations when you need to voice your displeasure at a service or product. When your complaint is serious, you usually need a written record of it. In fact, it is almost always better for your temper and your pocketbook to write down your complaint and send it out.

Letters of complaint, however, need to be thought through and worded so you receive the satisfaction you want—and deserve. (Reread "How to Complain" on p. 180 for further suggestions.) If you have ever tried to follow directions that were either inaccurate,

FIGURE 12.1   **A Sample Letter to a Prospective Employer, Block Style**

```
        707 Concord Street
        Monterey, California 93940


        November  20, 1988

        Mr. James Barrie
        General Manager
        Reilly Products
        Port Hope, Michigan  48468

        Dear Mr. Barrie:

        In response to your advertisement in today's Monterey Peninsula Herald
        for a knowledgeable, experienced computer salesperson, I am enclosing my
        resume for your consideration.

        I am currently completing my advanced classes in data processing at Monterey
        Peninsula College and will earn my A.A. degree next June. My grade point
        average is 3.25; my grades in data processing have all been A's and B's. I
        have achieved this academic record while working as a clerk at the James
        Hook, Inc. Computer Store twenty five hours a week.

        I am single, twenty-four years of age, and a 1983 graduate of Monterey High
        School with two years of Army service. You will find me neat, hard-working,
        and enthusiastic about a field in which I believe I can excel.

        My academic background and my work experience qualify me for the sales
        position you are seeking to fill. I look forward to hearing from you.


        Sincerely,

        Peter Pan

        Peter Pan
```

excessively complicated, or both, you will appreciate the parody of such direction in Figure 12.3 on page 196.

In Chapter One, we looked at the way language has changed. Language evolution does not involve just words. The mechanical rules governing writing change as well. Notice that the letter-parody in Figure 12.3 does not follow the block form of the Peter Pan letter. Instead each paragraph is indented and the complimentary close and signa-

FIGURE 12.2   A Sample Resume to a Prospective Employer

```
Peter  Pan
891 Great Ormond Street
Port Huron, Michigan 48060
(313) 555-7491
```

Education:

```
1980-1984:   Monterey High School

1986-1988:   St. Clair Community College  (3.25 grade point average)
```

Work Experience:

```
1986-1988:                       clerk
                                 James Hook, Inc. Computer Store
                                 614 Mermaid Way
                                 Port Huron, Michigan 48060


1984-1985:                       diet counselor
                                 United States Army
                                 7th Infantry
                                 Fort Ord, California 93941


1982-1983:                       truffle taster
                                 Creme de la  Creme
                                 780 Lighthouse Avenue
                                 Port Huron, Michigan 48060


1980-1981:                       counter person
                                 McDonald's Hamburgers
                                 980 Fremont
                                 Port Huron, Michigan 48060



References:                      James Hook
                                 James Hook, Inc. Computer Store
                                 614 Mermaid Way
                                 Port Huron, Michigan 48060

                                 Dr. Xerzes Xerox
                                 Chairperson, Computer  Science
                                 St. Clair Community College
                                 Port Huron, Michigan 48060

                                 Gen. James Beard
                                 United States Army
                                 7th Infantry
                                 Fort Ord, California 93941
```

FIGURE 12.3   **A Parody of a Letter of Complaint by H. F. Ellis, Indent Style**

Return address

Date

Inside address

Dear Sir:

    I have just been carefully following your directions. After half an
hour's preliminary work, I pushed the spindle R through the aperture BB.
Then I pulled the arm L sharply downward (Page 2) and retaining my hold on
R, worked DD gently past E, W and Q until it clicked into position at S.
Keeping L depressed as instructed, I now attempted, by means of the knurled
knob T at the side to raise the pinion at O until it engaged the horizontal
worm F.
    But there is no knurled knob at the side.
    Did you know that? There is a knob, fairly well knurled at the back, but
how can that be T? You can't reach it, for one thing, while still depressing
L, unless you let go of the end of the spindle R. And you know very
well-assuming you ever tried to assemble this thing yourself- what happens
then.
    On the off chance that I had all along been mistaking the back for the
side, I unclipped the two brackets U and U from what in this case would no
longer be the bottom, and fixed them on the old top- or front, rather. This
of course necessitated reversing the slotted panel HH (Page 1) and while I
was doing that, DD slipped out of S and a small bright part rattled down.
As far as I can tell from shining a torch through the floor boards, it is
either G or V.
    At this stage I turned to Page 3 and at once became convinced that
Diagram 9 is upside down. It is impossible to screw W to K, since the so-
called J would obviously be in the way if it had not already-through my
following Page 1 too carefully-been wrenched clean out of its socket.
Putting J back the other way round, so that the bent bit is to the top,
simply forces a small spring- would that be N or M? out of slot YY, and
there is a clang from insides that bodes, in my limited experience with this
kind of mechanism, no good. I had every right in my opinion, to find out
whether, by putting a foot on L, gripping R with my teeth and at the same
time giving a slight twist to this knurled knob of yours, I could induce the
spring to its original position. No one could possibly have foreseen that
this would cause the whole base plate-now, of course, on top-to buckle
upward and spew a number of brass screws into the fireplace. Nor was this
all. Even the worm F turned- and as to the pinion, all one can say for
certain is that it was no longer at O.
    When this happened, I took a cold chisel CC- not included in the
outfit- set it at about the point P and drove it through the apparatus from
A to Z, maintaining "a firm even pressure throughout" (Page 4). Then I
carefully tossed your directions out of a fourth floor window.
    May I suggest that it is now your turn to follow them?

        Sincerely,

        H. F. Ellis

        H.F. Ellis

---

ture are moved to the right. This is an older, more traditional style
that is rapidly being replaced by the easier-to-use, block style of the
Peter Pan letter.

FOR THOUGHT AND DISCUSSION

1. In a serious letter, what changes should H. F. Ellis make in the
   details used?

2. How effective would the final sentence be in a real business letter? Why?

Enough Is Enough!

Besides the murderous suggestion at the close of the letter, the writer was carried away by the intricacies of the "whatcha-ma-call-its" and "thinga-ma-bobs" he or she was working on. While you need to give enough concrete details to explain the problem adequately, you should not get carried away with details. Certainly such explanations do not produce cliff-hanger suspense, but they can be clear and concise enough to keep your reader's attention from wandering.

Two Useful Schemes

In organizing letters of complaints there are two basic schemes: begin with a complaint and then support the point with concrete details, or begin with concrete details and end with a generalized complaint. In choosing the method, always consider your audience: If the complaint is already familiar to the reader, begin with it. If the complaint is unusual or unfamiliar to the reader, begin with the concrete details.

How Much Is Enough?

When you are angry—as you often are when you have a complaint— your mind floods with a torrent of ideas and images. Because these ideas swirl around charged with emotion, it may seem capturing them on paper will be difficult. Wrong. Clustering will help you capture them. As you cluster, side issues will occur to you that you may later discard. Not to worry. Jot them down. Quite soon after you begin to cluster a lightbulb will go on in your brain, and you will understand the direction your complaint should take.

In the last chapter we discussed a fairly typical problem: getting a new car to work properly. The following is a clustering sample to help create and organize a letter of complaint about that car.

In the letter on page 199 written from the clustering on page 198, the writer had to include some terms that might be too technical for a general audience. As you read the letter, skim the technical material but do note the concrete documentation of the long Battle of the Lemon (or LeMon) as this model was aptly named.

FOR THOUGHT AND DISCUSSION

1. Which suggestions from "How to Complain" on p. 180 does the letter by Delta Dumpedon follow?
2. List words and phrases that are too technical for a general audience, but would be appropriate for I. A. Helpful?
3. What technique for concluding an essay (from Chapter Nine) does the letter use?
4. Could Delta Dumpedon explain this complaint as effectively by telephone? Why must she write it?

FIGURE 12.4   A Clustering Sample for a Letter of Complaint

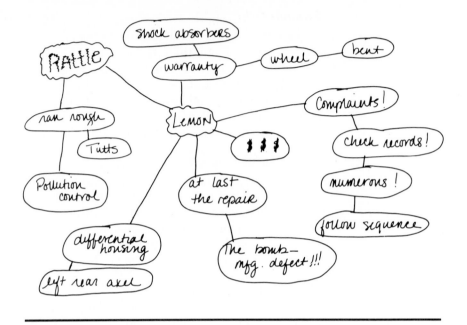

5. By the time Delta wrote her letter of appeal, she probably did not feel very polite toward either Melvin or Mohawk Motor Division. Would an angry, threatening letter have been as effective? Support your answer.
6. In the letter, Delta repeats certain phrases almost like a refrain. Is this effective? Why?
7. Which ideas from the clustering did Delta ignore in the letter? Why?
8. What information did Delta have to check after she finished clustering?

Of Thumbscrews, the Rack, and Our Purpose

After an experience such as Delta Dumpedon had with Melvin, you might allow yourselves to fantasize about medieval torture devices like thumbscrews and the rack. In fact, they might seem lenient for dealerships who make life complicated and unhappy. It is important, however, to keep your Purpose in mind when writing letters of complaint. As you write, imagine the impact of your words on their recipient. Will the words create anger—or action? Do you sound hysterical—or well-informed and intelligent?

FIGURE 12.5 A Letter of Complaint by "Delta Dumpedon"

26455 Ripped Off Avenue
Carmel, California 93923

August 6, 1988

I.A. Helpful, Director of Service
Mohawk Motor Division
Major Motors Corporation
Zero Mohawk Plaza
Mohawk, Michigan 431313

Dear Mr. Helpful:

Shortly after purchasing our Mohawk LeMon station wagon (#2D35U8B11600) from
Melvin Mohawk in Seaside, California, I complained to Melvin about a rattle
in the rear of the car. I also noted that the car ran roughly especially at
speeds approaching fifty-five miles per hour. Melvin said the problem was
caused by pollution control equipment, and they could do nothing about it.

Shortly after the warranty ran out, the problem became intolerable. At that
point, Melvin Mohawk said my problem was caused by a tire or wheel. They
rotated the tires, and inspected the wheels and brakes. The problem
persisted. I balanced the tires and aligned the front end—following
Melvin's advice. The problem persisted. I installed new shock—
absorbers following Melvin's advice. The problem persisted. Next Melvin
Mohawk told me the left rear wheel was bent and was causing the problem. I
replaced it. (See the enclosed copies of receipts for all this work.) Next
Melvin said my tires were out of round. I bought new tires. The problem
persisted.

At last Melvin Mohawk told me the differential housing was bent; the left
rear axle and bearings were worn because of this. They were sure this was
the solution to my problem. Estimated cost this time? $548.00. I appealed to
Melvin Mohawk and to your area service representative. (See enclosed copy
of my complaint letter.) Melvin ignored my letter. Your area service
representative said he could not help me. Furious with Melvin Mohawk, I took
my car elsewhere for repair. (A receipt is enclosed.) At last my car ran
properly.

Now—several years after my frustrating and fruitless battle—Mohawk has
recalled my car because of the very defect
I fought so long—and expensively—to have repaired.

Integrity and service are high on my priority list for automobile
dealerships. I found neither at Melvin Mohawk. However, I am hopeful that
Mohawk Motor Division is also concerned about integrity and service. I look
forward to a prompt refund of the money I spent to remedy the defect in my
car.

Sincerely,

Delta Dumpedon

Delta Dumpedon

The letter in Figure 12.6 on page 200 by humorist Jean Kerr is another example of a letter of complaint. Think about the way you would react had you received it, then answer the Thought and Discussion questions.

FIGURE 12.6   A Letter of Complaint by Jean Kerr

```
Return Address

Date

The All-Season Window Corporation
Mount Vernon, New York

Dear Sirs,

Listen, are you going to come out and put in those storm windows before we
are blown out into the damn Sound? You said Monday and here it is Wednesday.
We keep the thermostat up to eighty-five and still the toast is flying off
the plates. And I had to put mittens on to type this.

I hope to hear from you soon or never.

Sincerely,

Jean Kerr

Jean Kerr
```

FOR THOUGHT AND DISCUSSION

1. Describe Kerr's tone in the letter.
2. What line is intended to make its audience laugh?
3. When you are angry and someone makes you laugh, what happens to your level of anger?
4. Do you think Kerr's letter will help get her storm windows on? Support your answer.

When we are wronged, we often grow angry. Threatening a person or company, however, is usually not the most efficient way to get results unless, of course, you plan to follow through. For example, perhaps you actually plan to take someone to court if you do not get satisfaction; then you can say so in a letter. But before you make such a threat remember that, unfortunately, our courts move more like molasses in January than like greased lightning (to exercise some clichés). When possible, it is usually faster—and cheaper—to settle a dispute out of court.

As you read the first draft of your letter of complaint, slip into your reader's shoes—or reading glasses. How do you react to people who sound well-informed and reasonable? How do you respond to threats? Although you are at the top of your temper thermostat, think of the way you react to abusive language. Keep your *purpose* in mind. If you want your problem solved, consider the impact of your words on your audience. Remember, you can catch more ants with sugar than with vinegar.

Notice that Delta Dumpedon's letter of complaint is concise, concrete, and clearly organized. It contains the necessary details to help its readers act on her complaint.

WRITING ASSIGNMENT
Using What You Have Learned

For this assignment you have a choice. Write one of the following:

1. A letter of complaint
2. A letter of job application that includes a résumé

In your writing, be sure to do the following:

1. Use a prewriting activity to help formulate what you want to say.
2. Follow the standard format for letters and résumés.
3. When applying for a job, read the job description carefully, and make sure you tailor your comments about your talents and experiences to cover each point of the job description.
4. Get to the point quickly and make clear what your purpose is.
5. Make clear what action you want from the letter's recipient.
6. Include necessary information (such as model number) when you are not returning the actual item about which you are complaining.
7. In a complaint, use a firm, but nonthreatening tone unless you plan to follow through by taking the action you outline.
8. Put yourself in your reader's shoes and imagine in what way you would react to your letter.
9. If you need proof you sent your letter, use certified mail.
10. Keep a copy of the letter.

STUDENT STAR LETTERS
The Polished Product

***Remember: the authors of these essays used the following steps:

1. Prewriting
2. Writing

FIGURE 12.7   **A Letter to a Prospective Employer by Beverly Bonito**

```
          4321 Downtothesea
          Monterey, California 93940

          November 17, 1987

          Symanthia Elasmobranch
          Director of Education
          Monterey Bay Aquarium
          886 Cannery Row
          Monterey, California 93940

          Dear Ms. Elasmobranch:

          I am applying for a position as an aide in your elementary school education
          program. Both my educational and work experience qualify me for this
          position.

          I completed your sixteen-week aquarium-guide course in December 1986. Since
          then I have logged more than a hundred hours as a volunteer guide. I have
          also worked as a volunteer aide helping with shark-aging research in the
          laboratory of Dr. Gregory Cailliet of Moss Landing Marine Laboratories. In
          addition to my marine science experience, I worked as an aide at Sunset
          Preschool from 1985 through 1987.

          Currently I am completing my first year at Monterey Peninsula College where
          I am preparing for a career in environmental education.

          Sincerely,

          Beverly Bonito
          Beverly Bonito
```

FIGURE 12.8   A Resume to a Prospective Employer by Beverly Bonito

Beverly Bonito
4321 Downtothesea
Montery, Califoria 93940

Education

1984-1987   The York School
high School   9501 Salinas Highway
                                       Monterey, California 93940

1987-present   Monterey Penninsula College
student   980 Fremont
                                       Monterey, Califormia 93940

Work Experience

1986-present   Monterey Bay Aquarium
Aquarium volunteer guide   886 Cannery Row
                                       Monterey, California 93940

1985-1987   Sunset Preschool
educational aide   Sunset Drive
                                       Pacific Grove, California 93950

1986-1987   Dr. Gregory Cailliet
volunteer research aide   Moss Landing Marine Laboratories
                                       Moss Landing, California 95039

References

                                       Dr. Walter Webfoot
                                       Director of Volunteers
                                       Monterey Bay Aquarium
                                       886 Cannery Row
                                       Monterey, California 93940

                                       Dr. Gregory Cailliet
                                       Moss Landing Marine Laboratories
                                       Moss Landing, California 95039

                                       Ms. Nancy Nudibranch, Director
                                       Sunset Preschool
                                       Sunset Drive
                                       Pacific Grove, California 93950

3. Revising content
4. Proofreading and correcting mechanical errors

Notice the way the author of the letter in Figure 12.7 on page 202 makes herself sound like an attractive, qualified candidate despite her lack of actual paid work experience.

FIGURE 12.9   **A Letter of Complaint by Steve Howard**

1448 Old Post Road
Old Lyme, Connecticut 06371

November 23, 1988

U.R. Ajerk, President
Ajerk Tool Company
2 Longa Drive
Jipville, Nebraska 68977

Dear Mr. Ajerk:

I recently purchased from your company one Super A.T.C. orbital sander, model number 27005. I used it twice, and each time I carefully followed the manufacturer's instructions. The third time I used your sander, it did not go smoothly.

The sander was rotating too slowly for the job at hand, so I switched to a higher speed. I moved the speed control knob from the S-slow position to the M-medium position. The instant I did this, the sander accelerated to nearly 5,000 rpm. With the increased acceleration, both the backpiece and the spindle flew across the street. The smoke began to pour from the exhaust vent, and, after sparking briefly, the orbital sander stopped working.

I am sending you my purchase receipt and the sander. According to the warranty, the sander will either be repaired or replaced within two weeks. If you have any questions, please call me at (408) 555-0473.

Sincerely,

Steve Howard

Steve Howard

FIGURE 12.10   **A Letter of Complaint by A. I. Ariel**

A.I. Ariel
1631 Madrid Street
Tallahassee, Florida 32301

October 25, 1987

Junky Format Textbook Company
P.O. Box 1984
Lexington, Massachusetts 30200

Dear Sirs:

Currently I am enrolled in an intermediate algebra course at Florida State University in Tallahassee, Florida. The textbook we are using is called Intermediate Algebra for College Students (second edition) and is published by your company.

When I bought your book for $27.40 at the beginning of the semester, it was new. After the first three weeks of class, it began to fall apart. One by one, the chapters decided to go their separate ways; however, I managed to keep track of them by keeping them in a special pouch I purchased for another $4.22.

I am a neat, organized fellow. In fact I am a Navy veteran. I am kind to small children, animals and textbooks. As a matter of fact, this is the only book I have owned in my adult life that has fallen apart. I find little consolation in the fact that my book is not alone in this plight; approximately eighty percent of my class and our instructor are having the same problem.

Now we are three-quarters through the semester, and your textbook has suffered a complete nervous breakdown. Typical of those of my classmates, my book has large tears in the front cover and instead of one medium sized text, I now have fifteen little texts. Unfortunately there are only eleven chapters so my math book's division is not only inconvenient, it is inappropriate to its contents.

The educational material in the textbook is of value, but the poor workmanship and poor materials that went into binding interfere with the book's usefulness.

Like most college students, I work hard in and out of class. I expect fair value for my money, something I have not gotten from you. Our bookstore will not buy my book back at the end of the semester; I certainly cannot expect them to pay for a battered pile of papers. You, however, should return my purchase price. Please inform me where to send what is left of my book for a refund once the semester is over.

Sincerely,

A.I. Ariel

A.I. Ariel

HELP! FOR FURTHER WORK

Read the following letter by Alex Angry, and then answer the Thought and Discussion questions which follow it.

FIGURE 12.11   **A Letter of Complaint by Alex Angry**

987 Fixit Street
Sadsack, Michigan 48109

President
Tommy Tread Tennis Shoes
864 Hopeless
Echo, Nevada 89802

Dear Mr. Ripoff

Your tennis shoes may be selling like hotcakes, but they are an
over-priced disaster. I'm as mad as a hornet, and I'm climbing
the walls. Why can't you make a better product? I am telling
everyone I know not to buy your product which is so junky it
boggles the mind. The soles were being pulled away from the shoes
right after I bought them. In fact, I noticed a spot where the
sole was loose the first time I wore them. Don't you feel guilty
about cheating people out of their hard earned money? A penny
saved is a penny earned. Your shoes are more expensive than the
average tennis shoes. I am willing to pay for quality. However
$40 is a lot of money for a pile of junk. How can you
advertise that you make the best tennis shoes on the market?
Honesty is the best policy. Your ads are colorful and
attractive, but they are not true. Your company cannot
continue to rule the roost if it ignores quality. I hope you
will not turn a deaf ear to my complaint because I am going to
stick to my guns. I want my money back from you as quick as a
flash.

Sincerely,

Alex Angry

Alex Angry

FOR THOUGHT AND DISCUSSION

1. If you were the business person receiving this letter, what impression would you have of Alex after seeing the mechanical errors?
2. What changes in content does Alex need to make for his letter to be more effective?
3. When during the writing process should Alex have checked for mechanical errors?
4. Proofread Alex's letter and correct any mechanical errors he has made. After you read "Wordiness," beginning on p. 312, through "Clichés" in "The Final Touch: A Handbook," eliminate wordiness, clichés, and awkward passive-voice sentences.

13 INTRODUCING RESEARCH

"Who is the fairest one of all, and state your sources!"

Drawing by Ed Fisher; (c) 1984. *The New Yorker Magazine, Inc.*

Where there is much desire to learn, there of necessity will be much arguing, much writing, many opinions; for opinion in good men is but knowledge in the making.

John Milton, Areopagitica

CONCEPTS TO LEARN

- The usefulness of research for school and everyday life

- The way to identify a research question

- Where to find information for a research paper

- The way to properly credit sources of information, including formal and informal documentation

- The meaning of *plagiarism* and ways to avoid it

- The steps to follow in writing a research paper

- The way to summarize sources in your own words

KNOWLEDGE = POWER

This chapter will help you more quickly and efficiently do the research that will help you in your personal, academic, and professional lives.

RESEARCH FOR YOUR PERSONAL LIFE

A knowledge of research techniques will prove helpful in your personal life both while you are a student and long after you finish your formal education. English philosopher Francis Bacon wrote, "Knowledge itself is power." Indeed it is. I finished my college degrees many years ago, and yet I have found continuing need to seek knowledge—to research—a myriad of problems in my private life. For example, my younger son was having difficulties in school. The word *dyslexic* was being bandied about. To make the best decisions about my son's education I needed to learn a good deal about learning problems.

Dyslexia, I determined, was far more complicated than the tendency to reverse letters in words (wrods). Because of my research, I was better able to understand my son's learning problems and help him overcome them. As an extra bonus, I discovered that ten percent of people have some type of learning disability; because of my research, I began to recognize the symptoms of learning disabilities in my own students and am thus better able to help them.

Subsequently, research armed me with knowledge that gave me power in dealing with the threat of breast cancer. I learned nearly ten percent of American women develop this malady. If a breast lump my doctors thought was suspicious proved to be malignant, should I have a mastectomy? My library furnished me a variety of articles that updated me on the latest research about breast cancer. I was able to ask intelligent questions of my doctors—and I was able to make the best decision for me. I learned that breast cancer is very curable. If the cancer is caught early, the most knowledgeable doctors usually perform a simple operation that removes only the lump (a lumpectomy) and not the entire breast. While the cure rate for the simpler surgery is just as high as the cure rate for the mastectomy, the lumpectomy is much easier on the patient. As it turned out, my lump was benign, but during my research I found articles explaining the latest methods to avoid cancer. Therefore, my research has had continuing benefits.

My research skills have aided me in safeguarding my cats from cat leukemia (now Killer Number One among cat diseases). Research has helped me eliminate fleas from my cats, dogs, home, and formerly bumpy, itchy self. When my washing machine broke down, my odometer turned to 115,000 on my no-longer-trusty auto, and my flowers were attacked by mites, research came to my rescue.

RESEARCH EXERCISE
It's Your Turn

1. Make a list of three decisions you have to make in your private life in which more knowledge would be helpful to you.
2. Share this list with your classmates. Their lists often inspire additions to your own list.

RESEARCH FOR YOUR ACADEMIC LIFE

Atomic Courtesy

To smash the simple atom
All mankind was intent.
    Now any day
    The atom may
Return the compliment

Ethel Jacobsen

In addition to the personal usefulness of research skills, research papers are required in a cornucopia of courses ranging from astronomy to zoology. Not only our personal and academic lives will benefit from an ability to do research quickly and accurately. If we wish to live in a democratic society, in a world as wracked with problems as ours, Milton's "much desire to learn" becomes a survival necessity, not a mere intellectual luxury. The following is but a small sample of the multitude of questions we must answer to insure our continued life, liberty, and pursuit of happiness:

> Does increasing our stockpile of nuclear weapons make us safer—or does the burgeoning stockpile increase the chances these weapons will be used?
>
> What can we do to decrease our chances of getting cancer?
>
> How can be keep our air and water free from toxic materials?
>
> How do we guard our freedom of the press but protect our children from the exploiting and corrupting lens of the pornographer?
>
> Can we balance the demands of a growing population with the needs of the earth's fragile ecology?
>
> Should we continue to build nuclear power plants to provide the power to toast our bagels, perk our coffee, and run our televisions—and thereby expose ourselves to another Three Mile Island or Chernobyl disaster?
>
> Should we increase our dependence on the fossil fuels that pollute our skies and congeal on our coastal waters and beaches in a layer of black goo?

The answers to these questions are complex and difficult ones. And yet we answer many of these questions daily in selecting the food we eat, the insect sprays and other chemicals we use, and the political candidates we support. The arms race and Star Wars may seem to be issues far removed from our everyday world, and yet we work many days each years to pay for this race with our tax dollars—and we live with the threat: "Now any day/The atom may/Return the compliment."

In the following poem by John Updike, (author of Chapter Seven's "A & P") the poet makes concrete the threat of nuclear holocaust.

Sonic Boom

I'm sitting in the living room,
When, up above, the Thump of Doom
Resounds. Relax. It's sonic boom.

The ceiling shudders at the clap,
The mirrors tilt, the rafters snap,
And Baby wakens from his nap.

"Hush, babe. Some pilot we equip,
Giving the speed of sound the slip,
Has cracked the air like a penny whip."

Our world is far from frightening; I
No longer strain to read the sky
Where moving fingers (jet planes) fly.
Our world seems much too tame to die.

And if it does, with one more pop.
I shan't look up to see it drop.

John Updike

FOR THOUGHT AND DISCUSSION

1. Why does Updike speak to a baby in the third stanza of the poem? How would the poem change if he spoke the lines to an adult?
2. Which images in the poem are appropriate for an explanation to a child?
3. What is Updike's thesis in the poem?
4. How would the information in "Sonic Boom" differ had Updike decided to put its thesis in an essay instead of in a poem?
5. For "Sonic Boom" to be a convincing essay, what additional kinds of information should it contain?

ONE STEP AT A TIME

Let knowledge grow from more to more.

Alfred, Lord Tennyson

While most poems appeal primarily to emotions, most essays aim primarily at the intellect. Essays require specific facts and statistics to support a thesis. Since few are walking storehouses of information, we turn inevitably to research.

A research paper can seem an enormous task if you contemplate only the final product. When you look at the whole task, writing a research paper may make an ascent of Mt. Everest seem like a Sunday outing. Instead, borrow from the wisdom of Alcoholics Anonymous: take life one day at a time. You should write a research paper one step at a time. An effective way to attack the research mountain is by mastering a series of skills.

THE FIRST SKILL: IDENTIFYING A RESEARCH QUESTION

Sometimes instructors assign a specific research topic. More often, you will have to find one for yourself. Initially, you will probably not know exactly what it is you want to write about. Rather, you may have a general area of interest—for example, problems with education.

The problems with education are too vast and too complex to cover in a book, let alone a paper of a few hundred—or thousand—words. Your first step is focusing, that is, limiting your subject, as you learned to do in Chapter Eight.

One possible research topic under problems in education is dyslexia. What is *dyslexia*? What does the latest research show about the best method to help dyslexics learn? Unless you already know a good deal about a subject, you will have to read a comprehensive article or two before you even know what questions to ask about it. Once you are better informed about the issues surrounding your subject, you will be able to decide what aspect of the subject you wish to focus on.

After you have read some material about a subject, you can explore your thoughts and find a focus through prewriting. Brainstorming may be especially useful at this writing step, but you may want to explore clustering and freewriting as well to help you determine your focus.

WRITING EXERCISE
It's Your Turn

Write a thesis sentence that adequately limits your subject and states a supportable opinion on the following subjects:

1. Child abuse
2. Women's rights
3. United States foreign policy
4. Military spending
5. Computers
6. Education

For further review of the *crucial* skill of limiting and focusing a thesis statement, reread Chapter Eight.

SKILL TWO: FINDING INFORMATION IN THE LIBRARY

Vocabulary   **omnipresent:**   present everywhere at the same time

Actually, the first two skills overlap. You need to find information in order to determine your focus. Then you need to find yet more information to develop that focus. And as you learn more about your subject, you may find you need to limit and focus even more narrowly.

For almost every kind of research the following three research tools are very valuable: the reference librarian, the card catalog, and the *Reader's Guide to Periodical Literature*.

The Reference Librarian

Librarians rank very near the top of my list of Helpful People. Their purpose in life (professionally speaking) is to help you—and other library users. Librarians know an amazing amount of information. More importantly, they know where to look for information they do not know.

Librarians, however, are not **omnipresent**. A basic knowledge of library reference tools will help you fend for yourself when the librarians are fending for themselves or for someone else.

The Card Catalog

The card catalog lists information in three different ways: by subject, by author, and by title.

1. Subject.   Look in alphabetical order under the subject heading you are researching. The following example is an entry for a subject card:

FIGURE 13.1   An Example of a Subject Card

```
              LEARNING DISABILITIES.
    371.9
    Ros       Ross, Alan O.
                Learning disability : the unrealized
              potential / Alan O. Ross.   -- New York
              : McGraw-Hill, c1977.
                xviii, 202 p. ; 24 cm.

                Includes bibliographical references
              and index.

                I. Learning disabilities.   II. title.
```

2. Author.   If you know of an author who has written a book in your interest area, look in alphabetical order under the author's last name. Figure 13.2 on page 216 is a sample entry for an author card:

FIGURE 13.2   An Example of an Author Card

```
  371.9
  Ros          Ross, Alan O.
                  Learning disability : the unrealized
               potential / Alan O. Ross.   -- New York
               : McGraw-Hill, c1977.
                  xviii, 202 p. ; 24 cm.

                  Includes bibliographical references
               and index.

                     I. Learning disabilities.   II. title.
```

3. Title.   If you know the name of a book that will be helpful, look in alphabetical order for the title of the book. Figure 13.3 is a sample entry for a title card:

FIGURE 13.3   An Example of a Title Card

```
                  Learning disability : the unrealized
                  potential.
  371.9
  Ros          Ross, Alan O.
                  Learning disability : the unrealized
               potential / Alan O. Ross.   -- New York
               : McGraw-Hill, c1977.
                  xviii, 202 p. ; 24 cm.

                  Includes bibliographical references
               and index.

                     I. Learning disabilities.   II. title.
```

The Reader's Guide to Periodical Literature

Vocabulary   **periodical:**   published at regular intervals; a newspaper or magazine

Periodical articles are indexed in the extremely helpful research tool *Reader's Guide to Periodical Literature.* Because magazine articles are not indexed in the card catalog, you need to befriend *Reader's Guide* to benefit from the wealth of information published in periodicals. To keep up with the magazines it indexes, *Reader's Guide* publishes a supplement every two weeks. Larger volumes index articles published over longer periods of time. The cover of each volume will tell you which period of time it indexes. Figure 13.4 is a sample entry, from *Reader's Guide.*

You may need to look through several volumes of *Reader's Guide* since the articles that will help you may have been published during different months or years.

Reader's Guide lists articles published in one hundred and fifty popular magazines. Check the list in the front of *Reader's Guide* to see if a magazine you are interested in is included. Figure 13.5 on page 218 lists some abbreviations in *Reader's Guide.*

To save space, *Reader's Guide* uses abbreviations. In the front of each book *on two separate pages* is a list of abbreviations. One set of abbreviations is for magazine titles. For example, *Bull At Sci* is the abbreviation for what periodical?

Notice that *Reader's Guide* gives only the first initial of the author's first name, not the entire name. When you find an article you plan to use, be sure to write down the author's full name, so you will have it to properly credit your source. The proper method to credit your source will be covered later in this chapter.

Other Helpful Library Sources

You will also use many other sources in your research. Among them are almanacs, atlases, directories, encyclopedias, gazeteers, handbooks, statistical sources, yearbooks, and experts.

FIGURE 13.4   **A Sample Entry from the *Reader's Guide to Periodical Literature***

HOMELESS
See also
Refugee children
Hope for the homeless [cover story] D. Whitman. il
U.S. News & World Report 104:24-8+ F 29 '88
How attempts to help the homeless can backfire [treating
the mentally ill] il *U.S. News & World Report* 104:32-3
F 29 '88

FIGURE 13.5   Abbreviations from the *Reader's Guide to Periodical Literature*

*Better Homes Gard — Better Homes and Gardens
BioScience — BioScience
Black Enterp — Black Enterprise
Blair Ketchums Ctry J — Blair & Ketchum's Country
    Journal
Bull At Sci — The Bulletin of the Atomic Scientists
Bus Week — Business Week

Dept	Department
ed	edited, edition, editor
F	February
il	illustration,-s
Inc	Incorporated
int	interviewer
introd	introduction; introductory
Ja	January
Je	June
Jl	July

Almanacs.   Almanacs are a handy collection of useful information about countries, people, events, and a miscellaneous variety of other subjects. Almanacs give brief summaries of information with an emphasis on subjects associated with the country where they were published.

Atlases.   Atlases are collections of maps, usually of the earth's geography, but some atlases contain maps of other things like your anatomy or that of other creatures.

Geographical atlases are listed in the card catalog under the subheading of *maps* of a region such as "South America—Maps," for example.

Nongeographical atlases are listed under subject headings such as "anatomy—atlases" or "obstetrics—atlases."

Directories.   Directories give brief summaries of information about people or groups that have a common principle for classification such as having a telephone, for example. Again, the card catalog will help you find the directory you need. Look under the type of directory you need for instance, "Consumer Protection—Directories."

Encyclopedias.   Your library will have a variety of these. They can help get you started in your research because they summarize important information about a subject, for example capital punishment or fleas.

Gazetteers.   Gazetteers are dictionaries of geographical place names. Often they contain brief descriptive facts. Look in your trusty card catalog under "Geography—Dictionaries" to locate the gazetteers.

Handbooks.   Handbooks are collections of important information on a subject. They contain bibliographic references to document the sources from which their information is taken; therefore, they can help you compile your own list of reference sources in addition to containing helpful information themselves. Look in the card catalog under a subject heading such as "Nursing—Handbooks" to locate the handbooks on nursing.

Statistical sources.   It is handy to know the "how many" or "how often" or "how large" about a particular subject. Statistical sources give this information about a cornucopia of subjects ranging from geography to fertility. For example, *The Statistical Abstracts of the United States* will tell you how many Americans are overweight. It will also provide information about such diverse subjects as education, parks and recreation, state and local government, and insects like fleas. Look in your card catalog under the subject of interest combined with the subheading "Statistics" (for example, "United States—Statistics").

Yearbooks.   Yearbooks record information about a wide variety of subjects for a given year. They summarize information about trends and events. Look in the card catalog under the subject heading plus yearbook (for example, "Political Parties—Yearbooks").

The horse's mouth.   If you know someone who is an authority on your subject, interview him or her. Most people are *very* sympathetic to students who must write research papers. When you ask an expert for an interview, the worst that will happen is the expert will say no. Interviews can give you the latest information; interviews give your paper vitality.

SKILL THREE: IDENTIFYING YOUR SOURCES

If someone told you that he or she read an article about extraterrestrial aliens that have started a mushroom farm in the Catskill Mountains, you may be reluctant to believe that person. Where, you will probably ask, did he or she find the article? In a tabloid next to the supermarket checkout line, perhaps? If the story came from *The New*

York Times, Washington Post, or some other source you have learned to trust because of their past accuracy, you will react differently than you would if the story came from a tabloid that makes its money on stories of dubious truth.

Where information is from has a tremendous impact on whether or not you are willing to believe it. Certainly on our planet, very strange things do happen: A quiet little lake in Cameroon belches a gas bubble and nearly two thousand people die. An Air Force bomber accidentally drops a forty-two-thousand-pound hydrogen bomb and it lies in the twenty-five-foot crater it creates in the New Mexico desert for twenty-nine years until the *Albuquerque Journal* discovers government documents detailing the story. (Fortunately for New Mexico only the bomb's nonnuclear explosives detonated when it hit the ground.)

We are all interested in who did what to whom and when it happened. But we want our information from a source we have learned to trust.

Giving Credit Where Credit Is Due

You must tell your reader where you got your information in the following cases:

1. When you use a direct quotation
2. When you use a specific fact that is not common knowledge
3. When you use an idea not your own

Avoiding Crime

Unless you properly credit others for their words or ideas you are guilty of *plagiarism.* To *plagiarize* is to take someone else's words or ideas as your own. Of course, this is a borrowing sort of world, and along with milk, eggs, and flea spray, you borrow ideas from other people. Unlike the milk, eggs, and flea spray, you cannot return the ideas you borrow. Instead, you make sure the original owners of the ideas or words get fully credited for their work. As Samuel Johnson once said, "Your manuscript is both good and original, but the part that is good is not original and the part that is original is not good."

In a world filled with experts, we must use ideas that are not our own to make our writing up to date and authoritative. Recently, for newspapers and magazines, I've written articles about subjects as diverse as sharks, sea otters, diving suits—and fleas. Alas, I am an expert on none of these subjects, but—like your research papers—my articles needed to reflect the best thinking of the best people. I borrowed from their research and thinking very freely. Everyone who writes papers involving research does this, but all authors must be careful to give credit where credit is due. The following article by me, which appeared in the *San Francisco Examiner & Chronicle,* is the original source for the essays that follow it.

THE MENACE AND THE MYTH
Marlene Martin

The hundred-mile stretch of California coast from Ano Nuevo to Bodega Bay is the major shark attack zone in the world and the attacks have greatly increased over the past decade. Why? Is the great white shark—the predator in all human attacks in California coastal waters—actually becoming a more and more efficient machine, learning new and better ways to stalk swimmers? Or is the shark developing a preference for human flesh?

Hogwash, say those who know. The shark is a big, stupid animal with a walnut-sized brain whose reactions are entirely instinctual. The great white may be twenty feet long, but it's got the mind of an amoeba.

Scientists are sure the shark is dumb, but they know little else about it since it rarely comes to the surface for observation. Its numbers seem to be increasing, but scientists are not even sure of that—although, as one veteran shark observer put it, "There are either a lot more sharks in the waters out there or they are a lot hungrier than they used to be."

Dr. Gregor Cailliet of Moss Landing Marine Laboratories insists, however, that scientists cannot be sure of almost anything about the shark . . .

THE WRONG METHOD: THE ARTICLE PLAGIARIZED

Is the great white shark becoming a more efficient machine, learning new and better ways to stalk swimmers? Or is it merely developing a preference for human flesh? Whatever the answers to these questions, it is clear the shark has turned the hundred-mile stretch of California coast from Ano Nuevo to Bodega Bay into its favorite attack zone in the entire world.

Of the shark's increasing preference for human flesh—or its newly honed human-attack skills, shark experts say, "Hogwash!" The shark, in fact, is a big, stupid animal with a walnut-sized brain. While its body may be twenty feet long, it's got the mind of an amoeba.

THE RIGHT METHOD: PROPERLY CREDITED BORROWING

Note: the documentation in this essay is informal. For formal documentation, see page 224.

Despite our society's increasing concern for animals like the majestic whale or the teddy-bear-like sea otter, few have any response but fear for the toothsome terror of the seas: the great white shark. Over the last decade increasing numbers of great whites have traumatized swimmers, SCUBA divers, and surfers—especially along the earth's Number One shark attack zone, the hundred-mile stretch of California coast from Ano Nuevo Island to Bodega Bay. Pointing to the increasing number of attacks in this zone, Marlene Martin, in "The Menace and the Myth" in the *San Francisco Examiner & Chronicle*, asked a question on many minds: Why are there more shark attacks now than ever before in recorded history?

Her answer? Shark experts aren't sure. If fact, scientists like Dr. Gregory Cailliet of Moss Landing Marine Laboratories say we know very little about the shark, despite its penchant for taking us out to lunch.

Why Must You Credit Your Source

Although many papers requiring research do not need the formal documentation of a works cited list, it is still vital to give credit to the person whose words or ideas you use. There are two reasons to give credit:

1. To avoid plagiarism
2. To make your ideas more convincing when you cite an authority to support them

Be sure to check with your audience (your instructor) to find out if you can simply cite your sources informally within the article or if you need to credit your sources formally.

In the following excerpt from my article about sharks, I credited sources within the article since the audience, *Sea Frontiers*, does not use the formal method of documentation for its articles.

THE SHARK: MORE THREATENED THAN THREATENING?
Marlene Martin

For most people, "shark" conjures up images of hapless swimmers and, of course, of the *Jaws* movies. This popular image, however, is far from the truth, for in the contest of who-eats-whom, not only are humans way ahead, the shark is falling farther and farther behind. In fact, the annual California commercial shark catch—about 1,575 metric tons—is more than four times the catch of only decade ago, and during that same period the California drift gillnet fleet that catches sharks grew from fifteen to two hundred vessels. In 1983 alone, thresher shark landings exceeded 1,059 metric tons. According to Dr. Leonard Compagno of San Francisco State University, worldwide, people catch several million sharks each year. Yet, despite the increasing numbers of people using the ocean for swimming, surfing, and diving, the shark at most "catches" fewer than a dozen people—though as many as fifty serious assaults by sharks on humans occur annually.

Ancient fear of the shark, then, is rapidly being replaced by the taste for its succulent, white flesh—a preference spurred on by increasing awareness of the evils of the cholesterol abundant in red meat as well as the escalating cost of such terrestrially grown protein.

Before we become too elated by *Homo sapien*'s success, however, we need to look at the other fellow's—or species'—point of view, a look that in the long run might be to the advantage of those who fish for sharks commercially, those who like to dine on them, and those who seek to maintain the balance of nature within the oceans.

A USEFUL NEIGHBOR

While the shark lacks the teddy-bear appeal of the sea otter and the majesty of the whale, the shark is a useful resident of the oceans aside from its commerical value, for it plays an important role in maintaining the natural balance. Predators such as the great white shark, for instance, help control the numbers of seals, sea lions, sea otters, and other marine mammals. Without such predation, the populations of these animals might soon outstrip their food supplies. As Dr. John McCosker, director of Steinhart Aquarium, points out, "These mammals would then eat everything in sight, destroying much of their environment; after that they would starve to death—and that's a lousy way to go."

Already West Coast fishermen contend that the burgeoning sea-lion population is endangering their catch of commercially important species like salmon. At the same time, however, there are increasing numbers of attacks by great white sharks on sea lions around their rookeries according to scientific observers in such areas as Point Reyes Bird Observatory and Ano Nuevo Island off the central California coast: thus nature's check-and-balance system is in action.

Of course, the shark's bad-guy image has been unfair all along. According to Compagno, of the more than three hundred and fifty species of sharks in the world, only thirty-nine have ever been involved in attacks on humans. And of thirty-four species that are residents or occasional visitors to U.S. coastal waters, two species—the great white and the tiger shark—have been responsible for the majority of attacks.

REPELLENT RESEARCH

Unfortunately, however, in the past, funds for doing research on sharks have usually been tied to their man-eater image. The U.S. Office of Naval Research, for example, has funded projects that Compagno says have a lot more to do with human psychological fear of sharks than with reality. Hence, according to Compagno, "Scientists who wanted to study sharks have had to come hat-in-hand to granting agencies who aren't interested in learning what the animal is all about," but seek only to learn how to protect people from what is in actuality a remote chance of being attacked by a shark.

This lack of funding for basic research about sharks means we know very little about a creature the popular press portrays as a toothsome terror. Until recently, this ignorance did not pose a major threat: however with the burgeoning commercial shark fishery, ignorance has become a serious threat to the shark's well-being.

Scientists have learned that some commercially important species grow very slowly and become sexually mature late in life. While most bony fishes have a reproduction strategy that consists of producing large numbers of young, sharks have a long gestation period and few offspring; hence any damage done to shark populations by overfishing might take a long time to rectify— if the populations could recover at all. Currently, there is only minimal regulation of the commercial harvest; thus scientists are stepping up their research in the hope that learning more about sharks will help scientists to better advise lawmakers about the consequences of laws regulating the shark catch.

FOR THOUGHT AND DISCUSSION

1. Explain how the popular image of sharks differs from the truth about these animals.
2. How do I (an English instructor, not a shark expert) give credibility to my points about sharks?

Just in Case

If you do need to use formal documentation in a research paper, get a copy of an up-to-date guide to the new documentation methods that includes the 1984 MLA guidelines. Here is a minicourse in the new documentation:

(For an example of a "Works Cited" list used with an essay see the "Student Star Essays" section at the end of this chapter.)

1. At the end of your paper, list your sources in a "Works Cited" list.
2. Organize your "Works Cited" list in alphabetical order beginning with the author's last name, a comma, and the author's first and middle names (if any middle name or initial is given). Double-space "Works Cited" entries and double-space between entries. Figure 13.6 illustrates the proper format for listing a book, a magazine, and a newspaper.

Documentation Within Your Paper

Within your essay, simply state the author's last name along with the appropriate page number; put this information in parentheses immediately after the information, idea, or quotation you credit. If there is no author, use the first significant word of the title instead. For an example of this method of crediting your sources see the Student Star Essays at the end of this chapter.

SKILL FOUR: TAKING NOTES

Since you need to know where you got your ideas, facts, and quotations, you need a system to keep track of them. In addition, when you begin to write your paper, it will help you if you do not have to read through all of your notes to find the information you need for each section of your paper.

To organize your paper while you research, take notes on large index cards (approximately five-by-seven inches).

Source Cards

Use the following tips when you make source cards:

1. For every source write the information you will need on a small index card (about three-by-five inches).

FIGURE 13.6   Sample Entries in a "Works Cited" List

An article from a book

Newman, Edwin. Strictly Speaking. New York:
        Warner, 1975.

An article from a magazine

Shute, Nancy. "Stop Sneezing, Stop Wheezing."
        American Health July/August 1987: 85-94.

An article from a newspaper

MacDougal, A. Kent. "The Felling of Forests
        Takes Heavy Toll on Humanity." The Herald
        26 July 1987: 1B.

---

2. In the upper, right-hand corner of each source card write a
   number. Your first source of information will be number 1,
   your second number 2, and so on. Figure 13.7 on page 226
   shows examples of source cards.

Note Cards

Use the following tips when you make note cards:

1. Take notes on larger index cards (about five-by-seven inches).
2. In the upper, right corner of each note card write the number
   of the source card telling you where you got the information.
   The source number will help you quickly determine where
   you got information so you can properly credit it later.

FIGURE 13.7   Sample Source Cards

1

Kenneth Labich. "The Hunt is on for an Antifat Pill."
Fortune 18 August 1986: 37-42

2

Donna Haupt. "Feeling Good." Madamoiselle
November 1985: 82-3

3. Write only one kind of information on each note card. For example, if you are researching the environmental dangers faced by sea otters and you find information in one article about three threats to otters (oil threats, gillnets, and food shortage), you will need three separate note cards to record this information.

    If you simply lump all of your information together, you will have to search through all your notes to find information you need. If you put each type of information on a separate, titled card, the information will be easier to find later.

4. On the top line of your note card write a title for the card. The title reflects the kind of information your card contains.

5. Do put information into your own words as you take notes. Be sure to clearly mark any quotations so you can properly credit their sources.

6. Note the exact page number for any quotation or information so you can credit the source if you have to credit your sources formally.

7. As you read or interview each source, make a separate card. You will probably have several cards containing the same type of information, but from different sources. For example, in a paper about the disposal of waste products from nuclear power plants, several of your sources may discuss the problems involved with transporting radioactive waste materials. The information may differ so you will have several cards entitled "Dangers in Transportation." Of course, each card will have a different source number.

8. You may want to photocopy articles and then note important information with a highlighter. If you choose to do this, try color coding your highlighters to indicate a particular type of information. To help you find the information when you begin to write your paper, make a brief note card indicating you have this information. Highlighting the top of the note card in the appropriate color will help you find the highlighted information in the photocopied article. For example, you could highlight all information related to genetic causes of obesity in pink and highlight all material related to psychological causes in green. You could also cut up the photocopied article and glue the important parts to appropriate note cards. Figure 13.8 shows examples of note cards.

STEPS TO FOLLOW IN WRITING A RESEARCH PAPER

The following steps will help you in writing your research papers.

1. Reread "How to Write Fast"

"How to Write Fast" is in Chapter Eleven on page 175. Note the way

FIGURE 13.8   Sample Note Cards

Costly Failures   1

Americans spend $ 200 million annually on OTC weight drugs.   (37)

Billions on everything from fat farms to Jane Fonda tapes.   (37)

The cause of obesity: Psychological   1

Weight determined buy a complex set of systems of hormones, chemicals, and nerve signals that influence food intake, physical activity and metabolism.

Body sends messages to get person to consume food to maintain particular level of fat stores; level varies with individuals.

Dr. William I. Bennet, editor of <u>Harvard</u> <u>Medical</u> <u>School</u> <u>Health</u> <u>Letter</u> says "The person who is fat is responding to exactly the same signals as the person who is thin. The signals are just set at different levels."

FIGURE 13.8 (*Continued*)

1

The Cause of Obesity : Genetics

An intractable problem for so many.

Genetics -- greater role than previously thought U. of Penn researcher Dr. Albert Stunkard showed 80% of differences in body size = genetics.

(38)

author Alan Blackburn uses his right brain to help him with his research.

2. Go to the Library and Research Your Topic

After you decide on the general subject you will research, help your Right Brain do the work for you. Feed it some background information to acquaint it with the issues. While encyclopedias have some helpful, general articles, when your topic is a current one, encyclopedias will not be as up-to-date as magazines. The section on research sources in this chapter will help you locate current articles.

Check to ensure that you have a subject about which you can find information. (For the assignment at the end of the chapter, you need at least three sources.) If you do not find enough material, check with a reference librarian or your instructor to make sure you have not selected a subject so specialized that researching it will be very difficult.

As you read, think about your subject and jot down questions that occur to you. These questions can help you find your thesis.

3. Buzz Off

Once you are acquainted with the major issues surrounding your topic, follow Alan Blackburn's advice: Buzz off. Instead of contemplating the work that awaits you, give your Right Brain time to digest and organize the information. Your Right Brain will help you find a focus for your research paper if you relax and let it digest the information you have gathered.

4. Review Information and Prewrite with Your Right Brain

If you need to focus your information, review the questions you have jotted down. Then cluster, brainstorm, or freewrite. This will help you identify the issues involved with your subject.

5. Write a Preliminary Thesis

Once you have done the preliminary reading, thinking, and prewriting about your subject, write your preliminary thesis sentence. Proofread your sentence to make sure it does the following:

1. Limits the subject
2. States an attitude or opinion that can be supported with facts
3. Does *not* ask a question, but does make a statement (an initial question is a helpful guide, but before you begin to write, know the way you want to answer the question)

Note: This is a *preliminary* thesis. Keep an open mind; as you get more information, you may need to alter your thesis.

6. Write a Preliminary Outline

When you know the major issues involved in your subject, write a *preliminary* outline. Keep an open mind; as you do further research, you can modify your outline. If the word *outline* scares you, relax. You are simply making an informal list of points to support your thesis.

Your outline will serve as a map to keep you from getting sidetracked in your research. It will also help you break your work into steps. You can use even small amounts of time to work without wasting time trying to remember where you left off the last time you worked on the paper.

7. Return to the Reference Section of Your Library

With your *preliminary* thesis sentence and outline, return to the library and make a list of references available to help you. Notice that under many subjects there are numerous articles, but with your central point in focus, you will be able to select those that are most likely to be helpful for your paper.

8. Take Notes

Take notes using the time-saving method explained and illustrated under Skill Four.

9. Check Your Format and Write Your First Draft

Check to be sure you follow the format required by your instructor. When you have completed your research, make any necessary changes in your preliminary thesis and outline and launch yourself full-speed ahead into the writing process.

As you begin to write, remember to concentrate on getting ideas on paper. If you know there is documentation in your notes, do not interrupt the flow of your ideas to ferret it out. Underline or highlight a section that needs the information and return to it when you are ready for a break in writing.

To save time later, however, do insert documentation references in your draft when you are using documentation. For example, add "(1–28)" to a quotation that came from Source One, page 28. Then you will not have to search for the source information to properly document your source later.

10. Put Your Paper Away

Put your paper away for a few days to give your mind a break. Then, read it again. You will be more objective and able to make the changes it needs. Reread your paper aloud so you can check your audience's reaction. As you read, make sure you have done the following:

1. Concretely developed your points
2. Provided adequate transitions
3. Explained any technical terms your audience might not understand
4. Varied your sentence patterns
5. *Not* introduced a new idea in your conclusion

11. Edit with Your Left Brain

Now take your Left Brain out of the closet and put it to work editing your paper. Reread your paper again, checking to make sure you have done the following:

1. Properly credited your sources! Check to make sure all direct quotations have quotation marks and ideas and information not your own are credited to their rightful owners.
2. Corrected any run-ons or sentence fragments
3. Used proper punctuation
4. Checked any word about whose spelling you have even a *shadow of a doubt*
5. Ensured that your subjects, verbs, and pronouns agree
6. Made your sentences flow smoothly

WRITING ASSIGNMENT
Using What You Have Learned

Use your research skills to write a paper of at least six hundred words about a current, controversial issue. To make your task easier, be sure to do the following:

1. Select a current, controversial topic. (A current, controversial topic is a subject about which people disagree. Your subject must have been in the news in the last three years.)
2. Read an in-depth article or two to become familiar with the major aspects involved in your topic. If you know someone who is an expert on your subject, interview them.
3. Follow steps three through eleven in "Steps to Follow in Writing a Research Paper."
4. Along with your finished six-hundred-word essay, turn in your note cards and your source cards.
5. Be sure to include a "Works Cited" list with at least three sources.
6. Instead of using footnotes, place the last name of your source in parenthesis after the information from that source. If no author was given with your source, use the first word or two of the title. If you have already given the source within your paper, simply put the page number of the source in parenthesis. Read the Student Star Essays section at the end of the chapter for examples.
7. For a more thorough discussion of the research paper, refer to one of the following:

> Turabian, Kate L. *A Manual for Writers of Term Papers, Theses, and Dissertations* Chicago: The University of Chicago Press.
> *A Manual of Style* (also The University of Chicago Press).
> Check your bookstore for a book containing the 1984 *MLA* guidelines, for example, the *MLA Handbook.*

STUDENT STAR ESSAYS
The Polished Product

***Remember: the authors of these essays used the following steps:

1. Research
2. Prewriting and more research
3. Writing
4. Revising content
5. Proofreading and correcting mechanical errors

The essays are preceded by their thesis sentences and their outlines.

THESIS

Taking pills is an ineffective and often dangerous way to lose weight and maintain the loss.

Note: The outline for "Get Diet Pills Off the Counter" was altered several times during the research process as the author learned new information about her topic.

OUTLINE

1. Introduction
2. Amphetamines
   a. Effectiveness
   b. Dangers
3. Phenylpropanolamine (PPA)
   a. Effectiveness
   b. Dangers
4. Anesthetics
   a. Effectiveness
   b. Dangers
5. Bulk producers
   a. Effectiveness
   b. Dangers
6. The underlying problem with diet pills
7. Conclusion

GET DIET PILLS OFF THE COUNTER

"Lose weight quickly without hunger!" the diet ads proclaim, thereby creating an American dream, but that is all the ads deliver—a dream. Ten million Americans (90 percent of whom are women) currently use diet pills. By 1990 Americans will spend nearly six hundred million dollars in pursuit of a slim reality through antifat drugs (Labich 38).

Most of these pill packets promoting weight loss suggest a twelve-hundred calories-a-day diet and an exercise program. The diet and exercise programs are the only reason dieters lose weight. The sad truth is that no diet pill can take the weight off unless people consume fewer calories than they burn. Nevertheless, every year Americans spend two hundred million dollars on diet aids that don't work and may even be dangerous (38). Let's take a look at these marvels of modern medicine.

The amphetamines are the most common of the prescription appetite suppressants. Once doctors believed these stimulants suppressed the appetite center in the brain. Today doctors believe that the elevation in mood amphetamines cause is responsible for any decrease in appetite they bring. These drugs produce weight loss in a third of the people who use them, but this loss is not permanent—and it may be dangerous (Haupt 83). To maintain their loss, users must increase the dose of amphetamines; thus they run the danger of becoming dependent on these drugs. In addition, amphetamines can cause side effects such as nervousness, heart irregularities, damage to blood vessels, and even paranoia and other psychotic reactions (Raisz).

Since the 1940s, the most popular ingredient in over-the-counter appetite suppressants has been phenylpropanolamine (PPA). This drug is found in seventy different appetite suppressants and in nasal decongestants. The effects are similar to amphetamines because this drug also acts as a central nervous system stimulant. However PPA can cause strokes, seizures, hypertension, nervousness, and insomnia—even though the Food and Drug Administration's (FDA) original statement about PPA was that it was safe and effective for short-term weight control (up to three months) at doses of twenty-five milligrams taken three times a day (Hymes 15).

Anesthetics are another popular over-the-counter diet drug. Benzocaine, which is found in many spray antiseptics, is the key ingredient. Because of benzocaine's numbing effect, the drug was thought to be useful in interfering with taste. Several candy-type products are the result. Basically benzocaine puts the tongue to sleep. Unfortunately, it has no impact on appetite. Furthermore, its effects last only a few minutes and may interfere with swallowing. In addition, the drug doesn't produce permanent weight loss (Raisz).

Most of the bulk-producing diet pills contain methylcellulose to absorb liquid in the stomach. While methylcellulose will create a feeling of fullness, an empty feeling in the stomach is not the main reason people overeat. Rather overeating stems from boredom, frustration, or nervousness. The FDA says the bulk producers are safe, but they do not cause weight loss (Raisz).

According to studies at the University of Pennsylvania and Harvard University, the major problem with all these "miracle drugs" is they don't get to the basic cause of obesity. Research indicates that basic causes of obesity include psychological and behavioral problems, genetic predisposition, developmental and social problems, and nervous system disorders. Research also shows obese people eat more when they are upset or fearful, while people of normal weight tend to eat less under stress. Obese people may eat fewer meals, but they tend to overeat because food is a stimulus for them. Clearly because there are so many complex factors involved in causing obesity, any drug method for managing it is likely to fail (Labich 42).

More seriously, many diet pills are dangerous and untested. Many of these aids appear on the market without FDA approval because manufacturers contend the pills are food and therefore not subject to the premarket testing to which other drugs are subjected. Just how dangerous are these pills? Diet pills alone are responsible for ten thousand emergency room visits each year (Raisz).

For those who want to lose weight quickly, there is no magic solution. The tried and tested methods—sensible nutrition and regular exercise—still produce the only safe, permanent results.

VMB

WORKS CITED

Haupt, Donna. "Feeling Good." *Mademoiselle* November 1985: 82–3.

Hymes, Donna J., R.N. "Handle with Care!" *Current Health 2* January 1987: 14–5.

Labich, Kenneth. "The Hunt Is on for an Antifat Pill." *Fortune* 18 August 1986: 37–42.

Moffat, Anne Simon. "Obesity's Draft Age." *American Health.* July/August 1987: 142–44.

Raisz, Lawrence, M.D., Professor of Medicine. University of Connecticut Farmington. Personal Interview 4 September 1987.

Weber, Melva. "Weight-Loss Helpers." *Vogue* November 1984: 282.

THESIS

Everyone should wear a seat belt when traveling in a car.

OUTLINE

1. Introduction
2. Statistics about seat belt safety
3. The most common six reasons for not wearing belts and the response
4. Conclusion

DRESSING FOR DRIVING

"Nude, that's what I feel like when I don't have my seat belt on," said Porter Shimer in the January 1986 issue of *Prevention* (70). I feel the same way. I wear my seat belt not just because of the seat belt law but because I need the belt's protective cover. There are sixteen states that currently have laws making seat belts mandatory. Many other states are considering such laws. These states encourage seat belt use with fines of up to fifty dollars for noncompliance (Jacobsen).

Why should government dictate seat belt use? In 1983 there were 42,584 fatalities on highways in this country. Nearly thirty thousand of that total would be alive today if they had been wearing their seat belts (Jacobsen).

With such convincing statistics, why don't people buckle up? Most seat belt ignorers cite one of six reasons for their nudity. Let's examine these reasons, and the response of safety expert Diane Jacobsen to these reasons.

Reason Number One: It is best to be thrown clear of a serious accident.
Response: You must go through a windshield or door to land clear of an accident. Most of these trips—and landings—are far from happy.

Reason Number Two: Seat belts trap people in cars that are burning or sinking in water.
Response: People are often knocked unconscious from not wearing their seat belts. Conscious people obviously have a far better chance of surviving an accident involving submersion or fire.

Reason Number Three: At speeds of less than thirty miles-per-hour, seat belts aren't necessary.
Response: Even at a low speed, you can still bang your head on the windshield or the dashboard. At thirty miles-per-hour such a bang is equal to diving head-first from a three-story building to the sidewalk. Deaths have occurred at speeds as low as twelve miles-per-hour.

Reason Number Four: Seat belts are more of a nuisance than a help on a short trip near home.
Response: Seventy-five percent of all accidents occur within twenty-five miles of home.

Reason Number Five: Most seat belts fit too loosely to work properly.
Response: The slack in seat belts is there for comfort and ease of motion. If you tug at your belt as you would in an accident, the belt should function properly. If it doesn't, get it repaired.

Reason Number Six: Wearing a seat belt is fatalistic.
Response: Wearing a seat belt is certainly less fatalistic than accepting without protection the grim statistic that the average driver in this country can expect to be in an accident at least once every ten years (68–69).

Experts say that, in fact, there is no good reason for not wearing your seat belt (Peelo). So whenever you head off in a car, dress properly: buckle up.

Dan McLean

WORKS CITED

"Buckle Up California." The California Office of Traffic Safety, 1987.

"Can Seat Belts Be Death Traps?" *U.S. News & World Report* 25 August 1986: 10.

Jacobsen, Diane. "Buckle Up" Director. Monterey County Department of Health. Personal communication 24 September 1987.

Peelo, Officer David. California Highway Patrol. Personal communication 23 September 1987.

Shimer, Porter. "The Easiest Way to Live Longer." *Prevention* January 1986: 66–70.

"Use No Restraint in Buckling Up." *Prevention* July 1986: 10.

HELP! FOR FURTHER WORK

Read "The Working Mother," and then answer the Thought and Discussion questions which follow it.

THE WORKING MOTHER

In the passed, about 25 years ago, it was assumed a women has to stay home after she had a child. Now I have seen a data that indicates over half the women in this country work, and, after having a child, women can return to work without hurting there children. As a matter of fact, forcing a woman to stay home will probably make her feel sort of angry and resentful, etc. toward her child. Raising one can be and often is an isolating and lonely job.

Irregardless of her time away from her child, for the mother who is separated from her young one daily, its the quality of the care which counts, not the quantity. A mother and her child can enjoy each others company in two hours just as much from each other as they can in ten hours.

Besides mothers shouldn't always bear principle responsibility for raising a child, fathers should share more equally in the child care. Couples should of worked out schedules of equal responsibility even before the childs arrival. They can divide feeding and diapering and also share cuddling and playing time with their child.

If the child is too be taken to a day care center, both parents should research the places and people they'll be entrusting with the care of the child. Good care is important. Competent care for the baby would be one worker for every four children. The workers themselves should be well-trained, and than the center or sitter should be sure to make parents feel they are participating in there childs care. The center should also hold meetings with groups of parents and the staff; than particular problems can be discussed.

Parenting should be something one wrestles with: the adjustments and the problems. Their is not a perfect mother and the only kind of really bad mother is the kind that doesn't care about her baby.

FOR THOUGHT AND DISCUSSION

1. What is the central point at the beginning of "The Working Mother"?
2. Where does the author get off track from the central point?
3. Select a single thesis for the essay and list the kinds of evidence needed to support the thesis.
4. How much research is evidenced by this essay?
5. Indicate at which points in the essay the author should have given specific information to support her points.
6. What important social trends does the author ignore in her analysis of raising a child?
7. Correct the mechanical errors so they do not interfere with your analysis of "The Working Mother." Pay special attention to errors covered in "Formal and Informal Language," beginning on page 319, through "Spelling" in "The Final Touch: A Handbook."

14 WRITING IN THE CLASSROOM

© 1986 Universal Press Syndicate

Midway through the exam,
Allen pulls out a bigger brain.

Human history becomes more and more a race between education and catastrophe.

H. G. Wells

CONCEPTS TO LEARN

- The way to transfer good writing techniques to essay examinations
- Positive ways of viewing essay examinations

THE PROFITS OF WRITING ESSAY EXAMS

In this chapter, you will see the way the writing skills you have used thus far will help you to write more quickly, efficiently, and clearly in your academic life.

An important concept in this book has been to relax when gathering ideas for writing. Unfortunately, for some students the very word *examination*, to say nothing of *essay examination*, strikes more terror than Attila the Hun and King Kong could muster as a team. As you read the following poem watch for the details that recreate the atmosphere in a classroom during an examination.

Test

Across our silence the cool
neon tubes shine perfectly.
One hour, and the truth will be out,
monster named What We Do Not Know.
We listen to the humming light,
its one held note held perfectly,
and the teacher dreams of flat horizons
across this unfractured time.
So much perfection here, if
perfection means evenness,
the even whiteness of paper,
even blackness of the board.
But we are here, and our monster.
We shift, telling on ourselves,
scratching. Someone laughs, someone curses.
The clock clicks its heels perfectly.

Rich Linder

FOR THOUGHT AND DISCUSSION

1. What is the central mood of the classroom in "Test"?
2. Which details show the mood concretely?
3. List the examples of figurative language used in the poem.

4. When students are prepared for a test, why do they feel tension while taking it?
5. What does tension do to your ability to retrieve ideas from your memory?

BUGS BUNNY FEET AND BROOM HILDA BREWS

"Lovely," you say. "I really needed to be reminded about Test Tension. Here we are almost at the end of the semester, and Final Exams are breathing down my neck!"

Before you break out your magic potions and rabbits' feet, however, let's examine some test-writing suggestions that produce results just as magically, but far more reliably than Bugs Bunny feet and Broom Hilda brews.

We have all had times, when—like Allen in the cartoon—we needed a larger brain. The point of freewriting, brainstorming, and clustering is to get into what is, in a sense, another brain—a brain that will help us remember and organize information. Prewriting techniques help us get "another brain" by shutting off our Left Brain Critic with its suggestions like the following:

> You are going to clutch on this test.
> You are going to forget everything you know.
> You always blow tests.

While our Critic means well, in fact, it sets up a pattern of tension that interferes with our ability to think clearly and remember efficiently. An important concept to remember when we feel panicked about an exam was ably expressed more than three centuries ago:

> The mind in its own place, and in its self,
> Can make a Heav'n of Hell, and Hell of Heav'n.

> John Milton, *Paradise Lost*

In other words, we can—quite easily—convince ourselves that tests are Hell. We can also convince ourselves they are—well, perhaps not Heaven, but not all that threatening and unpleasant. How? Read on.

The Great Pretender

According to author Kurt Vonnegut, "We are what we pretend to be." Of course we are, and practice makes perfect. So to be a good test taker, you need to pretend—and practice in your imagination—to be a good test taker.

> They can because they think they can.

> Virgil

For psychologist Anthony Robbins, controlling the conflict between the various people that make up each of us is the key to achieving our goals—whether they be success in the business world or success on our next examination. Just as the health food advocate says "you are what you eat," so too we are what we tell ourselves we are.

EXCERPT FROM UNLIMITED POWER
Anthony Robbins

It is our belief that determines how much of our potential we'll be able to tap. Beliefs can turn on or shut off the flow of ideas. Imagine the following situation. Someone says to you, "Please get me the salt," and as you walk into the next room, you say, "But I don't know where it is." After looking for a few minutes, you call out, "I can't find the salt."

Then that someone walks up, takes the salt right off the shelf in front of you, and says, "Look, dummy, it's right here in front of you. If it was a snake, it would have bitten you." When you said, "I can't," you gave your brain a command not to see the salt. . . . Remember, every human experience, everything you've ever said, seen, heard, felt, smelled, or tasted is stored in your brain. When you say you cannot remember, you're right. When you say you can, you give a command to your nervous system that opens up the pathways to the part of your brain that can potentially deliver the answers you need.

So what do you do about nervousness that interferes with your ability to do your best? Ordering yourself to relax only increases your tension. Telling yourself you have a self-defeating attitude will, in fact, make your attitude even more self-defeating. Instead, why not reprogram yourself to do well? Such reprograming is free, painless, and *effective*.

How to Reprogram Yourself

As long as possible before an exam is an ideal time to begin to program yourself to remember material. Now is the time to convince yourself you *can* do well on examinations. If all this sounds more like a psychology course than a composition course, so what? What works is what works. The following suggestions—if you follow them—will work splendidly.

1. Interrupt your study with relaxing stretches. Just as we remember better when relaxed, we also learn better.
2. Several times each day take a deep breath and relax; stretch and yawn. Feel the tension ebb away. When you are relaxed, you are the most susceptible to suggestion. This is the time to tell yourself you *will* do well. But do not leave the suggestion at the *abstract* level. Remember the right brain thinks *concretely*. See yourself taking the test. See and feel yourself being

relaxed and doing well. Really get your senses involved. Take a few seconds to imagine yourself taking a test and doing well.

3. If you have a long pattern of telling yourself you will forget material during tests, you will have to spend time reprogramming these instructions you have been giving to your subconscious mind. Several times each day reprogram yourself for success. Tell yourself the following:

You are going to feel relaxed when taking tests.
You are going to do just fine on the next test.
Now you are in control of your memory.
Now you are in control of your ability to relax.
From now on, test taking will be a positive experience.

Of course, you do not have to limit yourself to this pattern. Simply remember the philosophy behind it: relax and reassure yourself. Make only positive suggestions to yourself. Are we repeating ourselves? You bet. Repetition of positive suggestions over a period of time is the key to your success.

THE MYSTERY SOLVED

You do not have to be Sherlock Holmes to figure out what an instructor wants in a writing assignment—whether the assignment is an essay question you must answer in class or an essay you write outside of class. The same principles of good writing apply whether you are writing a company memo or analyzing causes of World War I.

During an essay exam, be sure to read the questions carefully. Your instructors do not want you to reiterate all you know about a subject. Rather, they want the answer to a specific question. For example, when a sociology instructor asks you to analyze the changing function of the American family with the spread of industrialization, you must limit your subject to fall within those specific guidelines.

The Sunny Side

In structuring essay questions instructors do a good deal of your prewriting work for you. They help you limit your subject. They help you find the argumentative edge you need to develop.

The Next Steps

Once you are sure you have read the question carefully, let your Right Brain Creator take over as you begin prewriting exercises to plan your answer. In situations like tests, it is even more vital than usual that you write down the important ideas that occur to you. You do not have time to chase after those that escape you because you did not write them down. Once you think of an idea, trap it on paper.

Professional writers work under different conditions than you do in an essay test; however, the principles involved in the prewriting and organizational techniques are similar. Let's examine some essay-type questions to see in what way professional writers might handle them.

The Question: According to scientists Carl Sagan and Paul Ehrlich, what impact would a nuclear war have on our planet? In your answer, explain possible flaws in their theory.

Figure 14.1 is a sample of brainstorming for the answer. In Stage I, write down all your thoughts about the effect of a nuclear war. In Stage II, *after you have your ideas*, you can let your Left Brain swing into action to make a quick outline. Do not worry about being neat or fancy. Just get something down that will work for you. If you give it a chance, your Right Brain Creator will show you how to organize the material. The purpose of the outline is simply to help you remember what occurred to you as you rummaged around in your right brain.

Of course, you could use clustering to help you with the same question. Figure 14.2 is a sample clustering for the answer.

FIGURE 14.1   **A Sample Brainstorming for the Bomb Question**

3 kinds of effects : heat, blast, radiation
Bombs affect : people, structures, the
                whole environment.

effects of
  heat
  blast
  radiation
      on
        humans
        structures
        animals
        the earth's ecosystem.

FIGURE 14.2   A Sample Clustering for the Bomb Question

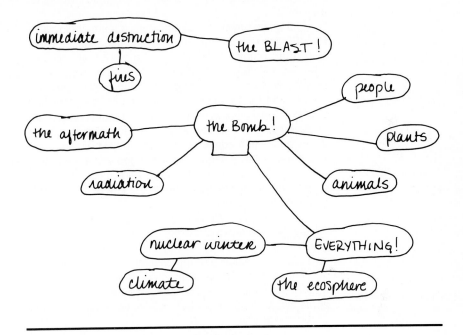

The Professional Answer
In the following article a professional writer answers the question.

THE NUCLEAR-WINTER THREAT
Thomas Levenson

Ever since Hiroshima and Nagasaki, most people have been grimly aware of the heat, blast, and radiation effects of nuclear weapons on human beings, structures, and the environment—and of the immensely greater holocaust that a full-scale nuclear war would bring. Now, two new studies suggest another catastrophic consequence of an all-out nuclear exchange, one that has been largely overlooked. At a meeting in Washington late in October, scientists warned that soot, smoke, and dust from the explosions of less than half of the superpowers' nuclear arsenals could blanket the earth, block out the sun, and cause a prolonged, bitterly cold "nuclear winter." This climatic upheaval, the scientists warned, could threaten the survival of the human species.

Planetary scientist Carl Sagan reported that he and several colleagues had run mathematical simulations showing that the pall from burning cities, forests, and fuel stocks would create a dense cloud that could screen much of the Northern Hemisphere from more than ninety percent of the sun's light for as long as a month. Within two weeks of detonation, the surface of the earth could cool to minus thirteen degrees Fahrenheit and remain that cold for several months. After several weeks, the cloud could reach the Southern Hemisphere as well. Full daylight and normal temperatures would not return for as long as a year.

Using the physicists' predictions, a team of biologists headed by Stanford's Paul Ehrlich gauged the ecological consequences of several levels of nuclear war. After a major conflict, involving more than three-quarters of the available strategic arsenal, the cold would devastate crops and other plant life, particularly if a war occurred during the spring or summer. Fresh water would freeze; hungry and thirsty animals would die. At the same time, the dark would limit photosynthesis, the process by which plants produce the chemical compounds necessary for life. In the oceans outside of arctic regions, the lack of sunlight would be felt immediately. There the food chain depends on microscopic plants that are extremely sensitive to changes in the amount of light they receive. On the land masses in the tropics, where most plants lack a reserve of stored energy, a substantial decrease in the amount of sunshine would quickly extinguish many species.

Says Ehrlich, "We doubt that these effects would kill off all humans immediately. But the survivors would face a radically different environment from that which they are used to." Over the decades that follow, he says, "we cannot exclude the possibility of the extinction of the human species."

These grim biological predictions depend on the accuracy of the mathematical techniques the physicists used to determine the climate changes, and some climate specialists have criticized Sagan's models for making too many assumptions about the behavior of smoke and soot particles in the atmosphere. Says Joseph Smagorinsky, retired director of the geophysical fluid dynamics laboratory at Princeton, "The models aren't suited for this kind of calculation. Most models attempt to predict small departures from the present. I don't doubt that a nuclear war would have some serious effects on the climate, but I don't know what those would be."

Stephen Schneider, an atmospheric scientist with the National Center for Atmospheric Research in Boulder, Colorado, agrees with Smagorinsky in part. "The three great uncertainties are how much, how high, how wide a cloud you get. There are no real calculations for these." But, Schneider adds, "there is an enormous amount of soot available. The results Sagan and Ehrlich discuss are all well within the range of possible consequences."

FOR THOUGHT AND DISCUSSION

1. According to Sagan how serious could the impact of fire be on the Northern Hemisphere? Support your answer with concrete material from the essay.
2. What percent of the superpowers' stored weapons would have to be exploded to cause the effects the scientists predict?
3. According to Ehrlich, what would happen to survivors of a nuclear war?
4. Do their scientific critics believe the Sagan-Ehrlich predictions are possible? Develop your answer concretely. (By the way, this would be a good essay question.)

Thinking It Through

If—in a geography, urban planning, or English composition class—we were asked to write an essay supporting the idea that a particular city was or was not a good place to live, how would we attack the essay? How do we make the idea of a "good" place to live concrete?

We know the principles of good writing call for limiting the subject. There are enormous numbers of things each of us could write about what makes a particular spot heaven or hell for its residents. We also know people do not agree on such abstract words as *good*, *bad*, and *ugly*. We need to come up with a list of *concrete* qualities to help us *limit* the subject.

The Question: What characteristics make a city a good place to live?

1. Begin with a prewriting technique to plan your answer.
2. To the proper bubble in the clustering sample in Figure 14.3, attach any additional traits you think a good place to live should have.

The Good, the Bad, and the Ugly: Places to Live

When Rand McNally's latest *Places Rated Almanac* was published, cries of delight—and anguish—resounded from Miami to Seattle. The following article, written by J. D. Reed, was reported by Kenneth W. Banta of New York, Charles Peltam of Yuba City, with other bureaus.

FIGURE 14.3   **A Sample Clustering for the Characteristics of a Good City Question**

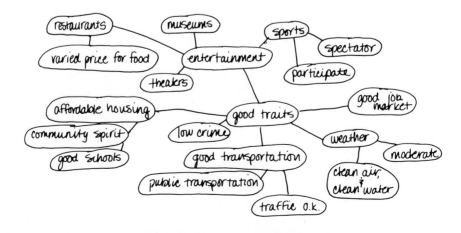

ALL RILED UP ABOUT RATINGS

A NEW BOOK EVALUATES 329 U.S. CITIES FOR LIVABILITY

Whether the subject is the beefiest burger or the biggest corporation, Americans have a penchant for making lists of the best and the worst, then arguing about the results. Since 1939, when Psychologist E. L. Thorndike devised a "goodness index" to rate U.S. cities, no rankings have inspired more disagreement than those about home sweet home. The latest edition of Rand McNally's *Places Rated Almanac* can only add to the controversy. According to the 449-page paperback released last week, the best all-round metropolitan area in which to live in the U.S. is Pittsburgh. The worst: Yuba City, California.

Pittsburgh boosters celebrated as if the Steelers had won the Super Bowl. "We've been the best-kept secret in the world," said Mayor Richard Caliguiri, "and now the secret is out." But in the Yuba City area (pop. 109,000), a farming center forty miles north of Sacramento, residents were mystified. Said Realtor Bill Meagher: "Our quality of living is excellent. Somebody's got their wires crossed."

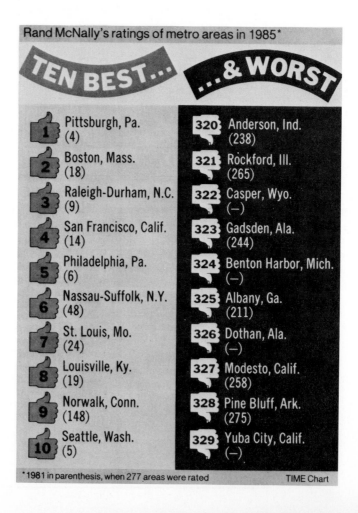

Rand McNally's ratings of metro areas in 1985*

TEN BEST... ...& WORST

	TEN BEST		WORST
1	Pittsburgh, Pa. (4)	320	Anderson, Ind. (238)
2	Boston, Mass. (18)	321	Rockford, Ill. (265)
3	Raleigh-Durham, N.C. (9)	322	Casper, Wyo. (—)
4	San Francisco, Calif. (14)	323	Gadsden, Ala. (244)
5	Philadelphia, Pa. (6)	324	Benton Harbor, Mich. (—)
6	Nassau-Suffolk, N.Y. (48)	325	Albany, Ga. (211)
7	St. Louis, Mo. (24)	326	Dothan, Ala. (—)
8	Louisville, Ky. (19)	327	Modesto, Calif. (258)
9	Norwalk, Conn. (148)	328	Pine Bluff, Ark. (275)
10	Seattle, Wash. (5)	329	Yuba City, Calif. (—)

*1981 in parenthesis, when 277 areas were rated   TIME Chart

The choices are far from the only revelations in the $14.95 *Almanac,* which ranks all of the nation's 329 metropolitan areas, where more than 75 percent of all Americans reside. Since 1981, when the first edition appeared, the fortunes of a number of cities have changed. One reason: this time around Authors Richard Boyer and David Savageau have refined their nine "livability" criteria. Data about climate, housing, health care, crime, transportation, education, culture, recreation, and economics are now weighted by such qualities as "fortunate circumstances of geography" and "outdoor recreational assets." Third-ranked Raleigh-Durham, North Carolina, moved up from ninth place, for instance, partly because it is "a genteel place to live." Atlanta, 1981's top city, fell to eleventh place, hurt by conditions at its zoo. Washington, second in 1981, slipped in rank to fifteenth, while the metropolitan Greensboro, North Carolina, area dived from third to forty-first.

Boston residents have their own theories on why Bean Town jumped from eighteenth to second place. Harvard Social Scientist David Riesman *(The Lonely Crowd)* thinks that media exposure helped. Doug Flutie, the former Boston College quarterback, he notes, "is quick, brainy, and made it on countless telecasts." John Updike, who lives in the exclusive suburb of Beverly Farms, cites the economic factor. "When I came to Harvard in the fifties, Boston was fairly grubby," says the novelist. "Now if you have the money, it's a nice place to live."

The almanac's most unexpected result: of the top twenty areas, only four are in the western part of the country. In the 1981 study, cities stood or fell on their own merits. Now the authors give smaller areas credit for the amenities of nearby major cities. Suburban Norwalk, Connecticut, for example, gained points for New York City's top standing in the arts and health care, but was not penalized for New York's last-place rating in crime. Thus Norwalk went from 148th place to ninth. New York's rank is twenty-fifth.

Boyer, a mystery novelist, and Savageau, a relocation consultant, worked for sixteen months to track down and verify new statistics. "Every call to a government agency," says Savageau, "uncovered ten other statistics we could use." The authors also devised their own formulas. To gauge climate, for example, they developed a complex scheme relating relative humidity to seasonal variations in temperature. To update the 1980 census, they turned to such sources as IRS change-of-address lists. One discovery: the Sunbelt may have oversold its desirability. Address changes for the past two years show the Northeast has been gaining population while the West has been losing it. Conclude the authors: "Not only did our [older] cities not die, they are undergoing a rejuvenation unparalleled in our history."

A rating of American metropolises, they write, "is like a snapshot of a moving target." No picture is fuzzier than that of No. One Pittsburgh. It received no outstanding marks in eight categories—its best was seventh in education—and it accumulated no low ones. "Pittsburgh is like the Steelers' front line," observes Boyer. "Not incredibly strong in any one area, but consistently good overall."

Cities in the basement are already contesting the criteria. By last weekend, Rand McNally was overwhelmed with outraged calls. One caller, Pat Lile, a Pine Bluff, Arkansas, development promoter, complained of Pine Bluff's 328th place rating: "They don't contact one person or make one phone call. Other people use their data, and the damage proliferates." Said Mayor Edward Bartholomew of Glens Falls, New York, which ranked 290th: "We're going to have a public burning of [Rand McNally's] almanac and all their maps." Responded Rand McNally Public Relations Director Conroy Erickson: "All we've done is supply the raw material. Readers need to make their own judgments."

Residents of Yuba City quickly did so. Apples and oranges, they said. "I don't see how they can compare cities like Pittsburgh and Yuba City," commented Fireman Ron Ruzich. "It's just a way for someone to sell books somewhere." Part-time Mayor Chuck Pappageorge, a grain merchant, looked for a way to capitalize on the city's bottom-rung prominence. Said he: "If we'd been second to last, no one would have noticed. This is a great opportunity. We'll get some yardage out of this." Better hold that line, Pittsburgh.

FOR THOUGHT AND DISCUSSION

1. Which beginning and ending technique from Chapter Nine did the authors of the article use?
2. List the criteria used in *Places Rated Almanac* that were not included in the clustering.
3. How would your own list of criteria differ from that used for the almanac?
4. What explanations do the authors give to insure this article will be understood by a general audience?

WRITING ASSIGNMENT
Using What You Have Learned

Write an essay that would be an appropriate response to an essay question in a class you are now taking or have taken in the past. In your essay be sure to use the following steps:

1. Practice the relaxation and self-suggestion techniques discussed earlier in this chapter. This will turn on your Right Brain Creator.
2. Limit your response to a specific question. Do not simply try to write an impressive amount of information somewhat related to a general topic.
3. Survey your ideas through clustering or brainstorming. (Hand this in stapled to the back of your essay.)
4. Write a thesis sentence that adequately limits your subject and makes a supportable point about that subject.
5. Provide transitions (see Chapter Eight) that help your reader to follow your thinking.
6. Use concrete details to support your central point. Remember, your instructor is trying to find out what specific information you have learned and whether or not you understand that information.
7. During an essay exam, save a few minutes to proofread your paper. Let your Left Brain out of its closet or cage (or wherever you keep it). As you do with all essays, take enough time to proofread your essay adequately.

STUDENT ESSAY EXAMINATION STARS
The Polished Product

***Remember: while time is often tight in an essay examination, the authors of the following essays budgeted time to use the following steps:

1. Prewriting
2. Writing
3. Revising content
4. Proofreading and correcting mechanical errors

THE IMPORTANCE OF THE RIGHT BRAIN

The Question: Explain the roles the right and left sides of the brain play in the composition process.

The right brain, which sees total objects or experiences, holds the key to creative thoughts and impressions. For example, when you describe a person using your right brain you might say, "It was wonderful to see Sharon again. She is so vivacious that her energy radiates throughout the room." If you had used your left brain, you might say, "It was wonderful to see Sharon again, but she really should get that chipped front tooth fixed." Your left brain, then, concentrates on one feature at a time, not on the total person. Your left brain keeps lists of details. And it likes to analyze, which is why it is good at telling you what is right and what is wrong.

Your right brain, on the other hand, will let you be free and have fun in your writing as long as the left brain isn't yelling instructions such as, "That's a stupid idea. Be more creative, and watch your spelling, grammar, and punctuation." If the left brain takes over in the initial stages of writing, it blocks the good ideas flowing from the right brain. When the left brain is not criticizing your writing, you are freer to formulate ideas, and your ideas are more interesting.

To awaken the right brain, it is important to be relaxed. To quiet the left brain and inspire the right brain, there are three major methods: clustering, free writing, and brainstorming. Clustering involves writing down a key word or phrase in the center of a blank sheet of paper. Circle this key idea and around it write any words or images that pop into your mind. Circle these and connect them to the central idea by a line. As you allow your mind to play with ideas that pop into your mind, yet more ideas will occur to you. Write and circle these under the idea that inspired them. Before long, you will have a flash of inspiration—rather like the lightbulbs cartoonists draw for their characters. When this flash occurs, your thoughts will come together. You will know what your want to say about your subject.

Freewriting is another method to help quiet your left brain and inspire your right brain. With this method, you simply write whatever pops into your mind about a particular subject. Using this method, you create what looks like an essay. This leads to the danger that your left brain will swing into action and issue warnings like, "Look up that word. It's spelled wrong. That sounds funny. Maybe it is a parallel structure error. Better read up on parallel structure." No matter how hard your left brain squawks, don't stop your thought processes to check on mechanics. Save that kind of editing until after you finish creating ideas.

Brainstorming lends itself to the same type of danger because with this method you list each idea that occurs to you. The left brain adores lists, so it wants to horn in on the writing process. Ignore it and keep writing down ideas. Don't allow yourself to be critical. Remember one idea leads to another. A bad idea often leads to a good one. If you stop to look up a spelling word, you may lose your train of thought.

Once you have finished getting ideas, let your left brain out of the closet. Invite it to make corrections. Let it be critical about sentence structure, spelling, grammar, and punctuation. After all, writing requires teamwork. Just remember to use your team members to your best advantages. Don't expect your defensive lineman to do the job of a nimble running back.

Judy Biddy

IT CAN BE DONE

The Question: Trace the steps in writing an essay.

An intriguing question—and an excellent one to answer before facing The Final Exam: How do you write an essay? Clustering might work to generate ideas for some people. Since there is a list of topics to include, however, brainstorming seems most helpful to me for this particular type of essay.

And logically, the first item on my brainstorming list is selecting a topic. The most efficient topic selection method is to choose a subject with which you are familiar. My ideas come from my children, classes, and family activities in addition to the newspapers and magazines I read. If you select a subject about which you know, you cut down on research time. When selecting a topic, remember your reader's interest. Our instructor, for example, has promised not to make us read any articles from her knitting magazines.

Once you select a topic, you must write a topic sentence with an argumentative edge. You need an angle you can support. Beware of the temptation to leave your topic sentence in question form. The question "Will the rain tomorrow contain radiation levels above normal?" does not give your essay the direction it needs. Similarly "Writing editorials allows an individual to express his opinion" is a fact and therefore leaves you nothing to prove to your reader.

Next your must organize supporting details in the most effective order. Some prefer the "Big Bang" method which presents the strongest argument first. The problem with this method is the paper fizzles out. It ends with a whimper after beginning with a bang. Remember the last time you held a sparkler? It was great at first. Then the sparkler just did the same thing to a lesser degree until it fizzled out. Don't let this happen to your paper.

The method that holds the reader's attention best is the "Add-a-Step" method which begins with arguments supporting your topic statement. Then it builds arguments one on another saving the best for last. Think of a mystery story. It slowly builds a step at a time toward a climax that keeps your interest. Like it, you want to hold your reader's interest to the very last word.

Finally you have presented all your arguments. What do you do next? Say "that's it" and stop writing? No! Picture each argument as a musician in a band practicing his part alone. Slowly the musicians get together in small groups to practice. For their performance to be effective, they must practice together to blend their music—just as through transitions and an effective conclusion, your development blends in perfect harmony.

When you feel the paper is ready for its opening night—stop! Go back and proofread to be sure you didn't hit any sour notes like run-on sentences or misspelled words. Check for changes in rhythm from three-fourths to four-fourths time that a tense change causes. Make sure misplaced punctuation doesn't throw off the beat.

Writing a paper and answering an essay question involve a complex process; however on opening night when the rave reviews roll in, it will have been worth the effort.

Christina A. Kroshl

WARTIME LEADERS

The Question: How were the leaders of the Confederate and the Union forces during the Civil War different from and similar to each other?

Two of the great men who fought in the Civil War had striking similarities, and yet they were essentially very different in their backgrounds and philosophies. However, both commanders were strong, not only in character but also in leadership.

Robert E. Lee was born to wealth and culture in Virginia, a member of one of the South's leading families. His father had been a general in the Revolutionary War, and two of his relatives had signed the Declaration of Independence. Lee attended West Point Military Academy and graduated with high honors. He later served as a colonel in the Mexican War.

The Declaration of Independence states "all men are created equal and endowed by their creator with certain . . . rights" including the rights to life, liberty, and the pursuit of happiness. Nevertheless, Lee felt there should be inequality in the social structure. A leisure class consisting of wealthy landowners, according to Lee, would bring forth a society with a strong sense of obligation to the land and to the community. This class would have nothing to gain for themselves, but would meet obligations placed on them because of their privileged status. From them the country would get its strong leadership. Lee, then, was an aristocrat who believed the landed nobility justified itself.

Ulysses S. Grant came from a very different background from Lee's, and Grant grew up with a philosophy derived from that background. Grant was the first of six children of a tanner on the Western frontier. Like Lee, Grant attended West Point, but Grant was only an average student. Unlike Lee, Grant did not like military life. During the Mexican War, Grant served as a lieutenant.

Also unlike Lee, Grant did not grow up with wealth paving the way for him. Instead of accepting the beliefs of an old, traditional society, Grant was one of a large body of Western frontier men who were obedient to no one but themselves, who cared little for the past but who had a good eye for the future. Their society had privileges not for those born to wealth, but instead for those who earned that privilege through hard work and ability. As the Western frontier expanded, so did each man have the opportunity to grow and better himself.

So Grant and Lee held very different views of America. Grant, looking to the future, saw the coming age of steel and machinery and masses of people in crowded cities. On the other hand, Lee's vision was limited to the past when American was a rural, agricultural society with individual ownership of large plantations.

Chris Widmann

HELP! FOR FURTHER WORK

Read the following question and essay, then answer the discussion questions which follow.

The Question: How is the computer age affecting Soviet society?

Soviet computers are currently being used in the schools, computers are also being used for industrial work. In the schools, 9th and 10th grade students are enrolling in computer classes. Not all the schools have computers now. Boris Goldenberg Soviet computer headmaster in Moscow wants to cooperate with schools in making personnel and equipment available until the Moscow schools all have their own personal computers. Vladimir Vaschenko, science organization administration director, says that the Soviets should buy their own assembly lines where they can assemble 1,000's of computers.

Computers are also used for industry by Soviets. 8% of all of the Soviet Union's enterprises have mainframe computers, according to William K. McHenry, a Georgetown University faculty member. The figure was higher among industrial plants that employ more than five hundred people—about thirty-three %. Computers are almost universally used in U.S. plants—nearly one hundred percent.

American authorities watch the Soviet Union's ability to concentrate enormous scientific and industrial resources, it almost assures some degree of success in their computer literacy drive. Still, nothing solves the computer problems facing the Soviet Union—not even all the spies they have in Silicon Valley.

FOR THOUGHT AND DISCUSSION

1. Reread the question. What does it ask the student to do?
2. Which material in the essay is appropriate as a response to the question?
3. Which material is not appropriate?
4. Indicate places where transitions are needed.
5. Write constructive criticism to help the student respond more appropriately to the question.
6. How could adequate prewriting have helped the student?
7. Correct the mechanical errors in the essay. Pay special attention to the errors covered in the "Word Problems" section of "The Final Touch: A Handbook," beginning on page 331.

THE FINAL TOUCH: A HANDBOOK

". . . but enough with the rhetoric."

INTRODUCTION

Once your ideas are captured on paper, and you have effectively developed and organized those ideas, it is time to make sure your reader is not mislead by mechanical errors in your grammar, punctuation, and spelling. The following handbook "The Final Touch" is a guide to help you correct your paper's mechanical weaknesses.

To help you find a particular mechanical skill, "The Final Touch" is organized into sections. Because students sometimes forget that mechanical rules exist to help them communicate effectively (and not to insure jobs for composition instructors), I have emphasized the content of the material that illustrates mechanical skills by relating that material to the contents of chapters of *Practicing the Process*. While you may not want to review mechanical skills in the order I list them, do notice that the material in "The Final Touch" corresponds to the *Practicing the Process* chapters indicated in the following list:

DICTION AND SPELLING

WORD PROBLEMS

THE BASICS: LEFTY IN THE LIMELIGHT

If you show up for a job interview wearing dirt-splattered jeans and a grease-stained, rumpled shirt, chances are your friendly, knowledgeable personality will not shine through. You probably will not get the job. Similarly if your ideas show up in grimy, wrinkled dress, they will not get their job done. It is not enough that your ideas are good ones; you must communicate those ideas properly if they are to be effective.

ITEM 1   THE GRADING CHART

The standard correction symbol for grading chart is *grade*. (For a complete list of standard correction symbols, see the inside back cover of this book.)

Study the following chart to see the interaction of left and right brain skills for grades A through F. While this chart is not tailored to any specific essay, it reflects the usual strengths and weaknesses of papers getting these grades. See Chapter Two if you need to review right- and left-brain functions.

Grade	What You Say
A or B	You have thought beyond the obvious to come up with something worthwhile to say. You have supported your clearly stated central idea with convincing, relevant, and specific examples. If you did not already know enough about your subject, you did enough research to obtain the necessary information.
C	You do have a central point, but you have not thought very deeply about it. Some of your ideas are too obvious. Your support of your ideas needs to be more detailed and convincing.
D or F	You need a central focus. Since you do not have one, your support cannot convince readers. The support you do offer is too sketchy and abstract. Review *abstract* and *concrete* in Chapter Four.

Grade	How You Make Your Point
A or B	You have organized your ideas so they relate clearly to each other. Your transitions help readers move from idea to idea. The development of your ideas is arranged effectively.
C	Although your ideas are organized, they are not arranged in the most effective order, and your transitions need to be smoother and more varied.
D or F	You need to organize your ideas more effectively and you need to more more clearly indicate the interrelationship of your ideas.

Grade	Your Mechanics
A or B	Your word choice is original and appropriate, your sentences are effectively varied. You have used standard spelling, punctuation, and grammar.
C	You have selected appropriate words, but you need to consult a dictionary or thesaurus to help you vary your word choice and ensure you have the very best word for your meaning. In addition, review sentence variety. You may need to vary your sentence types. Proofread with greater care. Review the "Word Problems" section on page 331 of "The Final Touch," paying particular attention to any errors you repeat.
F	Your word choice is not always appropriate. You sometimes use nonstandard or unidiomatic language. You need to pay more attention to grammar, punctuation, and spelling. You make so many errors, your meaning is sometimes lost. If your school has an English learning or tutorial center, take advantage of it. Such places provide a marvelous opportunity to get help tailored to your specific needs.

ITEM 2   HELPFUL HINTS FOR PROOFREADING

By the time you finish a paper, your brain is ready for a break. It is tired of reading those same ideas over and over, so it reads what you *think* you wrote, and it sometimes misses errors. You need to wake up your brain and give it a fresh view of your writing. To do this, proofread your paper by putting a sheet of paper under the last line and reading the paper backwards, line by line. The sheet of paper will help you concentrate on each line.

Know Thyself

Keep a list of your mechanical errors and try to pinpoint your weaknesses. If spelling is a weakness, double-check every word that could possibly be wrong. Give your paper a separate reading during which you concentrate only on spelling. Similarly, if you have trouble with run on sentences or fragments, you should do a special reading looking only for these errors. This method means you will be proofreading your paper several times.

A Friend in Need

Spotting other people's errors is much easier than spotting your own. Trade papers with a friend (or better yet with several friends) and help each other proofread.

ITEM 3   MANUSCRIPT FORMS

The standard correction symbol for manuscript form is *ms* and for titles is *title*. (For a complete list, see the inside back cover.)

Abide by the following commandments when you write a final draft of a paper.

1. Unless your instructor requests a different format, write your name, the course title, the section number, the date, and the assignment name in the upper right-hand corner of the first page, as shown in the following example:

> William Shakespeare
> English 201
> Tuesday Section
> September 23, 1992
> Name of Essay Assignment

2. Type your papers. If you do not know how to type, learn now. Typing will be useful to you in your academic life, your professional life, and your personal life. Among the benefits of knowing how to type are the following:

   a. Computers are here to stay. If you do not already use a computer at work, chances are that eventually you will. Knowing how to type is an enormous advantage for people who use computers.

b. Typed papers are easier to read than handwritten papers—even when handwritten papers are neatly written.

c. Once typing is mastered, even slow typists can type ideas several times faster than they can write them in longhand.

d. Typing is easier on your hands than writing. Typing leaves your hands uncramped and ready for other exciting activities—for example, turning the pages of textbooks. Read first the handwritten version and then the typed version of the following passage from William Zinsser's *On Writing Well*. Next ask yourself which communicated to you more quickly and effectively.

Short paragraphs put air around what you write and make it look inviting, whereas one long chunk of type can discourage the reader from even starting to read. A newspaper paragraph generally shouldn't have more than two or three sentences. You may worry that such frequent paragraphing will damage the logical development of your ideas. Don't worry. The gains far outweigh the dangers.

Short paragraphs put air around what you write and make it look inviting, whereas one long chunk of type can discourage the reader from even starting to read. A newspaper paragraph generally shouldn't have more than two or three sentences. You may worry that such frequent paragraphing will damage the logical development of your ideas. Don't worry. The gains far outweigh the dangers.

3. Under extreme circumstances (for example, if you have been kidnapped by terrorists), you can write an essay in cursive instead of typing it. When you cannot type your essay, write *neatly* in black ink on 8½ by 11-inch paper. Be sure to use standard cursive writing. Papers printed in all capital letters are not acceptable because capital letters communicate important information to your reader—

information that cannot be communicated when your whole paper is in capitals. For more information on capitalization, read "Capitalization," on page 284.

4. Double-space both handwritten and typed papers and leave one-inch margins at the left, right, and bottom of each page. Write on only *one* side of the paper. (Incidentally, when you double-space your rough draft, you have more room for revision and corrections. Doing so makes your next draft easier. Many writers even triple-space rough drafts to get extra revising space.)

5. Give each paper a title. Skip a line between the title and the first line of your essay. Do not underline the title or put it in quotation marks!

6. Number pages after the first. Some computers number the first page too. (Do not worry about things you cannot control.)

PRACTICE LEADS TO PERFECTION

1. What is the difference between an A-B and a C paper in content?
2. What is the difference between an A-B and a C paper in mechanics?
3. Explain how to proofread a paper to ensure you look at it word-by-word.
4. Make a list of the mechanical errors you think you need to watch for most carefully when you proofread.
5. In your own words, list the six commandments for proper manuscript format.

THE SENTENCE

A sentence is a team of words that expresses a complete idea. The trick in writing is to make sure your reader knows which team of words should be working together as a sentence. If essays were athletic contests, the words in each sentence could wear uniforms to distinguish them from the other sentences. Since it would be a bit tricky to outfit all of your words in little suits, it is important that you learn about the signals that will help your reader figure out which groups of words belong to which team.

Just as teams have people who play different positions, so too, sentences have words that fill different functions. Just as there are rules that indicate when a game is over, so too there are rules that help you indicate to your readers that a sentence is over. This section will help you review the basic rules that govern the creation of sentences. Mastery of these rules will help to insure that your readers will know when you have, in fact, scored a point by expressing a complete idea.

ITEM 4   FINDING THE SUBJECT AND THE VERB

Most students have studied the parts of speech since elementary school. After many years of studying the parts of speech, many students want to scream, "EEEEEK enough is enough is enough!"

There is Something New Under the Sun?

You will not be asked to learn any of the grammatical rules in this section simply for the sake of knowing them. Everything you learn will help you avoid mechanical errors in your writing. (If you actually mastered finding subjects and verbs in those thrilling days of yesteryear, you can zip through this section and feel superior to your classmates who need a review of subjects and verbs.)

Certainly you have a right to ask *why* you are once again searching for the elusive parts of speech.

Among the reasons you need to recognize subjects and verbs are to help you do the following:

1. Identify sentence fragments
2. Identify comma splices and other run-on sentences
3. Make your subjects and verbs agree
4. Vary your sentence patterns

We will deal with fragments, run-on sentences, and subject-verb agreement in later sections of this handbook, but feel free to read ahead if you want to see why identifying subjects and verbs will be helpful in your writing.

✳ ✳ ✳   **NOTICE:** The *subject* of your sentence is what it is about.

The *verb* in your sentence tells what the subject is or did.

The Method

Look first for the verb. Most sentences contain several nouns or pronouns that could be the subject, so pin down the verb first. Consider the following sentence:

English changed rapidly in the days before the printing press.

Did something in this sentence do anything? Yes, something changed. *Changed* is a verb. Next ask yourself *who* or *what* changed. The answer to *who* or *what* plus the verb will get you the subject. The subject of the sentence is "English."

✳ ✳ ✳   **NOTICE:** If you put *who* or *what* after a verb, you will not get a subject. The order of your words is important. For example, read sentence 3 in the "Practice." *Influenced* what? The answer is "English"—which is not the subject. What *influenced*? The answer is "words"—which is the subject.

PRACTICE LEADS TO PERFECTION

Using the *who* or *what* plus the verb method, find the subjects and verbs in the following sentences:

1. In 1066, William the Conqueror defeated Harold at the Battle of Hastings.
2. William spoke French, not English.
3. French words influenced English.

Often a verb does not do anything; it merely exists. Words such as *is, are, was, were, seems, appears, can, might, could, would* do not really show action, but they are also verbs. In fact, they are some of the most common verbs used.

For example

William **was** king.

French **was** the status language in England.

The English **seemed** uncivilized to their French conquerors.

The Test

To check to see if a word is a verb, try the following test: Put the word in the following sentences. If the word "fits," it is a verb.

- Yesterday I **verb.**

- Today I **verb.**

- Tomorrow I **will verb.**

Verbs change form to indicate time.

For example

Yesterday I **learned** about William the Conqueror.

Today I **learn** about William the Conqueror.

Tomorrow I **will learn** about William the Conqueror.

✳ ✳ ✳   **NOTICE:** Words like the following are never part of the verb: *always, not, never, often, only, now,* and *usually.*

Often sentences contain more than one subject and verb.

For example

Chaucer and **Shakespeare** are two of the greatest English writers.

Shakespeare **wrote** plays and poems and **acted** in plays.

Chaucer **wrote** poetry and **worked** as a diplomat and tutor.

PRACTICE LEADS TO PERFECTION

Underline the subjects once and the verbs twice in the following sentences:

1. a. In the fourteenth century, Chaucer wrote in English.
   b. Chaucer was proud of being English.
   c. Chaucer's English is called *Middle English.*
   d. The French and the Normans greatly influenced Middle English.
2. a. In 1564, Shakespeare was born.
   b. This was 164 years after Chaucer died.
   c. English changed very slowly after Shakespeare's day.
   d. The printing press helped to standardize the language.
3. a. *Romeo and Juliet* and *Hamlet* are two Shakespearian tragedies.
   b. Romeo and Juliet fell in love.

c. Their families hated each other and feuded openly.
d. Tragedies, comedies, and histories are the three types of plays Shakespeare wrote.

Tense Equals Time

To indicate time, verbs have different tenses. In tenses called participles, the verbs need a helping verb (also called an "auxiliary" verb). To learn more about verb tenses, read "Shifts in Tense," on page 300 of this handbook.

Present	Past	Past Participle	Present Participle
learn	learned	(had) learned	(are) learning

Other helping verbs include *am, is, are, was, were, may, could, might, should, would, will,* and *have.*

Subtle information about time can be indicated by combining helping verbs, as shown in the following sentence: I *had been learning* a lot about Chaucer and Shakespeare until I fell asleep:

✳ ✳ ✳ **NOTICE:** Words ending in *ing* must have a helper. If they have no helper, they are not being used as a verb.

For example

Reading "The Final Touch" **is exciting.**

✳ ✳ ✳ When the word *to* appears before a verb it is not being used as a verb.

For example

I am eager **to read** more in this **stimulating** book.

PRACTICE LEADS TO PERFECTION

Underline the subjects once and the verbs twice in the following sentences:

1. Queen Elizabeth I had been well educated before becoming queen.
2. Like many of her countrymen, Elizabeth attended Shakespeare's plays.
3. Elizabeth's father Henry VIII was proud of his daughter's intellect.

4. However, Henry VIII wanted to have a son.
5. In his pursuit of a son, Henry VIII was married six times.

ITEM 5   BEFRIENDING THE PREPOSITION

Taken apart, *preposition* becomes *pre position*. In fact, most prepositions indicate position in space—though a few indicate time or idea relationships. The prepositions in the following paragraphs are in bold.

✻✻✻ **WARNING:** If you think cartoons are only for kids, this cartoon exercise may seem juvenile. The following exercise, however, helps make the abstract concept of *preposition* into a concrete image. As an ancient Chinese philosopher once said, "What works is what works, even if it uses a cartoon.

If Tweety Bird stays **in** the cage, he can fly **at** the bars, sit **on** the perch, fly **to** the top, rest **under** the swing, fly **into** his mirror as he goes **after** his reflection, or move restlessly **from** side **to** side.

During his time **in** the cage, he can move **in** the following directions: **up, down, around, within,** and **across.**

Prepositions are words that link nouns and pronouns to other words in a sentence. After a preposition, you will find a noun or a pronoun that is its *object*. Why is this important to you? It is important because if you mistake an object for the subject of a sentence, you may incorrectly choose a verb to agree with the object instead of the subject. You may also select the wrong pronoun for a subject. For instance, which is correct: "between you and I" or "between you and me"? The answer? "Between you and me." More about this later.

English sentences are often filled with prepositions. One way to help you recognize most prepositions is to think of Odie's position relative to Garfield. Where can Odie run to escape?

For example

He can run **under** the table or **behind** the couch.

Memorize prepositions like the following because they do not fit the "Where can Odie run?" or "Where Can Tweety Bird Fly? tests: *during, except, like, of, since,* and *until.*

Prepositional Phrases

A *prepositional phrase* is a preposition plus the noun or pronoun following it. It also includes any modifying words attached to that noun or pronoun.

For example

during the thunder storm
in the slimy, green moat
through the heavy, metal door
under the brackish, black water

PRACTICE LEADS TO PERFECTION

Underline the subjects once and the verbs twice in the following sentences. (Hint: cross out the prepositional phrases first.)

1. One of the reasons to improve your writing skills is to get a good job.
2. Soldiers at all levels need to communicate better in writing.
3. As a recipient of hundreds of press releases, memos, and letters each week, Sylvia Porter can testify about bad writing.
4. According to Maryann Piotrowski, "The hours spent on teaching employees to write well will be repaid." (Hint: a subject does not have to be a single-word idea. It may be a many-word idea.)

ITEM 6   FINISHING THE FRAGMENT

The standard correction symbol for fragmentary sentences is *frag.* The symbol for transition is *trans.* (For a complete list, see the inside back cover.)

A *fragment* is a sentence whose message is incomplete. Usually students who write fragments have written all the words they need, but the words are punctuated incorrectly. Fragments signal that a thought is complete when, in fact, the thought is not complete.

Independent Clauses

An *independent clause* contains a subject and a verb that delivers a complete thought. A more familiar name for *independent clause* is *sentence.*

Dependent Clauses

A *dependent clause* is a group of words that contains a subject and a verb. However, a dependent clause is introduced by a word that makes the clause rely upon an independent clause to make sense. By itself, a dependent clause does not deliver a complete thought.

Put words like those in the following list in front of a sentence and presto! you create a dependent clause. If you do not attach a dependent clause to an independent clause, your reader will be mystified because your meaning will be unclear.

after	if	when	while
although	since	whenever	who
as	than	where	whom
because	that	wherever	whose
before	though	whether	why
even if	unless	which	
even though	until	whichever	
how	what		

The following is an example of an independent clause and two dependent clauses.

For example

I read about the right and left sides of the brain.

After I read about the right and left sides of the brain,

Until I read about the right and left sides of the brain,

✳ ✳ ✳   **NOTICE:** When a dependent clause comes in front of an independent clause in a sentence, separate the two with a comma.

For example

After I read about the right and left sides of the brain, I understood
the creative process better.

Until I read about the right and left sides of the brain, I did not
realize how to separate my critical and creative sides.

If you place a period after a dependent clause, you signal to readers
that your thought is over. Your reader is puzzled because your message is, in fact, incomplete.

A Good Idea Whose Time Has Come

Once you are familiar with the list of words that turn sentences into
fragments, *do not* avoid these words. Make friends with them. They
serve as *transitions* to help you link your ideas. Use the transition
words to introduce your ideas. They help you create more interesting,
mature sentences. In addition, transitions signal to readers what to
expect in the clause that follows them; your readers, therefore, understand your ideas more easily.

In the following exercise, notice the way transition words help
show the relationship between the ideas.

PRACTICE LEADS TO PERFECTION

Add an independent clause to make the following phrases into
sentences:

1. When I am criticized,
2. If we do not turn off our Critic Brain when we are creating ideas,
3. Although I have many good ideas,
4. Before we worry about mechanical errors,

Create three sentences of your own. Begin each sentence with a
dependent clause followed by an independent clause.

Not all sentence fragments are dependent clauses. Some are just
groups of words missing either a subject, a verb, or both.

✳ ✳ ✳   **NOTICE:** Essays containing sentence fragments often have all the
words necessary for complete thoughts; however, the
words are punctuated incorrectly and therefore are
fragments.

PRACTICE LEADS TO PERFECTION

Make the following into complete sentences:

1. Criticized all the time. People get discouraged. And feel like giving up. After all, why keep trying? When everything you do seems wrong.
2. It is very sad. That people in authority like bosses and parents. Don't realize that people respond better to positive comments. People want to try harder when they are successful. When they see they can do something well. People are often enthusiastic about improving their performance.
3. Thinking about writing an essay. All my ideas seem jumbled. Clustering helping me survey what I know.
4. The student addressed in "What I Did Last Summer" upon getting the essay back. Feeling indeed discouraged. The student probably will decide to never again. Write about something so intensely personal and painful. Even though writing often helps people clarify their thoughts and feelings. This is tragic. When a little encouragement and acknowledgment about what a profound and devastating experience this must have been.

ITEM 7   REMEDYING THE RUN-ON

The standard correction symbol for run-on sentences is *RO*. (For a complete list, see the inside back cover.)

Run-on sentences (also known as "fused sentences") are, in a sense, the opposite of fragments. Fragments need an independent clause. Run-on sentences have two or more independent clauses punctuated as one; thus they are really two sentences fused together. These sentences usually occur when their ideas are so closely related that their author thinks of them as one unit. Readers think of run-on sentences as confusing.

For example

Wrong

In his poetry, Langston Hughes used the rhythms of the blues and the ballad these poems were often documentary in tone.

Right

In his poetry, Langston Hughes used the rhythms of the blues and the ballad. These poems were often documentary in tone.

De-fusing the Run-on Sentence

You have four choices for repairing a run-on sentence.

Method one. Simply place a period at the end of an independent clause (a sentence) and capitalize the first letter of the first word of the next independent clause.

For example

Wrong

Langston Hughes was one of the few black students at Columbia University his poem "Theme for English B" records his feelings about his similarities to and differences from other students.

Right

Langston Hughes was one of the few black students at Columbia University. His poem "Theme for English B" records his feelings about his similarities to and differences from other students.

Method two. Place a semicolon between the two independent clauses.

For example

Wrong

Journals do not just record events they record an author's reaction to these events.

Right

Journals do not just record events; they record an author's reaction to these events.

✳✳✳ **NOTICE:** Do not capitalize the word after a semicolon unless the word is a proper noun. Proper nouns are always capitalized.

✳✳✳ **WARNING:** Commas and semicolons are not the same! To find out the difference between a comma and a semicolon read "The Semicolon," on page 286. When you use a comma between two sentences you commit a sin called a *comma splice.* Commas by themselves cannot separate two sentences. Stay tuned for further information about comma splices under Method Four.

Method three. Glue the ideas in the sentences together with a glue word (better known as a *transition*). Be sure to notice whether the transition you use requires a semicolon or a comma. The following transitions require a semicolon when they come between independent clauses:

also	moreover
consequently	nevertheless
finally	otherwise
furthermore	then
however	therefore
likewise	thus

✳✳✳ **WARNING:** Do not automatically use a semicolon with the words in the list. Make sure they come between independent clauses first.

When a transition word introduces a sentence, put a comma after it.

For example

Right

Anne Frank was an intelligent, sensitive, young Dutch girl; **however,** she had the tragic misfortune of living in Holland when Hitler conquered it.

Also right

The Nazis wanted to execute Jewish people. For a long time, **however,** friends of the Frank family hid them from the Nazis.

✳✳✳ **NOTICE:** Transitions help ideas flow more smoothly and sound more sophisticated.

Method four. Place a comma and one of the following words between the independent clauses: *and, or, but, for, yet,* or *so.*

✳✳✳ **NOTICE:** To tell the transition words requiring semicolons from those requiring commas, count their letters. Notice the words requiring commas have three or fewer letters.

✳✳✳ **WARNING:** Do not automatically use a comma when you see these words. Make sure the words come between independent clauses.

Do not simply put a comma between the independent clauses. You must also use *and, or, but, for, yet,* or *so.*

For example

Wrong

The Indians of Guatemala are often treated as second-class citizens, they are descended from the proud Mayans.

✳✳✳ **NOTICE:** This type of run-on sentence is also known as a "comma splice" because a comma tries, but fails (alas!) to separate the sentences properly.

Right

The Indians of Guatemala are often treated as second-class citizens, **but** they are descended from the proud Mayans.

Which Way Is Right?

Since you have a number of methods for correcting run-on sentences, how do you choose which one to use? Good question. You need variety in your sentence patterns. The most common method to divide sentences is the old standby of Method One. But using only one method is boring. In addition, many students overuse the "comma plus *and* or *but*" in Method Four. Be adventurous. Try something new from time to time; try a semicolon, for example. When you use a semicolon, you signal to readers that your ideas are closely related; make sure this is true.

Use a method that will help your ideas flow smoothly, a method that will help readers understand the connection between your ideas.

PRACTICE LEADS TO PERFECTION

Correct the following run-on sentences:

1. The most famous journal ever written was *The Diary of Anne Frank* however Anne had no idea anyone else would ever read her journal.
2. Tragically, Anne was shipped off to a concentration camp by the Nazis then she and the rest of her family except for her father died in the camp.
3. We are horrified when we learn the Nazis killed six million people simply because they were Jewish born when we read Anne Frank's diary the statistics about these murders become more meaningful.

4. Keeping a journal helped Anne cope with her thoughts and feelings about growing up it helped her understand herself better.
5. When Anne's father returned to the apartment where his family was captured by the Nazis, he thought everything of value was gone then he discovered his daughter's diary.

Write a sentence using a transition word requiring a semicolon. Write a sentence using a comma and *or*, *for*, *yet*, or *so*.

PUNCTUATION AND CAPITALIZATION

Punctuation marks are the road signs of the world of writing. Like road signs, some punctuation marks (for example, the period) tell us to stop. Some (like the comma) tell us to slow down. Others (like the colon) tell us what to expect down the road of the written page. The point is writers must be careful what signal they give to their readers. When you use the wrong punctuation mark you will mislead your reader—just as an incorrect road sign will mislead drivers.

ITEM 8   THE COMMA CLARIFIED

The standard correction symbol for comma is *c*. (For a complete list of standard correction symbols, see the inside back cover of this book.)

The comma story is a sad one. Commas are small marks given a big job by the gods of Punctuation Rules. Commas try hard to meet their job description, but, quite frankly, they find it frustrating because people ignore the comma job description and keep giving commas more and more tasks to perform. You, of course, do not want to contribute to the trials of the comma, so be sure when you use a comma, you know *why* you are using a comma.

The major problem most people have with the comma is remembering the 6,247 comma rules Ms. Smeltzer taught them back in fifth grade. The American philosopher Henry David Thoreau wrote some advice about life in general that applies beautifully to comma rules, "Simplify, simplify, simplify."

The 6,247 rules can be condensed into four basic uses of the comma.

Comma Use Category One: Let Me Introduce You

The comma is like a butler. It introduces. It announces a word, phrase, or clause that comes before the main subject and verb.

1. Use a comma to introduce words like *yes*, *no*, and *well*. (Avoid beginning a sentence with *well*, but if you must, use a comma after *well*).

For example

Yes, the poem "Fueled" points out that we often take the environment for granted.

2. Use a comma after phrases coming before the subject and verb.

For example

After reading the section on concrete and abstract language, I realized I often ask for a concrete example when I don't understand an idea.

3. Use a comma after a dependent clause that begins a sentence.

For example

Because I had just read "Room for One More," I walked the seventeen flights to my dentist's office instead of taking the elevator.

Comma Use Category Two: Let Me Interrupt You

Just as it takes two people to tango, it takes two commas to separate an interrupting word, phrase, or clause in the midst of a sentence.

1. To create variety and save words, information is often inserted into a sentence. When such information is not essential to understanding the main part of a sentence, separate it from the sentence with commas.

For example

Aesop, **who had been a slave,** became a celebrity because of his fables.

✻ ✻ ✻   **WARNING:** Before you set off an interrupter with commas, make sure your interruption is not essential to the meaning of your sentence.

For example

The wolf **in the grandmother's bed** was wearing a nightcap.

The wolf in the sentence does not have a name or any other identifying detail except the phrase "in the grandmother's bed." Since you cannot identify to what particular wolf the sentence refers, the phrase is needed. Therefore, do not set off "in the grandmother's bed" with commas. Without the phrase you would not know whether the sentence refers to the wolf in grandmother's bed or the wolf who was watching *Saturday Night Live* in the kitchen.

Another example

The house in James Thurber's "The Night the Ghosts Got In" was a real residence, 77 Jefferson Avenue, Columbus, Ohio. Thurber wrote "I deliberately changed the address for the simple reason that there *was* a ghost. . . .

You do not know which of Thurber's stories is meant so the title is essential to the sentence and cannot be set off by commas.

2. Often you interrrupt yourself with words or phrases like *for example, furthermore, however, in fact, nevertheless,* and *on the other hand.* If these words come in the middle of a sentence, separate them from the rest of the sentence with commas. If these words come between sentences, review Method Three for correcting run-on sentences on page 274.

For example

Fables, **in fact,** have been found in Egyptian tombs dating back more than three thousand years.

James Thurber, **however,** drew his ideas for fables from contemporary life.

3. Parts of dates and addresses can be thought of as interrupters. If you say May 5, you need to say what year. Place a comma between the day and the year and another between the year and the rest of a sentence.

For example

James Thurber was born on **December 8, 1894,** in Columbus, Ohio. Thurber died on **November 2, 1961,** in New York City.

4. Addresses also fit into the category of interruptors. Put a comma between the street and the city. Put another comma between the city and the state. To which Forest Lane are you referring?

For example

Red's grandmother purchased a charming cottage at 718 Forest Lane, **La Selva, Ohio,** on May 16, 1989.

5. Often you interrupt yourself to quote someone else. When you do this, separate your words from the quoted material.

For example

Professor Higgins said, "James Thurber did much to establish the style of *The New Yorker.*"

"James Thurber was a humorist who began working for *The New Yorker* shortly after it was founded in the 1920s," Professor Higgins said.

Comma Use Category Three: Coordination for Fun and Profit

Commas also act as coordinators between two independent clauses, but they can do this only with the help of *and, or, but, for, yet,* or *so.*

✳ ✳ ✳   **NOTICE:** *Independent clause* is another term for *sentence.*

For example

A painting is concrete, **but** its beauty is abstract.

✳ ✳ ✳   **WARNING:** You must have two independent clauses before you use a comma with *and, or, but, for, nor, yet,* or *so.* Often these words appear within a clause where no comma is needed.

For example

We often overlook miraculous things in nature **and** do not appreciate them.

Comma Use Category Four: Learn about Linking

Commas help to link words together.

1. Use a comma after items in a series.

For example

Penny Plump nibbled on lettuce leaves for breakfast, lunch, and dinner.

2. Use a comma between equally important adjectives describing a word or phrase.

For example

Penny Plump always saw a frumpy, pudgy lady in the mirror.

> Use a comma to separate adjectives if (1) the position of the adjectives can be reversed (pudgy, frumpy lady) or (2) the word *and* can be inserted between the adjectives (frumpy **and** pudgy lady). Should the adjectives in the sentence, "Penny would not even taste Mom's delicious apple pie" be separated by commas? Why?

3. As you become increasingly adept at writing, you will begin to link modifying words and phrases to your sentences. Use a comma as a link between a sentence and a modifier.

For example

Finally Penny Plump disappeared, having dieted herself out of existence.

PRACTICE LEADS TO PERFECTION

In the following sentences, add commas where they are needed:

1. "The Lioness" being the queen of beasts believed in quality not quantity.
2. Ann cooked cleaned washed and ironed trying to please Frank.
3. Yes Frank was born at 140 Peter Pan Lane in Neverneverland Virginia on April 1 1969 and his mother immediately placed him on a velvet cushion.
4. After getting over the trauma of her divorce Ann lived happily and productively.
5. For their meals wolves eat mice other rodents and weak caribou but rarely eat anybody's grandparent.
6. However countless fables like "The Little Girl and the Wolf" depict wolves in a common though unenlightened manner.

ITEM 9 QUOTATION MARKS

The standard correction symbol for quotation marks is *quot.* (For a complete list of standard correction symbols, see the inside back cover.)

Quotation marks are hams. They attract attention to the words they enclose. Therefore, they add life to writing. Like commas, however, quotation marks have several different functions, and several rules apply to quotation marks.

1. Quotation marks enclose the exact words you are quoting.

For example

"Where is the money you promised me?" the student asked the loan officer.

✳ ✳ ✳   **WARNING:** Do not use quotation marks when you are not using a speaker's exact words. For instance, when you use the word *that*, you signal you are not quoting exact words. Do not use quotation marks around words introduced by *that*.

For example

The student said **that** he wanted his money.
The student asked if he could have the money promised to him.

✳ ✳ ✳ **NOTICE:** Begin a new paragraph with each change of speaker.

For example

"I can just imagine the scene after the little girl shot the wolf in her grandmother's bed," Tanya said.

"Yes, she was undoubtedly arrested for carrying a concealed weapon in her basket of cookies," Sally agreed.

"She shouldn't have shot the wolf!" Fred exclaimed.

Sally frowned. "Why?" she asked.

"Wolves are helpful creatures. Haven't you read *Never Cry Wolf* by Farley Mowat?" Fred asked.

2. When you use quotation marks within quotation marks, use single marks.

For example

"James Thurber wasn't trying to say, 'Wolves are evil,' " Tanya said. "He was merely retelling the old folk tale 'Little Red Ridinghood.' "

3. Use quotation marks around titles of works less than a whole volume long. Magazines, newspapers, and books are a whole volume, so their titles are italicized. Short stories, most poems, articles, and chapter titles, are less than a volume. Their titles are enclosed in quotation marks.

For example

For poems such as "Mending Wall" in his book *North of Boston*, Robert Frost drew from his experiences as a New England farmer.

4. If a quotation is more than four lines long, omit the quotation marks and indent the quotation ten spaces from the left margin. Double space before and after long quotations.

John Steinbeck often wrote about his native area of central California. Descriptions like the following passage from *Of Mice and Men* show Steinbeck's awareness of the natural world.

For example

On the sandy bank under the trees the leaves lie deep and so crisp that a lizard makes a great skittering if he runs among them. Rabbits come out of the brush to sit on the sand in the evening, and the damp flats are covered with the night tracks of 'coons and with the split-wedge tracks of deer that come to drink in the dark.

5. Quotation marks must also follow particular rules with other punctuation marks.
 a. Commas and periods always go inside quotation marks.

For example

Reread the examples for the second and third rules about quotation marks.

 b. Colons and semicolons *always* go outside quotation marks.

For example

One of my favorite poems is "Two Tramps in Mud Time": Frost was correct that we should strive to unite our vocation and our avocation.

 c. Question marks and exclamation marks go inside quotation marks when a quotation is a question or exclamation.

For example

In "Snow" one of Frost's characters asks, "But how much better off are we as it is?"

✳✳✳ **NOTICE:** The preceding example is a statement, not a question. However, the quotation asks a question, so the question mark is inside the quotation marks.

 d. When question marks and exclamation marks refer to an entire sentence, put question marks and exclamation marks outside quotation marks.

For example

Did Frost write "Stopping by Woods on a Snowy Evening"?

ITEM 10 ITALICS

The standard correction symbol for italics is *ital.* (For a complete list of symbols see the inside back cover.)
 Because few typewriters can type in italics, you can also indicate italics by underlining.

1. Use italics for the titles of books, newspapers, and magazines.

For example

Frost's "Nothing Gold Can Stay" appears in his book **New Hampshire.**

✳✳✳ **WARNING:** Do not punctuate the title of holy books like the Bible, Talmud, or Upanishad or any of their parts.

2. Use italics for the titles of television series, works of art, trains, ships, and airplanes.

For example

In 1915, Frost returned to the United States from England after living there awhile. Fortunately, he did not take the *Titanic.*

3. Use italics for words, numbers, and letters used *as* words, numbers, and letters.

For example

When Frost sent his first poem to *The Independent* for publication, he misspelled it *Independant* with an incorrect *a.* "Learn to spell the name of our magazine," the editors told Frost.

4. Use italics for foreign words and phrases.

For example

Vaya con Dios is a lovely expression.

5. Use italics (very sparingly) to create emphasis.

For example

Never put quotation marks around an italicized title.

ITEM 11 CAPITALIZATION

The standard correction symbol for capitalization is *cap.* (For a complete list, see the inside back cover.)

Capital letters (alias upper case letters) are signals to readers. WHEN YOU CAPITALIZE ALL OF THE WORDS IN A SENTENCE YOUR READER MIGHT MISS INFORMATION LIKE, FOR EXAMPLE, THE FROST YOU ARE DISCUSSING IS A PERSON, NOT A COLD-WEATHER PHENOMENON. Use capital letters in the following situations:

1. Capitalize the first word of a sentence and a direct quotation that is a whole sentence long.

For example

John Steinbeck wrote, "**The** profession of book-writing makes horse racing seem like a solid, stable business."

2. Capitalize all words in titles or names of works of art, but do not capitalize prepositions less than five letters long or connecting words (like *and, or,* and *but*). Always capitalize the first and last words of a title. A list of prepositions appears on page 268.

For example

Because he could not get his poems published in the United States, Robert Frost moved to England in 1912. *A Boy's Will* and *North of Boston* were published in England and were so well received that when he returned to America in 1915 Frost was considered one of the best poets in the United States.

3. Capitalize all proper names and words derived from proper names.

For example

When he was trying to get into **Harvard, Robert Frost** worried that he had neglected the study of **Greek,** but he felt well prepared for **English, French,** physics, astronomy, algebra, and geometry. **Frost** had been co-valedictorian at **Lawrence High School** with **Elinor White,** whom he later married.

4. Capitalize the name of a specific class.

For example

One of my favorite college courses was a botany course entitled **The Biology of Plants and Man.**

5. The sections of the United States are proper names. Capitalize them.

For example

Robert Frost was born in the **West,** but he spent most of his life in the **East** although he taught for a time in the **Midwest** at the **University of Michigan.**

6. Directions like north, south, east, and west are not capitalized.
7. Summer, spring, winter, and fall are not capitalized, but holidays like Fourth of July, Thanksgiving, and Mother's Day are.
8. Remember that company and organization names and products are proper nouns—for example, Kleenex, United Nations, and Ford Motor Company.

9. If you are a person who believes in democracy, you are a demo-crat. Robert Frost's father was an organizer for the Democratic Party in the San Francisco area. He was a Democrat.
10. Name-substitutes can be tricky. If you replace a name with a word like *mother*, *father*, *brother*, *sister*, *aunt*, or *uncle* then you capitalize that word. If you put a word like *my* or *his* in front of the name-substitute, however, you do not use a capital letter.

For example

When his **father** died, Frost wrote, "We moved to New England where **Mother's** family lived and where she could get a teaching job."

PRACTICE LEADS TO PERFECTION

Punctuate the following sentences with quotation marks or italics. Add capital letters where necessary.

1. born in india of english parents, kipling made good use of his indian experiences in books like barrack-room ballads which contains such famous poems as gunga din and mandalay.
2. i read a fascinating article entitled robert frost and new england in national geographic.
3. did you know mark twain visited hawaii in 1866? sam asked.
4. in his book letters from hawaii, mark twain wrote of the saddle: there is no seat to it—one might as well sit in a shovel.
5. of the li'o (the hawaiian word for horse), twain wrote that he preferred a li'o that was sick, asleep, or dead. he wanted a li'o with no spirit whatsoever.

ITEM 12   THE SEMICOLON

The standard correction symbol for semicolon is ;. (For a complete list, see the inside back cover.)

Semicolons look like a cross between a comma and a period; however, they are most closely related to the period.

1. Until you are on intimate terms with the semicolon, use it when you would use a period. The semicolon tells readers, "Stop." The period tells readers, "Stop!"

In other words, when a sentence has ended, but you want to signal to readers that the next sentence is very closely related, use a semi-colon. Review Method Two in "Remedying the Run-on," on page 272 for more about this use of the semicolon.

For example

Bubba Smith has stopped doing beer commercials; he believes his commercials are a bad influence on young people.

✳ ✳ ✳   **NOTICE:** The word after a semicolon is not capitalized unless it is a proper name.

2. Occasionally you get yourself into a a jam in your sentences. You write a sentence containing several commas, and then you want to add another sentence with another comma plus *and, or, but, for, nor, yet,* or *so.* In this rare event, use a semicolon to signal a stronger pause than a comma indicates.

For example

When she was a child, Maya Angelou lived at various times with her father, her grandmother, and her mother; **but** Bailey, her younger brother, helped provide stability in her life.

3. Another writing muddle is sometimes created when the parts of a series contain commas, and you need to signal a stronger pause than another comma would indicate.

For example

Among the places Maya Angelou has lived are Stamps, Arkansas; St. Louis, Missouri; and San Francisco, California.

ITEM 13   THE COLON

The standard correction symbol for a colon is :. (For a complete list, see the inside back cover.)

Your mother was wrong. Sometimes it is polite—and correct—to point. Use a colon to point out your meaning in the following situations:

1. Use a colon to introduce a quotation.

For example

Of Maya Angelou's book James Baldwin wrote: "*I Know Why the Caged Bird Sings* liberates the reader into life simply because Maya Angelou confronts her own life with such a moving wonder, such a luminous dignity."

2. Use a colon to introduce a list at the end of a sentence *if the list is not preceded by a verb.*

For example

Chapter Six, "Describe a Person" contains the following important words: *narcissistic, permeate, dogmatism, edibility,* and *Gallic.*

3. Use a colon to mark the end of a sentence when the second sentence explains the first.

For example

Of Maya Angelou's book *I Know Why the Caged Bird Sings,* *Newsweek* reviewer Robert A Gross wrote:

> Miss Angelou's book is more than a tour de force of language or the story of childhood suffering: it quietly and gracefully portrays and pays tribute to the courage, dignity, and endurance of the small, rural community in which she spent most of her early years in the 1930s.

✶✶✶ **NOTICE:** Because the quotation is long, it is indented instead of enclosed in quotation marks.

ITEM 14   THE QUESTION MARK

The standard correction symbol for a question mark is ?. (For a complete list, see the inside back cover.)

Question marks are probably the easiest puncutation mark to use correctly. Put a question mark after a question. Is that clear?

To review the use of question marks with quotation marks, see page 281 of "Quotation Marks."

For example

Have you read any of Hemingway's novels?

ITEM 15   THE EXCLAMATION MARK

The standard correction symbol for an exclamation mark is !. (For a complete list, see the inside back cover.)

Think of the exclamation mark as the chili powder of the punctuation world. A little adds zest to your writing.

For example

Use the exclamation mark sparingly! When you overuse the exclamation mark, it loses impact! Your readers no longer think your sentence is emphatic when you overuse this mark! Instead you sound either silly or hysterical!

To review the use of exclamation marks with quotation marks, see page 281 of "Quotation Marks."

ITEM 16　THE DASH

The standard correction symbol for a dash is *dash*. (For a complete list see the inside back cover.)

Dashes are twice as long as a hyphen. On a keyboard, dashes require two, unspaced strokes of the hyphen key.

For example

Dash: —

Hyphen: -

While they look somewhat alike, dashes and hyphens actually have opposite functions. Hyphens join words, thereby signaling a single idea. Dashes signal an abrupt change in thought. Dashes help to make writing sound more conversational—since ideas are often interrupted in speech.

For example

From childhood the Durrell brothers—especially Lawrence and Gerald—had an exceptional talent for expressing themselves in writing.

✳ ✳ ✳　**NOTICE:** There is no space between the dash and the words before and after it.

ITEM 17　THE HYPHEN

The standard correction symbol for a hyphen is *hy*. (For a complete list, see the inside back cover.)

Hyphens may look a little like dashes, but hyphens function very differently from dashes.

1. Use a hyphen to connect words acting as a single, descriptive idea.

For example

Growing up on the Greek island of Corfu, Gerald Durrell developed a life-long fascination with the natural world.

2. Use a hyphen with the prefixes *ex*, *self*, and *all*.

For example

The French count was **self**-indulgent.

3. Use a hyphen to prevent confusion when you join two identical letters in a prefix.

For example

The count's narcissistic behavior was not **anti-inflammatory.** The Durrell family found him to be an unpleasant guest.

4. Use a hyphen in the words for numbers from twenty-one to ninety-nine.

For example

By the time Hemingway was **twenty-one,** he was writing about his World War I experiences.

5. Use a hyphen with the suffix *elect*.

For example

John F. Kennedy was the **president-elect** until a few months before Hemingway died in 1961. Kennedy was president when Hemingway died.

ITEM 18 PARENTHESES

The standard correction symbol for parentheses is *par.* (For a complete list, see the inside back cover.)

Parentheses are similar to dashes, but parentheses get less attention from readers. (Honestly, do you always pay attention to words enclosed in parentheses?)

ITEM 19 ELLIPSIS POINTS

The standard correction symbol for ellipsis points is . . . . (For a complete list, see the inside back cover.)

Ellipsis points have the following two purposes:

1. To mark an omission from a quoted passage.
2. To indicate a reflective pause.

For example

Original passage

When I see her [Nga Che] during the day, my usual, hectic inner pace slows down under her calming influence.

Omitted material marked by ellipsis points

When I see her [Nga Che] during the day, my usual . . . pace slows down under her calming influence.

PRACTICE LEADS TO PERFECTION

Place semicolons, colons, question marks, exclamation marks, dashes, hyphens, parentheses, ellipsis points, or periods where necessary.

1. Like May Swenson I have watched as pigeons flocked around a person feeding them then when the food was gone I have watched the pigeons fly away
2. It is not strange Hemingway wrote about an old man caught up in the disruptions of war Hemingway was involved in several wars
3. Why do you think Hemingway focused on the problems of the old man war brings more spectacular changes than he experienced
4. Jim Murray makes good use of amusing, concrete details to show the contrast between the legendary Bubba and the real person in fact Bubba at least when he is not playing football is a sensitive, intelligent giant
5. Nga Che like so many refugees has needed patience, courage, and strength to rebuild her life hasn't she

ITEM 20   THE APOSTROPHE

The standard correction symbol for an apostrophe with contraction is *apos-c*. The standard correction symbol for an apostrophe with possession is *apos-p*. (For a complete list, see the inside back cover.)

Apostrophes look like commas trying to be acrobats. And—like the comma—they serve several different functions.

When Apostrophes Show Possession

Use an apostrophe to show that a noun owns something. If the owner-noun does not end in s, simply add 's and presto! the noun is the proud owner of whatever you want to write about.

For example

Washington Irving wrote "The Legend of Sleepy Hollow." Irving's famous story is often on television near Halloween.

The big problem with apostrophes is where to put them. This may be your lucky day, for if you follow one simple rule with your possessive nouns your apostrophes will always be in the right place. Ask "to whom or what does the possessed belong?" If the word that answers this question ends in s, simply put an apostrophe after the s.

For example

After Irving's fiancee died, he went to Europe for seventeen years.

To whom did the fiancee belong? To Irving. *Irving* does not end in s, so to form the possessive of *Irving* add 's.

Irving's parents were well-to-do. His parents' money helped to ease his way as a writer.

To whom did the money belong? To the parents. *Parents* does end in s, so to form its possessive we add only '.

✳ ✳ ✳   **WARNING:** Be sure a noun owns something before you attach an apostrophe. Many words that end in s own nothing. In the previous "For Example" which nouns ending in s own nothing? (If your answer was *years* and the first *parents* you are correct.)

✳ ✳ ✳   **NOTICE:** Many words that end in s are not plural—for example, *James, Charles, kiss,* and *grass.*
Many words that do not end in s are plural—for example, *lice, mice, moose, children, men,* and *women.*

Forget about the rules that ask you to first decide if a word is singular or plural before you add an apostrophe. As Henry David Thoreau said: "Simplify, simplify, simplify."

✳ ✳ ✳   **WARNING:** Remember the possessive form is often used for words that do not actually own anything. For example, "Chapter Six's poem is about an injured hawk."

When Pronouns Possess

Some pronouns present problems when you use an apostrophe. Pronouns like *mine, yours, its, his, hers, theirs, ours,* and *whose* come with built-in possession. *Do not* use an apostrophe with these words.

When do you use a possessive apostrophe with a pronoun? Use apostrophes to show possession with pronouns that do not refer to a specific person; for example, pronouns containing *one* or *body* require an *'s* to show possession. Words like *anybody, anyone, everybody, everyone, somebody,* and *someone* require an *'s* when they own something.

For example

Anyone**'s** sympathy would be aroused by the plight of the hawk. Its wing was shattered. It's sad Jeffers had to shoot the hawk.

When Apostrophes Do Not Show Possession

Apostrophes do not show possession when used to form contractions. When you drop the end of one word and connect it to another word, use an apostrophe as a bandage to cover the wound where you cut out the letter. The following list shows common phrases and their contracted forms:

are not	aren't
could not	couldn't
does not	doesn't
is not	isn't
it is	it's
who is	who's
will not	won't (the only oddball)
you are	you're

✳✳✳ **WARNING:** *Should have* is contracted *should've* even though it sounds like *should of,* which is *always* wrong. It best to avoid contractions like *should've, could've,* and *would've* in formal writing. Save them for dialogue. Because it is so easy to make a mistake with words like *it's, you're,* and *who's,* always say *it is, you are,* and *who is* when you write *it's, you're,* and *who's.*

When Apostrophes Indicate Plurals

In the following specific cases *'s* can be used to form plurals:

1. Indicate the plural of a lowercase letter with an apostrophe and an *s*. To indicate the plural of uppercase letters either *C's* or *Cs* is correct.

For example

Dot your i**'s** and cross your t**'s.**

2. Indicate the plural of abbreviations containing periods with **'s.** If the abbreviation contains no period, use either s or **'s.**

For example

B.A.**'s**, M.D.**'s**, D.V.M.**'s**

VIP**'s**, or VIP**s**

3. To indicate the plural of numbers, use either s or **'s.**

For example

5**s** or 5**'s**

PRACTICE LEADS TO PERFECTION

Add apostrophes where they are needed in the following sentences:

1. How many s are in Jeffers name?
2. Does Jeffers poem argue for euthanasia?
3. The poems language is very powerful, and its language is concrete.
4. Youre going to understand "Hurt Hawk" better after you study it.
5. The rodents tail looked like a toothpick.
6. The superintendents attitude toward the rodent was sympathetic although his action was not.
7. Sammys hometown was too conformist and conservative for his taste.
8. Its residents did the same things over and over. They even ate the same kinds of foods and wore similar types of clothing.

VERBS

There are two basic kinds of verbs:

1. Those that show action. These verbs do something such as *hop, skip, jump,* or *slither*. These verbs *run* marathons, *bake* muffins, or *write* essays.
2. Those that are couch potato verbs. These verbs simply exist. Often they are forms of the verb *to be* such as *is, are, was,* and *were.* Sometimes they *seem, appear,* and *feel.*

   The important thing to remember is to put the right verb form with the subject it matches. This matchmaking is the subject of the following section.

ITEM 21 MAKING SUBJECTS, VERBS, AND PRONOUNS AGREE

The standard correction symbol for subject-verb agreement is *agr-v.* The standard correction symbol for pronoun agreement is *agr-p.* (For a complete list, see the inside back cover.)

What is meant by *agreement?* Certain subjects, verbs, and pronouns go together like peanut butter and jelly. Others go together like mustard and chocolate chip cookies. Before going on to bigger and more exciting parts of the agreement dilemma, let's quickly review pronouns.

Pronouns

	Singular	Plural
First Person	I	we
Second Person	you	you
Third Person	he, she, it, one	they

✳✳✳ **NOTICE:** Although there are four third-person pronouns, each uses the same subject, verb, and pronoun agreement pattern. When adding an *s* to a word, we usually think *plural.* In fact, when adding an *s* to a noun we *are* making it plural— for example, *river* plus *s* is *rivers.*

ITEM 22 REGULAR VERBS AND IRREGULAR VERBS

The standard correction symbol for tense is *T*. (For a complete list, see the inside back cover.)

Present Tense

Adding *s* to a noun is the regular way to form plural nouns. When a regular verb has an *s* added, however, the verb must be used with a third-person-*singular* subject.

For example

In Woody Guthrie's poem, Juan **wades** the river. Juan and Rosalita **wade** the river.

∗ ∗ ∗   **NOTICE:** Regular present tense verbs form the third-person-singular by adding an *s* to the verb.

Past Tense

One of the nice things about English is, except for a few disorderly verbs (called *irregular verbs*), you do not have to worry about subjects and verbs agreeing in the past tense. Regular past tense verbs end in *ed* no matter what their subjects are.

The following chart shows the conjugation of the verb *to use*:

The Regular Verb *To Use*

Present	Past	Past Participle	Present Participle
I use	used	(have) used	(am) using
you use	used	(have) used	(are) using
he, she, it, one uses	used	(has) used	(is) using
They use	used	(have) used	(are) using

∗ ∗ ∗   **NOTICE:** Regular verbs form the present tense, third-person-singular by adding an *s* and form the past tense for all persons by adding *ed*.

For example

He walks. He walked.

With one unfortunate exception, even the irregular verbs obey the *s* rule in the past tense. The exception? The wild and crazy, but very common, verb *to be*. The following chart shows the conjugation of the verb *to be*:

The Irregular Verb *To Be*

Present	Past	Past Participle	Present Participle
I am	was	(have) been	(am) being
you are	were	(have) been	(are) being
he, she, it, one is	was	(has) been	(is) being
they are	were	(have) been	(are) being

Both regular and irregular verbs use the same past tense verb for the first and second person (both singular and plural) and for the third person plural. The only exception is for the verb *to be*.

For example

I/ We/ You/ They studied hard on weekends.

I was. **We** were. **You** were. **They** were.

You pick up almost all grammar by imitation. Given a new regular verb, you will automatically—without having to think about the rules—be able to form its tenses.

PRACTICE LEADS TO PERFECTION

I have made up a word to show you how you automatically deal with a new regular verb. *Gork* is a nonsense word. I frequently gork in the summer. Fill in the blanks with the proper form of the verb *to gork*.

1. Yesterday I _____ all afternoon.
2. He _____ every time he feels tense.
3. You are _____ a lot these days.
4. I have _____ every day this week.

Common Irregular Verbs

The present participle of all verbs is always the stem form plus *ing*. Except for *to be*, the present tense is the stem form.

Despite the length of the following list, most verbs are regular. If you are unsure of the verb you need and it is not on the list, check its stem form in your dictionary to find its tenses.

Stem Form	Past	Past Participle
become	became	become
begin	began	begun
break	broke	broken
bring	brought	brought
build	built	built
buy	bought	bought
catch	caught	caught
choose	chose	chosen
come	came	come
cost	cost	cost
do	did	done
draw	drew	drawn
drink	drank	drunk
drive	drove	driven
eat	ate	eaten
feel	felt	felt
fight	fought	fought
find	found	found
forget	forgot	forgotten
get	got	got, gotten
give	gave	given
go	went	gone
hang (a person)	hanged	hanged
hang (an object)	hung	hung
have	had	had
lay (to place)	laid	laid (See page 332)
lead	led	led
lie (to rest)	lay	lain
ride	rode	ridden
ring	rang, rung	rung
see	saw	seen
set (to place)	set	set
shake	shook	shaken
shine (with light)	shone	shone
shine (with polish)	shined	shined
sit (to rest)	sat	sat
steal	stole	stolen
swim	swam	swum
teach	taught	taught
tear	tore	torn
throw	threw	thrown (See page 325)
write	wrote	written

✳ ✳ ✳ **WARNING:** Beware of the prepositional phrase between your subject and verb. Often a noun immediately in front of a verb is part of a prepositional phrase and therefore not the subject of a sentence.

In the following example, the verb *is* agrees with the subject *one* rather than with the object of the preposition *topics*. Read "Befriending the Preposition," on page 268 to review prepositions.

For example

One of Woody Guthrie's topics **is** the plight of the migrant workers.

A Golden Opportunity to Make Your Mother Feel Guilty

When learning to talk, no one gives you a book of rules to follow. Instead you imitate those around you. (That is why John F. Kennedy and Jimmy Carter pronounced words strangely—unless you were from Boston or Georgia.) If your family did not use a standard subject-verb agreement pattern, you probably are using the same nonstandard agreement pattern. You will need to pay special attention to break the old nonstandard patterns. Old habits *are* hard to break, but you can do it.

Three More Problems with Subject-Verb Agreement

1. Usually collective nouns are singular because they act as a single unit. They are plural when their individual members act separately. Examples of collective nouns include *committee, covey* (of quail), *family, group, herd, pod* (of whales), *raft* (of sea otters), and *team.*

For example

Singular

The **team was** gathered around the computer.

Plural

The **team were** arguing about the computer's advice.

2. When a subject follows a verb, there are often errors in subject-verb agreement.

Wrong

There is many uses for the computer in baseball.

Right

There are many uses for the computer in baseball.

3. Sentences, like life itself, can get complicated. Sometimes a sentence has a singular and a plural compound subject. Then what do you do? Match the verb to the nearest subject.

For example

Neither the **players** nor the **coach likes** to rely on computers.

ITEM 23 SHIFTS IN TENSE

The standard correction symbol for a shift in verb tense is *shift-v*. (For a complete list, see the inside back cover.)

Do not shift from one verb tense to another verb tense unless you clearly mean to indicate a different time.

For example

Wrong

Computers **have** numerous possible uses in baseball. They **are** useful for keeping track of both major and minor league players. They **were** also helpful as a teaching tool.

Right

Computers **have** numerous possible uses in baseball. They **are** useful for keeping track of both major and minor league players. They **are** also helpful as teaching tools.

PRONOUNS

Just between you and I—or should I say "between you and me"?
Before I go on, let's find out. Pronouns come in several basic types
called *cases*. A pronoun's *case* is its job description. Some pronouns
can act as subjects of sentences; others can act as the object of a preposition. Just as you would not hire a brain surgeon to fix your television—or a television repairperson to do brain surgery—you need to
select the right pronoun for the following jobs:

ITEM 24   PRONOUN AGREEMENT

The standard correction symbol for pronoun agreement is *agr-p*. (For
a complete list, see the inside back cover.)

A pronoun must agree with its antecedent (the word to which it
refers). If the antecedent is third person singular, the pronoun must
also be third person singular.

For example

The **mouse** was old-fashioned. **She** needed to update **her** image.

Sex, Scandal, and Pronoun Agreement

None of us wants to be accused of being sexist. However, we run into
a problem because we do not know the sex of *singular* indefinite pronoun subjects like *anybody, each, either, neither, everybody, one,* and
no one. In the olden days when I first started teaching, the rule was
to use the generic masculine pronouns (*he, him,* and *his*) when we did
not know to which sex we were referring. Now we want to avoid the
generic masculine, but we also want to avoid ugly, awkward constructions like *he or she* and *him or her.*

An awkward example

Everyone had decided that **he** or **she** would like **his** or **her** career to
be in a company like IBM.

To avoid sounding like a chauvinist pork chop or a long-winded
wimp, multiply your subjects. *They* and *their* are sexless.

For example

The **students** had decided **they** would like **their** careers to be in a
company like IBM.

PRACTICE LEADS TO PERFECTION

Make the subjects, verbs, and pronouns agree in the following sentences. Avoid sexism.

1. Long before man could read and write, he told stories.
2. A ballad was the best form for oral stories because they had rhythm and rhyme and therefore was easier to remember.
3. Stories like *Beowulf* celebrates the exploits of heroes.
4. One of the migrant workers were Woody Guthrie's grandfather.
5. Everyone should treat their workers like human beings.

ITEM 25 POSSESSIVE CASE PRONOUNS

The standard correction symbol for pronoun case is *ca*. (For a complete list, see the inside back cover.)

Possessive case pronouns are pronouns that possess. We have already looked at the possessive case pronouns in "The Apostrophe," on page 291. Possessive pronouns like *mine*, *hers*, *his*, *its*, and *yours* show possession.

ITEM 26 NOMINATIVE CASE PRONOUNS

When a pronoun is a subject it is a nominative case pronoun. Nominative case pronouns serve as the subject of a verb or mean the same thing as a word that is the subject of a verb. Nominative case pronouns are the following: *I*, *he*, *she*, *it*, *we*, *they*, and *who*.

For example

Nominative case as subject

I read Lewis Carroll's book *Alice in Wonderland*.

Nominative case meaning the same thing as the subject

The white rabbit in *Alice in Wonderland* is *he*. (The sentence means, "He is the white rabbit." *He* and *rabbit* mean the same thing in the sentence.)

* * * **WARNING:** Often we drop words and assume readers will understand our intent. When you omit the final words in comparisons containing *as* or *than*, be sure you choose nominative pronouns.

For example

The pitcher outsmarted the batter. The pitcher was more clever than he *was*. (We often drop the verb in such comparisons in both speaking and writing.)

ITEM 27　OBJECTIVE CASE PRONOUNS

When a pronoun is an object, it is an objective case pronoun. Objective case pronouns are the following: *me, him, her, it, us, them,* and *whom.* The following is a quick rundown of the objective case pronoun's jobs:

Back to Prepositions

If you have, alas, forgotten about prepositions, review ("Befriending the Preposition," on page 268. The pronoun that goes with a preposition is called an "object of the preposition."

For example

Just **between you** and **me,** I find most *Mad Magazine* articles amusing.

Direct Objects

To find a sentence's subject, first find the verb and then ask *who* or *what* plus the verb. (See "Finding the Subject and the Verb," on page 264.)

For example

Paradoxes puzzle readers.

(*Who* or *what* puzzle readers? *Paradoxes* must be the subject.

To find a direct object, change the question around to ask, puzzle *who?* Puzzle readers. *Readers* is the direct object. Serving as a direct object is another function of an objective case pronoun.

＊＊＊　**NOTICE:** Many sentences have neither a direct nor an indirect object.

Indirect Objects

An indirect object is a word that tells readers *for* or *to whom* the verb was acting.

For example

John Kennedy gave the world the Peace Corps.

Subject	Verb	Indirect Object	Direct Object
John Kennedy	gave	the world	the Peace Corps

Do not worry about which job an objective case pronoun is performing. All you need to know is the pronoun is not a nominative case pronoun, and you will not confuse possessive case pronouns with nominative and objective case pronouns. Such a mistake would sound silly to you.

For example

His wants to use computers in baseball.

ITEM 28 PRONOUN REFERENCE

The standard correction symbol for a pronoun reference is *ref.* (For a complete list, see the inside back cover.)

There are three pronoun reference problems that can occur.

1. One type of pronoun reference problem occurs when you use an orphan pronoun, that is, a pronoun with no antecedent. (An *antecedent* is the word to which a pronoun refers.)

For example

Wrong

In much of the Third world, **they** really appreciate the Peace Corps. (Who is the *they* of the sentence? It is impossible to tell.)

Right

Many people of the Third World appreciate the Peace Corps.

Another example

Wrong

I have always admired people who go into the Peace Corps, and I have decided to become **one.** (*One what?*)

Right

Because I have always admired Peace Corps Volunteers, I have decided to join the Peace Corps.

2. Another type of reference problem arises when readers cannot figure out who said what to whom. The best way to clarify such a
sentence is to use a quotation.

For example

Wrong

Jim told his father that he would profit from studying the Japanese
educational system. (Who would profit—Jim or his father?)

Right

Jim told his father, "You would profit from studying the Japanese
educational system."

or

Jim told his father, "I would profit from studying the Japanese
educational system."

3. A third type of reference problem occurs when you use *it, that,
this,* or *which* without a clear antecedent.

For example

Wrong

Medical experts disapprove of fried foods and smoking **which** can
lead to heart disease. (What leads to heart disease—smoking? fried
foods? Both.)

Right

Medical experts believe **both** eating fried foods and smoking can
lead to heart disease.

ITEM 29 SHIFTS IN PRONOUNS

Yet another problem with pronouns occurs when you refer to the
same individual, but you switch persons—for instance, from first person (*I*) to second person (*you*) or the third person (*he, she,* or *it*). You
also create a problem when you switch from singular to plural—for
instance, when using the singular *I,* you switch to the plural *we* without explaining why.

For example

Wrong

When **one** thinks about Mother Teresa's dedication to the poor, **you** feel a sense of awe and admiration.

Right

When **people** think about Mother Teresa's dedication to the poor, **they** feel a sense of awe and admiration.

✳ ✳ ✳ **WARNING:** When you use the pronoun *you*, make sure that you mean your reader. Informally, in conversation, *you* is often used to mean "all you folks out there" (or "you all" in some parts of the United States.) Be sure that in writing you substitute words like *one*, *people*, or *a person* when you do not really mean *you*.

For example

You should experiment with using the beginning and ending techniques in Chapter Nine, "Beginnings and Endings."

PRACTICE LEADS TO PERFECTION

Correct the pronoun problems in the following sentences:

1. MTV has written guidelines on sex and violence which are civic-minded pieties.
2. Mary told Danielle she would benefit from self-defense training.
3. Reading the Gloria Steinem article made me think journalism would be an exciting career, and now I have decided to become one.
4. Since Japan is such an important country, people should know more about it. You should make a point to read articles about it.
5. When the Nobel Peace Prize was awarded to Mother Teresa, they gave her a lot of money which she spent to help poor people.

MODIFYING PHRASES

At the age of five, I was left an orphan. Because I was so young, I had no idea what to do with the orphan.

Modifiers add descriptive information to sentences. As in the example above, misplaced modifiers can mislead readers. When you have a modifying phrase, be sure to put it next to the idea it modifies.

ITEM 30   MISPLACED MODIFIERS

The standard correction symbol for a misplaced modifier is *mm*. (For a complete list, see the inside back cover.)

The following sentences are examples of misplaced modifiers and their corrections.

For example

Wrong

E. B. White sent several manuscripts to the recently founded *New Yorker* **beginning his career as a journalist.** (Because *beginning his career as a journalist* should modify *E. B. White*, it must come next to *E. B. White*.)

Right

Beginning his career as a journalist, E. B. White sent several manuscripts to the recently founded *New Yorker*.

Wrong

The furnace in Robert Hayden's house **almost** gave **no heat** at night. (Because *almost* should modify *no heat*, it must come next to that phrase.)

Right

The furnace in Robert Hayden's house gave **almost no heat** at night.

Wrong

My family **on our video recorder** watched *Hannah and Her Sisters.* (Because *with our video recorder* should modify *watched Hannah and Her Sisters*, it must come next to that phrase.)

Right

My family watched *Hannah and Her Sisters* on our video recorder.

PRACTICE LEADS TO PERFECTION

Correct the misplaced modifiers in the following sentences:

1. Many people think of E. B. White as a children's author having read *Charlotte's Web* and *Stuart Little*.
2. My sons became Woody Allen fans having watched his movie *Sleeper*.
3. Recently our video recorder has almost broken down on every Woody Allen film we have rented.
4. After being told to be thrifty over and over at an early age, the fable "Frugality" really appeals to me.

ITEM 31   DANGLING MODIFIERS

The standard correction symbol for a dangling modifier is *dm*. (For a complete list, see the inside back cover.)

Like their cousins misplaced modifiers, dangling modifers leave the reader wondering who or what is being modified. While sentences with misplaced modifiers have all the necessary information, however, sentences with dangling modifiers omit the word or phrase that is being modified.

For example

Wrong

After studying Michael Korda's formula for success, the need for ethical values in the formula was apparent. (Who studied Korda's formula for success?)

Right

After studying Michael Korda's formula for success, **I** felt a need to add ethical values to the formula.

Wrong

In 1987 E. B. White died. At age eighty-seven, the world felt a great loss.

Right

In 1987 at age eighty-seven, E. B. White died, and the world felt a great loss.

PRACTICE LEADS TO PERFECTION

Correct the dangling modifiers in the following sentences:

1. From an early age, the concept of trying to be perfect is drilled into society.
2. After reading Michelle Brinsmead's essay about perfection, the role it plays in my life is clearer.
3. Reading Michael Korda's definition of *success*, the lack of considerations in some big companies for human values became clear.

STYLE

Just like the pieces of a jigsaw puzzle, the words we choose and the way we put them together determine whether or not our final product works. With a puzzle, if the pieces go together wrong, the result is a jumble. With an essay, if the pieces go together wrong, the result for the reader is also a jumble.

For example

Wrong

Being confused between you and me indeed to help our ideas to our readers clearer to appear, in the correct order we must put them.

Right

In other words, when we put our ideas together properly, they appear clearer to our readers.

This section of "The Final Touch" discusses several errors to watch out for when you are putting your ideas together.

ITEM 32 PARALLEL CONSTRUCTION

The standard correction symbol for parallel construction is *paral.* (For a complete list, see the inside of the back cover.)

When you have ideas of equal importance, you must express them with similar words, phrases, or clauses. If one of the equal ideas is expressed with a word such as a noun, verb, or adjective, the other equal ideas must be expressed with the same part of speech. If the first equal idea is expressed with a prepositional phrase—or some other type of phrase—the other equal ideas must be expressed the same way. If an idea is expressed in an independent—or dependent—clause, the other ideas must be similarly expressed. If you violate parallel structure, your ideas will get off track.

For example

Wrong

According to Horace, he has gained every vote who has mingled profit with pleasure by delighting the reader **and also to instruct him.**

Right

According to Horace, he has gained every vote who has mingled profit with pleasure by delighting the reader **as well as instructing him.**

✳✳✳ **NOTICE:** A phrase is a group of words without a subject and verb.

For example

Wrong

Edwin Brock says people have killed others by nailing them to crosses, running them through with swords, suffocating them with poisonous gas, and **people have killed each other with bombs.**

Right

Edwin Brock says people have killed others by nailing them to crosses, running them through with swords, suffocating them with poisonous gas, and **dropping bombs on them.**

✳✳✳ **NOTICE:** A clause is a group of words with a subject and verb.

For example

Wrong

The brain starts with chaos. It **likes to end** with order.

Right

The brain starts with chaos. It ends with order.

PRACTICE LEADS TO PERFECTION

Correct the parallel structure errors in the following sentences from "How to Write Fast":

1. The brain juggles the teeming data, and then it is allowing them to shape their own patterns.
2. Like a Labrador retriever, the brain delights to chase after birds, nuzzle around in the underbrush of your neurons, and startling you with distant memories which it dumps, tail wagging at the feet of your consciousness.
3. The brain sniffs for the sequined, the dangerous, horrible things, and the sensual.
4. Pull out the stops for *efficiency*. Make sure your typewriter works, your files are in order, and all reference sources lie at hand.

ITEM 33 AWKWARD CONSTRUCTION

The standard correction symbol for awkward construction is *awk*, and for not clear is *NC*. (For a complete list see the inside back cover.)

Odd indeed this sentence sounds. It is an awkward sentence, or awkward is this sentence. Reread your sentences aloud to avoid awkward phrases.

The *NC* signal means your readers are lost. If your paper is handwritten, your writing may be a puzzle. Reread "Manuscript Forms," on page 261. If your writing is legible, your meaning may be a muddle. Rephrase your idea.

PRACTICE LEADS TO PERFECTION

Rewrite the following sentences to correct any awkward and unclear construction.

1. A difficult and puzzling man was Milton.
2. Although he was a Puritan, twice was Milton divorced.
3. A paradoxical mix were self-discipline and idealism along with arrogance, passion, and pride in Milton's character.

ITEM 34 WORDINESS

The standard correction symbol for wordiness is *wdy*. (For a complete list, see the back inside cover.)

The secret to successful writing is not churning out as many words as possible. The cliché says, "two heads are better than one"; however, one word is better than two—or more words—when one word conveys your meaning.

"Brevity is the soul of wit" Shakespeare wrote nearly four centuries ago. Your readers—just like Shakespeare's readers—do not want to search through a verbal jungle to ferret out your idea. Long, pompous phrases put your reader to sleep. Sleeping readers miss your point.

George Orwell illustrated Shakespeare's point about brevity when he imitated pompous, abstract, wordy writing in the following passage from "Politics and the English Language":

Objective consideration of contemporary phenomena compels the conclusion that success or failure in competitive activities exhibits no tendency to be commensurate with innate capacity, but that a considerable element of the unpredictable must invariably be taken into account.

Once you figure out what he meant, rewrite Orwell's parody in your own words.

Now compare your version to the original, clear, unwordy document in the following passage which Orwell turned into an abstract, wordy jumble. (Note the original is from the King James version of the Bible which was written in Shakespeare's era.)

I returned, and saw under the sun, that the race is not to the swift, nor the battle to the strong, neither yet bread to the wise, nor yet riches to men of understanding, nor yet favour to men of skill; but time and chance happeneth to the all.

Ecclesiastes, Chapter 9, Verse 2

How many words does the Orwell parody contain? How many words does the Ecclesiastes quotation contain? Which version is easier to understand—the Orwell version written in modern English or the Biblical version written four centuries ago? What makes the Bible version easier to understand?

Verbal Hedges to Prune out of Your Writing

Wordy	**Not Wordy**
1. because of the reason *or* the reason is because	because
2. large in size	large
3. old in age	old
4. green in color	green
5. tall in height	tall
6. proceeded to drive proceeded to (plus a verb)	drove Just use the verb. Exterminate *proceeded to!*
7. I personally believe *or* In my opinion	If you are writing the opinion, it is obviously your opinion. Just state your opinion and skip the fanfare.
8. in our modern society today	today
9. in this day and age	today
10. at the present time *or* at this point in time	now

11. very unique	*Unique* means "one of a kind." Something cannot be very unique. Something could be almost unique.
12. in the morning at 10 a.m.	at 10 a.m.

To get into the swing of pruning your verbal hedges, you need to question your meaning and ask yourself, "Can I say this with fewer words?"

PRACTICE LEADS TO PERFECTION

Eliminate wordiness in the following sentences:

1. At this point in time it seems to me that I would be an especially efficient employee because of the fact that I possess some very unique skills that would be of some special value to your firm.
2. Due to the fact that the incorrect article you sent me is red in color instead of green in color, I am returning it to you. Besides the fact that the article is the wrong color, it is also too large in size. Please send me the correct color and size that is one size smaller than the too large article I am returning. I fully expect that your response will be in a quick manner.
3. After writing to your local dealer to complain about the problem with my Mohawk LeMon station wagon, I proceeded to write to your area service representative to complain about the problem with my Mohawk LeMon station wagon. It seems to me that in my opinion your company has not responded very quickly in time to my especially important and serious complaint about the problem with my LeMon station wagon. Because of the fact that my station wagon is not old in age, I would like you to refer back to my service record to review for yourself all the numerous times I have tried without success to have a problem fixed that should not have been wrong with my car in the first place.
4. I personally believe you are going to have increasing problems competing with foreign imports when you are so slow in speed in dealing with customer complaints. I myself will certainly hesitate each and every time I shop for a new car in the future before I purchase a car made by your car company.

ITEM 35 PASSIVE VOICE VERSUS ACTIVE VOICE

The standard correction symbol for passive voice is *pass*. (For a complete list, see the inside back cover.)

Passive voice does not mean "past tense." Passive voice signals that something is being done to the subject. *Active voice* signals that the subject is acting. Active voice sentences are less wordy and more lively; they are, in fact, more active.

For example

Passive voice

Emily Dickinson's poetry **was studied** by the students.

Active voice

The students **studied** Emily Dickinson's poetry.

Passive voice

The life and work of Emily Dickinson **are discussed** in Cynthia Griffin Wolff's biography *Emily Dickinson*.

Active voice

Cynthia Griffin Wolff's biography *Emily Dickinson* **discusses** the life and work of Emily Dickinson.

Passive voice

More than 1,700 poems **were written** by Emily Dickinson, but only seven poems **were published** by her during her lifetime.

Active voice

Emily Dickinson **wrote** more than 1,700 poems, but during her lifetime she **published** only seven.

✱ ✱ ✱   **NOTICE:** A clue you may be heading for passive voice trouble is a form of the verb *to be* plus a verb ending in *d, ed,* or *t.*

Unless you are told not to use the first person (I), do not strive to avoid it. Avoiding *I* can lead to some strange-but-not-wonderful sentences, many of which are passive voice.

When Can You Use Passive Voice?

1. Use passive voice when you do not know or do not want to say who or what is responsible for the action.

For example

Abraham Lincoln **was elected** President when Emily Dickinson was thirty years old. (In the sentence we do not care who elected Lincoln. The emphasis is on the fact that Lincoln was elected.)

New biographies of Emily Dickinson will continue to **be published.** (In the sentence we do not know who will publish the biographies.)

2. Use passive voice in some scientific journals. The following example is from John Martin and Michael Gordon's article "Northeast Pacific Iron Distribution in Relation to Phytoplankton Productivity," in *Deep Sea Research:*

For example

Inshore and offshore iron distributions **were evaluated** in relation to the phytoplankton requirement for this essential element.

✳✳✳ **NOTICE:** Although passive voice is correct in certain circumstances, strive to write active voice sentences.

PRACTICE LEADS TO PERFECTION

Replace passive constructions with active ones in the following sentences. Eliminate wordiness where possible in the revisions.

1. There is disagreement among biographers about Emily Dickinson's last words. "I must go in, the fog is rising" is thought by some to be her final words. "Oh, is that all it is" is thought by others to be her final words.
2. Instructions were left by Emily Dickinson to destroy her unpublished poems after her death.
3. The decision to destroy the poems was made by Emily's sister Lavinia and Emily's friend Mabel Loomis Todd.
4. A feud was caused by the affair Emily's brother Austin was having with her friend Mabel Loomis Todd.
5. A box containing poems by Emily Dickinson was willed to Millicent Todd Bingham by her mother Mabel Loomis Todd. These poems were not published until 1945.

ITEM 36   CLICHÉS

The standard correction symbol for triteness is *cliché.* (For a complete list, see the inside back cover.)

Clichés are expressions that have lost their first blush of youth. In fact, clichés are like the old car that is scratched and dented from years of use. Once you felt a special thrill from seeing that car and experiencing its efficiency and power. Now you scarcely think about it. It is simply a vehicle you hope will get you where you are going. Because of its age, however, it is not as reliable as it once was. Sometimes it does not get you to your destination efficiently.

Similarly, clichés were once bright, shiny stars that sparkled in their readers' minds. Now they do not deliver their message very effectively because they are burned out. When you read about someone who is as cool as a cucumber, you no longer get an image of a crisp, cool, moist vegetable. Because this cliché is no longer crisp and fresh, it does not help make a point effectively.

Examples of Clichés

a shot in the arm	fresh as a daisy
beyond the shadow of doubt	green with envy
blind as a bat	happy as a lark
boggles the mind	head over heels
burn the midnight oil	played his cards right
center of attention	proud as a peacock
climb the walls	raining cats and dogs
clumsy as a bull in a china shop	ruled the roost
cool as a cucumber	set the world on fire
flat as a pancake	turn a deaf ear

In contrast to the flabby impact of clichés, notice the image called up by the following passage and poem:

> I do not know whether my present poems are better than
> the earlier ones. But this is certain; they are much
> sadder and wiser, like pain dipped in honey.

> Heinrich Heine

Apartment House

> A filing-cabinet of human lives
> Where people swarm like bees in tunneled hives,
> Each to his own cell in the towered comb,
> Identical and cramped—we call it home.

> Gerald Raftery

PRACTICE LEADS TO PERFECTION

Replace the clichés in the following sentences with fresh expressions:

1. The inefficiency of my Mohawk Motors dealership boggled the mind.
2. Beyond a shadow of a doubt, my complaint was valid.
3. I felt so frustrated when the dealership ignored my complaints, I was climbing the walls.
4. Because I played my cards right, I received a refund from Mohawk Motors.
5. I was as happy as a lark about the success of my complaint letter.

DICTION AND SPELLING

Essays are a little like those boxes that you open to find smaller boxes which you open to find smaller boxes that contain still smaller boxes. In essays the smallest boxes are the individual letters.

Because our ideas consist of clusters of words that are made up of clusters of letters, we can sometimes come up with the wrong word when we are expressing an idea. Of course, when we are generating ideas, we need to focus on the idea and not on the individual letters and words that help us express it. However, once we have captured the idea, it is time to read it word for word—and letter for letter—to make sure those words are, in fact, the words we want for the job they are supposed to fill. The following section is designed to help you get your words—and their letters—in apple pie order.

And one man in his time plays many parts.

Shakespeare

ITEM 37   FORMAL AND INFORMAL LANGUAGE

The standard correction symbol for formal language is *formal* (For a complete list, see the inside back cover.)

Just as we have different types of clothing for different activities, we have different sets of language for different situations. I *do not* use the same language with my mother that I use with my husband and close friends. Similarly, I have a vocabulary I reserve for business situations, another vocabulary I reserve for my children, and yet another for my dogs.

Dictionaries reflect the different types of language with usage labels. Words like *corny, shucks,* and *gee whiz* are colloquial; thus these words should be reserved for informal situations.

Writing for business situations and for classes should use *formal* language. *Formal* language follows the forms or rules of standard (sometimes called *proper*) English.

PRACTICE LEADS TO PERFECTION

In the following sentences, replace informal words with words appropriate to formal writing:

1. The author of ''Sonic Boom'' raps with his kid about a loud racket.
2. I told several of the folks in my class about my hunch that dyslexia would make a rad research topic.

3. Because the guy who sits next to me in class is a surfer, he was scared to death of sharks before he read the shark article.
4. I chipped in with my idea that sharks make yummy eating.

ITEM 38   CONFUSING WORD PAIRS

The standard correction symbol for diction is *D*. (For a complete list, see the inside back cover.)

Like much of life, language can tricky. Words that look or sound alike can have very different meanings. To help you avoid mixups, this section contains a list of especially tricky words.

1. **a, an**

The Vowels are *a, e, i, o,* and *u*. The Consonants are the rest of the alphabet except for the vowels.

Use *a* before a word beginning with a consonant sound.

Use *an* before words beginning with a vowel sound.

✳ ✳ ✳   **WARNING:** When *u* is pronounced *u* as in *unicorn, union, use,* use *a* before it—for example, **a** *unicorn,* **a** *union,* and **a** *use.* If it is not a long *u*, use *an* before it—for example, **an** *umpire,* **an** *umbrella,* and **an** *ulcer.*
When an *h* is silent, use *an* before it—for example, **an** *heir,* **an** *honor,* and **an** *hour.* If an *h* is not silent, use *a* before it—for example, **a** *helper,* **a** *hanger,* and **a** *hand.*

2. **affect, effect**

Affect is a verb. *Affect* means to "influence."

Effect is usually a noun. As a noun, *effect* means "something brought about by a cause." If words like *an* or *the* come first, the word you want is *effect.* Occasionally *effect* is used to mean "to bring about."

For example

Sharks have a valuable **effect** in keeping a balance of life in the oceans.

The article **effected** a change in attitudes about sharks.

Mankind's fear of sharks has **affected** the kind of research done on them.

3. **all ready, already**

If you can drop *all* without changing your meaning, use *all ready.* Otherwise, use *already.*

For example

I was **all ready** to turn in my paper. I had **already** properly credited my sources.

4. all right

All right is always two words, just as *all wrong* is two words. Since you would not write *alwrong*, you must NEVER write *alright*.

5. around

Around refers to direction. *Around* does not mean *about* or *approximately*.

For example

Wrong

I used **around** ten sources for my research paper.

Right

I used **approximately** ten sources for my research paper.

A good example

I looked **around** the library to find the reference librarian.

6. bad, badly versus good, well

Bad and *good* are adjectives. *Badly* and *well* are adverbs. (Many adverbs have *ly* endings). Forms of the verb *to be* and verbs like *seems, appears, smells, feels, tastes* require the adjective form to follow them. Do not use an adverb after these verbs.

For example

Wrong

I felt **badly** when I couldn't find the article I wanted for my paper.

Right

I felt **bad** when I couldn't find the article I wanted for my paper.

* * *   **NOTICE:** You would not say you felt *well* about finding the article, right? Substitute the adjective *good* and the adverb *well* if you are not sure if you need the adjective or adverb form.

7. being as, being that

Avoid both *being as* and *being that*. Instead use *because*.

8. capital, capitol

A *capitol* is the building where laws are made. Use *capital* unless you mean that building.

9. complement, compliment

Complement is related to *complete*, but *compliment* is the kind of remark I like to hear. I like compliments.

10. contractions

We would sound strange if we did not fill our conversations with contractions. In formal writing, however, use contractions sparingly. Unless you are using a quotation, use only contractions like the following on the few occasions when you have decided you should use a contraction: *aren't, can't, doesn't, don't, won't, it's, isn't, let's, wasn't,* and *weren't*. Always avoid the following contractions in formal writing except in quotations: *could've, should've, would've, you're, they're,* and *we've*.

11. could of, could've

Could of is always wrong. You mean *could've*. Avoid *could've* in formal writing. Use *could have*.

12. data

Data is plural. *Datum* is singular.

13. fun

Fun is a noun, not an adjective.

For example

Wrong

It was a **fun** paper to write.

Right

The paper was **fun** to write.

14. its, it's

These are a troublesome twosome. Always mean *it is* when you write *it's*. It's too easy to confuse these words otherwise. Your point loses part of *its* punch when you misuse *it's* or *its*. For further information, see the section on contractions in "The Apostrophe," on page 291.

15. kind of, sort of

Use these words only in informal writing. They sound sloppier than words like *somewhat* and *rather*.

16. lay, lie

While it may seem these verbs were invented by a sadist, in fact, they evolved their confusing pattern all by themselves.

> ***To lay:*** to put or place something
> ***To lie:*** to rest or recline

The Verbs *To Lie* and *To Lay*

Present	Past	Past participle	Present participle
lay	laid	has laid	is laying
lie	lay	has lain	is lying

For example

After reading the article, I **laid** it on the table.
After working on my paper for four hours, I **lay** down for a nap.

17. **less, fewer**

Their meanings are related, but these words are not interchangeable. *Few* answers the question, How many? Use *few* with things you can count.

Use *less* with things you cannot count. *Less* answers the question, How much?

For example

After I read "How to Write Fast," I needed **less** time to write my papers.

I needed to spend **fewer** hours writing my paper because of the good advice contained in the article.

18. **passed, past**

Passed is an action.

For example

I **passed** the reference librarian on my way into the library.

Past has to do with either time or position.

For example

The reference librarian said, "I think you have a book that is **past** due."

19. **principal, principle**

The main thing is the *principal* thing. The principal of a school is its main administrator. Handily, both *main* and *principal* contain an *a*.

Principles are rules. When you write, you need to understand the *principles* of punctuation. Both *principle* and *rule* end in *le*.

20. **set, sit**

The problem with these verbs is closely related to the problem with *to lay* and *to lie*.

To set: to put or place (unless you are a hen, in which case you cannot read but you can *set* on eggs.

To sit: to rest on the hindquarters.

The Verbs *To Set* and *To Sit*

Present	Past	Past participle	Present participle
set	set	has set	is setting
sit	sat	has sat	is sitting

For example

I had **set** all the reference books within easy reach.

I **sat** at the table taking notes for my paper about over-the-counter diet pills. My reference books were **sitting** all around me.

21. **should of, should've**

See *could of* on page 332. *Should of* is always wrong. You mean *should've*. Avoid *should've* in formal writing. Use *should have*.

22. **than, then**

I suspect much of the trouble with this pair would be corrected if people misusing them looked more carefully at these words. One little difference in letters makes a big difference in meaning. Use *than* in comparisons.

For example

I found more information about current events in *Reader's Guide to Periodical Literature* **than** I found in the card catalogue.

Use *then* to refer to time or to consequence.

For example

I followed the steps in "How to Write Fast. " **Then** I got an A on my beautifully organized, well-documented paper. I was happier with the A **than** I was with the C I had gotten on my previous paper.

23. **their, there, they're**

Review the section on contractions in "The Apostrophe," on page 291. Because these triplets sound the same, they are sometimes used for one another. However, they do not mean the same at all.

1. Whenever you write *they're*, read it as *they are*. Except in a quotation, do not use *they're* in formal writing.

2. When you use *their* make sure it is showing possession.
3. Write *there* when you are pointing something out.

For example

There on my desk was the book the librarians had claimed was overdue. "Other students need that book to help with **their** research papers," the librarian had told me. "**They're** in here everyday asking if the book has been returned."

24. threw, through

These words confirm the suspicion that English spelling can be irrational at times. However, life itself is not rational, and complaining about this irrationality is not productive. So stiffen your upper lip. The distinction between this pair is easy to master.

Threw is an action verb. It is the past tense of the verb *to throw*.

Through has a variety of meanings—everything from *finished* to *by way of*. When you do not mean the past tense form of to *to throw*, use *through*.

For example

My roommate *threw* away my research notes.

In the past most of the funding for shark research has come **through** agencies primarily concerned about the shark's man-eater image.

25. till, until

This is a chance for you to exercise your creative genius. Take your choice. Both are correct. However *'til* is not correct.

26. to, too, two

Two is the easiest to master of this trio. *Two* is always a number. *Too* means *an excess* or *also*. Use *to* for all other occasions.

For example

Dr. John McCosker, director of Steinhart Aquarium, and Dr. Leonard Compagno, a San Francisco State University Professor, are **two** experts on sharks. These **two** scientists are worried that fishermen may be catching **too** many sharks for the shark **to** sustain its population at a healthy level.

27. which, who

Which refers to things, not people. *Who* refers to people.

For example

Many people **who** use the ocean to surf or swim fear the great white shark, **which** is the culprit in most shark attacks on people.

28. **whose, who's**

This pair is related to *its, it's.* Use *who's* only when it makes sense
to say *who is.*

29. **would of, would've**

See *could of, could've* and *should of, should've* on pages 322 and
324. *Would of* is always wrong. You mean *would've.* Avoid *would've*
in formal writing. Use *would have.*

30. **your, you're**

Always mean *you are* when you write *you're.* Avoid *you're* in formal writing except in a quotation. When you are indicating possession, use *your.*

For example

John McCosker tells surfers, "You must put the danger of shark
attack in perspective. **You're** in more danger in **your** car on the way
to the ocean than **you're** in when **you're** surfing."

PRACTICE LEADS TO PERFECTION

Correct the errors in the following sentences:

1. Being that I enjoyed "Sonic Boom" and "A & P" so much I decided
   to read other John Updike works to.
2. I all ready had an little background about Updike's life and writing,
   but their was one data that I especially wanted to investigate:
   Updike was sort of young (still in high school) when he started
   writing. What factors effected his desire to become an author?
3. I should of realized Updike's experience as editor of his high
   school paper would be sort of important in helping him decide to
   be a writer.
4. Of course, Updike's mother, which published a number of short
   stories, was one of the principle influences in his life.
5. They're other important early influences on Updike's career choice
   to—such as his years at Harvard when he was the *Lampoon's* leading wit.
6. Updike loved and respected his father, which was a high school
   math teacher, but his mother was a stronger career influence then
   his father.
7. Updike has written about feeling isolated from his peers because
   he suffers from psoriasis. In his youth Updike and his mother laid
   in the sun even in the winter as their was no other treatment for
   this skin disease when Updike was growing up in the 30ies and
   40ies.

ITEM 39   SPELLING

The standard correction symbol for spelling is *sp.* (For a complete list, see the inside back cover.)

Each semester I have a few students for whom spelling comes easily. For their own protection, I do not release their names to their classmates for whom spelling is as natural and easy as swimming the English channel, running the four-minute mile, or climbing Mt. Everest. I have some good news for the majority of you, however, for whom spelling is *not* a cinch. Just because spelling is tricky does not mean you must misspell words.

True Confessions

Although I have published numerous articles in newspapers and magazines, and although I have taught college English for a decade and a half, I do not find spelling easy. It is a struggle. But through my struggles, I have come up with some tips to help you in your battles with spelling.

Martin's Handy Guide to Successful Spelling

1. Involve as many of your five senses as you can in learning to spell. Do not just look at a word that gives you trouble; write that word while saying the letters out loud. Furthermore, write the troublesome part of the word larger, or in different colored ink to help you recognize the difficult spots.

For example

Original Spelling	**Correction**	**Correct Rewriting**
r e p i t i t i o u s	r e p^ei t i t i o u s	repetitious

2. Use a memory scheme. My grandfather used to say the following:

   Remember, it is *i* after *l* and *e* after *c.*
   Just keep that *lice* running through your head.

   Grandpa Cameron's lousy scheme works beautifully with words like *receive, deceive, conceive, relieve,* and *believe.*

3. *All right* is a snap to remember if you think of *all wrong.*
   You would not write *alwrong,* and you must not write *alright.*

✱ ✱ ✱ **NOTICE:** When you misspell a word, think of an association that will help you remember the way to spell that word correctly.

4. Learn a few helpful rules. Grandpa Cameron's Lice Rule is related to the following rule:

   i before *e* except after *c* or when sounded like *a* as in *neighbor* and *weigh*

   The exceptions to this rule can be crammed into the following odd, but helpful, sentence:

   Neither leisured foreigner seized the weird heights.

PRACTICE LEADS TO PERFECTION

Fill in the blanks with the proper *i e* sequence.

1. r__ndeer   4. n__gh   7. fr__ght
2. effic__nt   5. hyg__ne   8. anc__nt
3. br__f   6. v__n   9. misch__f

5. Learn this rule for doubling consonants. When you add *ed*, *er*, or *ing*, double the final consonant when
   a. the word ends in a single consonant,
   b. the consonant is preceded by a single vowel,
   c. and the word is accented on its last syllable.

Remember: *a*, *e*, *i*, *o*, and *u*, are vowels. All other letters are consonants.
   (This is one of my personal favorites among spelling rules—simply because this rule helps me out so often.)

PRACTICE LEADS TO PERFECTION

Add *ed*, *er*, or *ing* to the following words:

1. return   4. creep   7. begin   10. spell
2. wed   5. permit   8. occur   11. fight
3. benefit   6. plan   9. put   12. eat

KEEP PRACTICING

The following is a list of the most frequently misspelled words. Have someone test you, and then use one or more of the methods in this spelling unit to learn those you miss.

101 Troublesome Words on the Misspelling Parade

1. absence	31. description	61. mischievous
2. acquaintance	32. desirable	62. necessary
3. across	33. desperate	63. ninety
4. adequately	34. disappoint	64. ninth
5. aggravate	35. disastrous	65. noticeable
6. alcohol	36. eighth	66. occasionally
7. alleviate	37. embarrass	67. parallel
8. all right	38. environment	68. permissible
9. a lot	39. existence	69. preceding
10. amateur	40. familiar	70. prejudice
11. analysis	41. February	71. privilege
12. apparent	42. finally	72. proceed
13. argument	43. gauge	73. psychology
14. athlete	44. government	74. pursue
15. awkward	45. grammar	75. recommend
16. benefit	46. guarantee	76. repetition
17. bureaucracy	47. harass	77. religious
18. business	48. humorous	78. rhythm
19. calendar	49. independent	79. ridiculous
20. category	50. intelligence	80. sacrifice
21. cemetery	51. interfere	81. secretary
22. certain	52. knowledge	82. separate
23. committee	53. laboratory	83. sergeant
24. competition	54. library	84. shining
25. conscientious	55. license	85. significant
26. conscious	56. length	86. similar
27. consistent	57. loneliness	87. sincerely
28. continuous	58. maneuver	88. sophomore
29. criticize	59. mathematics	89. straight
30. definitely	60. medicine	90. succeed

91. surprise	95. truly	99. vacuum
92. thoroughly	96. unanimous	100. villain
93. though	97. undoubtedly	101. Wednesday
94. tragedy	98. unfortunately	

WORD PROBLEMS

The final touch in this handbook is a potpourri of rules that focus on individual words.

ITEM 40 SINGULAR AND PLURAL WORDS

The standard correction symbol for singular is *sing*, and the standard correction symbol for plural is *pl.* (For a complete list, see the back inside cover.)

Singular means just one. *Plural* means more than one. Check in a dictionary to make sure you have used the proper form. Some nouns do not indicate their plurals by adding *s*.

For example

Singular	Plural
child	children
datum	data
goose	geese
mouse	mice
moose	moose
man	men
woman	women

For more information about agreement, read "Making Subjects, Verbs, and Pronouns Agree" on page 295.

ITEM 41 DIVISION OF WORDS

The standard correction symbol for division of words is *div.* (For a complete list, see the inside back cover.)

If you cannot fit the whole word on a line, it is best to write the word on the next line. However, if you must divide a word, be sure to divide it at a syllable. Check the syllable division in your dictionary to verify symbols.

ITEM 42   WRONG WORDS

The standard correction symbol for a wrong word is *ww*. (For a complete list, see the inside back cover.)

Some words sound a lot like other words. (Read "Diction and Spelling" on page 319 for more information.) An unintentional, funny use of a wrong word is called a *malapropism*. Mrs. Malaprop is a character from *The Rival*, a play written in 1775 by Richard Sheridan. Her misuse of words adds to the fun of the play. Check your friendly, helpful dictionary for guidance when you have the least doubt about a word—lest you create a malapropism. Of course, not all wrong words are humorous, but for a bit of comic relief, we will practice detecting wrong words with malaprops. *The New Yorker* magazine has fun with malaprops appearing in print—as you will see in the following exercise.

PRACTICE LEADS TO PERFECTION

Replace the malaprops in the following sentences with a more appropriate word:

1. In the "American Dream" the attacks on suburban *morays* and values is too heavy handed.
2. Sixty-five million years ago the dinosaurs vanished in what some astronomers believe was a *comic* catastrophe that could recur today.
3. Critics have wondered how Asquith could base an entire book on fruit tarts. She, in turn, is amazed by that reaction. "It is almost *infinitesimal*, the things you can do," she said.

ITEM 43   ABBREVIATIONS

The standard correction symbol for an abbreviation is *ab*. (For a complete list, see the inside back cover.)

While we often abbreviate words in informal writing, formal writing has strict rules about when we can and cannot abbreviate. The following abbreviations are always acceptable:

1. *Mr., Mrs., Jr.,* and *Sr.,* used with a person's name
2. *Dr., St., M.D., Ph.D., M.A.,* and other similar degrees, used with a person's name
3. *Col.* and other military titles, used with a person's name
4. *a.m., p.m., A.D., B.C.*
5. Names of organizations you are sure your audience will recognize—for example, CIA, FBI, KGB, IBM, NAACP, and SPCA

If you are not sure your audience will recognize the abbreviation, you can abbreviate the name of an organization you plan to mention repeatedly by first giving the full name and then giving the abbreviation in parenthesis. After mentioning its full name, you can then use its abbreviation.

For example

California Department of Fish and Game (CDFG)

While some abbreviations are acceptable, make sure the following abbreviations are written out, as shown:

Wrong	**Right**
&	and
etc.	*and so forth*

Make sure readers have a clear idea of what you mean when you write *and so forth*. If readers will not have a clear picture, do not use the expression.

Abbreviation	**Abbreviation Written Out**
lbs.	pounds
′ , ″	feet, inches
Eng.	English
N.Y.	New York (write out all states)
U.S.	You can use U.S. as an adjective, but write out *United States* when it is a noun.

For example

The health of the **U.S.** economy is important to the economic health of the rest of the world. In the **United States,** many people are very worried about the balance of payments.

ITEM 44   NUMBERS AND NUMERALS

The standard correction symbol for numbers and numerals is *num.* (For a complete list, see the inside back cover.)

While the rules vary about when to write out a number and when to use a numeral, use the following three guidelines in writing for the humanities.

1. Write out the word, not the numeral for numbers you can express in one or two words.

Yes, technical and scientific writing as well as newspapers and magazines follow a different rule, but this is the rule for formal writing in the humanities.

For example

The poet John Milton lived for **sixty-two** years (from **1608** to **1674**).

Places Rated Almanac evaluates the livability of **329** cities.

2. Use numerals for pages, time followed by *a.m.* or *p.m.*, units of measurement, percentages, decimals, and comparing numbers. Avoid shifting between numbers and figures within a sentence.

For example

By **11 a.m.,** I had moved my entire collection of Milton's works to my office. The books must have weighed **50** pounds.

3. Do not begin a sentence with a numeral.

For example

Seven hundred sixty-three people attended the reading of Milton's poetry.

Last night, **763** people attend the reading of Milton's poetry.

PRACTICE LEADS TO PERFECTION

Write out any words in the following sentences that should not be abbreviated:

1. In Eng. 102, I studied Milton & Shakespeare, & etc.
2. In my Crim. Justice class we studied the history of the CIA, KGB, and FBI.
3. Our instructor was Agatha Christie, Ph.D., from Atlanta, Ga.
4. Kurt Vonnegut, Jr., is one of my favorite authors.
5. Doctor Paul Ehrlich was one of the first scientists to warn people in the U.S. about the dangers of nuclear weapons.
6. 614 students enrolled in the class about Milton.
7. By age 44, Milton was blind.

ACKNOWLEDGMENTS

PHOTOGRAPHY ACKNOWLEDGMENTS

All photos not credited are the property of Scott, Foresman and Company.

PAGE CHAPTER 4

57   Reproduced with permission: The Putnam & Grosset Group.

59   Copr. 1940 James Thurber. Copr. 1968 Helen Thurber. From *Fables for Our Time* published by Harper & Row.

63   Courtesy of Therese M. Markarian.

PAGE CHAPTER 5

73   Courtesy of Hawaii Visitors Bureau.

PAGE CHAPTER 8

127   (1) Chuck Solomon/Focus on Sports.
(r) Focus on Sports.

PAGE CHAPTER 9

137   "The Far Side" cartoon by Gary Larson is reprinted by permission of Chronicle Features, San Francisco.

141   MAD Magazine © 1985. Reproduced with permission of E. C. Publications, Inc.

PAGE CHAPTER 11

173   Kimble Pendleton Mead.

181   Illustration by Lane Smith.

PAGE CHAPTER 12

191   From John Welter, "More Letters from Papa," *Saturday Review*, January–February 1984.

PAGE CHAPTER 14

239   "The Far Side" cartoon by Gary Larson is reprinted by permission of Chronicle Features, San Francisco.

248   Reprinted with permission. Time, Inc.

PAGE FINAL TOUCH: A HANDBOOK

255   Reprinted by permission: Tribune Media Services.

268   © 1987 United Feature Syndicate.

269   © 1984 United Feature Syndicate.

Cover   *Tidal Wave II*, 1978, Jennifer Barlett. Oil on two canvases. Courtesy Paula Cooper Gallery, New York. Private Collection, Zurich, Switzerland.

LITERARY ACKNOWLEDGMENTS

PAGE CHAPTER 1

5   Lt. Col. Charles G. Cavanaugh, Jr., "The Write Way to Do It," *Soldiers*, August 1985.

6   From "Managers Need to Write Well" by Sylvia Porter as appeared in *Monterey Peninsula Herald*, April 30, 1986. Copyright © 1986 Los Angeles Times Syndicate. Reprinted by permission.

10   From *Growing Up* by Russell Baker. Copyright © 1982 by Russell Baker. Reprinted by permission of Contemporary Books, Inc.

PAGE CHAPTER 2

19   Marjorie Holmes, Excerpt from *Writing the Creative Article*.

20   "Gone Forever" by Barriss Mills from *Elizabeth IV*. Copyright © 1963 by The Elizabeth Press. Reprinted by permission.

22   From *The Inner Game of Tennis* by W. Timothy Gallwey. Copyright © 1974 by W. Timothy Gallwey. Reprinted by permission of Random House, Inc.

23   From *Writing the Natural Way* by Gabriele Rico. Copyright © 1983 by Jeremy P. Tarcher, Inc., Los Angeles. Reprinted by permission of St. Martin's Press.

24   "The Hands She Wore" by Marcia Kruchten, *Writer's Digest*, August 1985. Reprinted by permission of the author.

26   "Take Me out of the Ball Game" by John Leo, *Time*, August 15, 1983. Copyright © 1983 Time Inc. All rights reserved. Reprinted by permission.

28   "What I Did Last Summer" by Dick Albert from *Inside English*. Reprinted by permission of the author.

30   From *Scott, Foresman Advanced Dictionary*. Copyright © 1988 Scott, Foresman and Company.

PAGE CHAPTER 3

39   "Theme for English B" from *Montage of a Dream Deferred* by Langston Hughes. Copyright 1951 by Langston Hughes. Copyright renewed 1979 by George Houston Bass. Reprinted by permission of Harold Ober Associates Incorporated.

40   From *The Journal of Charlotte Forten: A Free Negro in the Slave Era*. Copyright 1953 by The Dryden Press, Inc. Reprinted by permission.

42   From *I, Rigoberta Menchu: An Indian Woman In Guatemala*, edited and introduced by Elisabeth Burgos-Debray, translated by Ann Wright. © Verso Editions, 1984. Reprinted by permission.

43   From *Writing Without Teachers* by Peter Elbow. Copyright © 1973 by Oxford University Press, Inc. Reprinted by permission.

PAGE CHAPTER 4

51   Sheridan Warner Baker, *The Practical Stylist*, Fifth Edition. New York: Harper & Row, 1981, pp. 4, 84.

52,53 From *Scott, Foresman Advanced Dictionary*. Copyright © 1988, Scott Foresman and Company.

54   "Fueled" from *Serve Me a Slice of Moon*, copyright © 1965 by Marcie Hans, reprinted by permission of Harcourt Brace Jovanovich, Inc.

56   From "The Current Crop of Ghost Stories" by Bennett Cerf in *Famous Ghost Stories*, edited by Bennett Cerf. Copyright 1941 and renewed 1972 by Random House, Inc. Reprinted by permission of the publisher.

57   Illustration by Fritz Kredel reprinted by permission of Grosset & Dunlap from *Aesop's Fables*, copyright 1947, copyright renewed © 1975 by Grosset & Dunlap, Inc.

59   "The Little Girl and the Wolf" by James Thurber. Copyright 1940 by James Thurber. Copyright © 1968 by Helen Thurber. From *Fables for Our Time*, published by Harper & Row.

PAGE CHAPTER 5

69   "Once by the Pacific" by Robert Frost. Copyright 1928 by Holt, Rinehart and Winston, Inc. and renewed 1956 by Robert Frost. Reprinted from *The Poetry of Robert Frost* edited by Edward Connery Lathem, by permission of Henry Holt and Company, Inc.

70   From *Travels With Charley* by John Steinbeck. Copyright © 1961, 1962 by The Curtis Publishing Co., Inc. Copyright © 1962 by John Steinbeck. All rights reserved. Reprinted by permission of Viking Penguin, Inc.

71   From *Blue Thirst* by Lawrence Durrell. Copyright © 1975 by Lawrence Durrell. Reprinted by permission of Capra Press, Santa Barbara, CA.

73   Marlene Martin, "Volcanic Beauty."

PAGE CHAPTER 6

86   "Pigeon Woman" by May Swenson is used by permission of the author. Copyright © 1962 by May Swenson, first printed in *The New Yorker*.

88   From I Know Why the Caged Bird Sings by Maya Angelou. Copyright © 1969 by Maya Angelou. Reprinted by permission of Random House, Inc.

90   Ernest Hemingway, "Old Man At The Bridge" from *The Short Stories of Ernest Hemingway*. Copyright 1938 Ernest Hemingway; copyright renewed © 1966 Mary Hemingway. Reprinted with the permission of Charles Scribner's Sons, an imprint of Macmillan Publishing Company.

92   From "Soft-Spoken Bubba Once a Synonym for Stark Terror" by Jim Murray. Copyright © 1988, Los Angeles Times. Reprinted by permission of Los Angeles Times Syndicate.

94   From *Fauna and Family* by Gerald Durrell. Copyright © 1978 by Gerald Durrell. Reprinted by permission of Curtis Brown Group Ltd., London on behalf of Gerald Durrell.

PAGE CHAPTER 7

102   "Hurt Hawks" Copyright 1928 and renewed 1956 by Robinson Jeffers. Reprinted from *Rock and Hawk: A Selection of Shorter Poems by Robinson Jeffers*, by permission of Random House, Inc.

108   "Tale of the Rodent" by Roger Starr, *The New York Times*, August 2, 1981. Copyright © 1981 by The New York Times Company. Reprinted by permission.

110   "A & P" Copyright © 1962 by John Updike. Reprinted from *Pigeon Feathers and Other Stories* by John Updike, by permission of Alfred A. Knopf, Inc.

PAGE CHAPTER 8

119   Sheridan Warner Baker, *The Practical Stylist*, Fifth Edition. New York: Harper & Row, 1981, pp. 4, 84.

120   "Plane Wreck at Los Gatos (Deportee)" lyric by Woody Guthrie, music by Martin Hoffman. TRO copyright © 1961 (renewed 1963) Ludlow Music, Inc., New York, NY. Used by permission.

122   Pete Axtheim, "A Star Flunks His Test," *Newsweek*, January 5, 1987.

123   From "Who Said Minnie Was Mousy?" *Newsweek*, February 24, 1986. Copyright © 1986 Newsweek, Inc. All Rights Reserved. Reprinted by permission.

123   "Confessions of a Nicotine Freak" by Jack E. White, *Time*, April 18, 1988. Copyright © 1988 Time Inc. All rights reserved. Reprinted by permission.

125   "Seeing the Future at Work at IBM" by Lani Luciano, *Money*, November 1985. Copyright © 1985 Time Inc. All rights reserved. Reprinted by permission.

126   From "Computers in the Dugout" by Steve Boros, *Discover*, October 1984. Copyright © *Discover*, 1984, Family Media, Inc. Reprinted by permission.

129   Sharon Begley, "A Cosmic Birth Announcement." *Newsweek*, January 19, 1987.

PAGE **CHAPTER 9**

138   "Pitcher" from *The Orb Weaver* by Robert Francis. Copyright 1953 by Robert Francis. Reprinted by permission of Wesleyan University Press.

141   From "Filling a Bottle With Integrity: A Hot New Business Trend" by Dave Barry as appeared in *The Monterey Peninsula Herald*, March 16, 1986. Reprinted by permission of the author.

142   Wayne Scheer, "Creative Grading or How I Decided to Stop Worrying and Love My Gradebook." *Innovation Abstracts*, January 24, 1986.

142   From "Women Learn to Fight Back" by Mary Tesoro, *Monterey Peninsula Herald*, November 3, 1985. Reprinted by permission.

143   Cliff Jahr, "Marie Osmond: On her own at last." *Ladies' Home Journal*, November 1985.

143   From "Dolly Parton" by Gloria Steinem, *Ms.*, January 1987. Reprinted by permission of the author.

144   From "Stop nagging him, he's trying to quit" by Mike Royko, as appeared in *San Jose Mercury News*, December 9, 1985. Reprinted by permission: Tribune Media Services.

144   From "Fortunes in missing masterpieces" by John Lee and Miriam Horn with Andrea Gabor, *U.S. News & World Report*, August 10, 1987. Copyright © 1987 by U.S. News & World Report, Inc. Reprinted by permission.

145   Barbara Grizzuti Harrison, "The Stubborn Courage of Mother Teresa." *McCall's*, August 1985.

145   Marlene Martin, "Angler's All." *American Way*, 1986, p. 12.

145   From "After a turbulent youth, the Peace Corps comes of age" by Nancy Shute, *Smithsonian*, February 1986. Reprinted by permission of the author.

146   Stuart M. Berger, "How What You Eat Can Add Years to Your Life." *Parade*, March 30, 1986.

147   From "The Pleasures of Being an Astrophysicist: An Adventure in Science" by Richard A. Muller, *The New York Times Magazine*,

March 25, 1985. Copyright © 1985 by The New York Times Company. Reprinted by permission.

147 From "Traveler's Update" by Emily Praeger, from *Penthouse* November, 1985).

147 Schiller, Diane P. and Walberg, Herbert H., "Japan: The Learning Society." *Educational Leadership*, March 1982. Reprinted with permission of the Association for Supervision and Curriculum Development and the authors. Copyright © 1982 by ASCD. All rights reserved.

147 Eric Gelman, et al., "MTV's Message." *Newsweek*, December 30, 1985.

148 David Galvin and Sally Toteff, "Toxics on the Home Front." *Sierra*, September/October 1986, p. 48.

149 From "Cocaine Con" by Gabe Mirkin, *Health*, January 1985, p. 8. Copyright © 1985 by Family Media, Inc. Reprinted by permission.

150 From "Our Insatiable Brain" by Joann Ellison, *Annual Editions: Psychology*, 1985/1986. Reprinted by permission.

150 From "Will Spelling Count?" by Jack Connor, *The Chronicle of Higher Education*, 1980. Copyright © 1980, The Chronicle of Higher Education. Reprinted by permission.

PAGE CHAPTER 10

158 "Those Winter Sundays" is reprinted from *Angle of Ascent, New and Selected Poems*, by Robert Hayden, by permission of Liveright Publishing Corporation. Copyright © 1975, 1972, 1970, 1966 by Robert Hayden.

160 "On Frugality" from *Without Feathers* by Woody Allen. Copyright © 1975 by Woody Allen. Reprinted by permission of Random House, Inc.

161 "Defining Success" From *Success! How Every Man and Woman Can Achieve It* by Michael Korda. Copyright © 1977 by Success Research Corporation. Reprinted by permission of Random House, Inc.

PAGE CHAPTER 11

171 "Five Ways to Kill a Man" from *Invisibility is the Art of Survival* by Edwin Brock. Copyright © 1972 by Edwin Brock. Reprinted by permission of New Directions Publishing Corporation.

172 "Ten Typewriter Problems You Can Correct Yourself" by Wayne Gash, *Writer's Digest*, October 1984.

175 From "How to Write Fast" by Alan R. Blackburn, *Writer's Digest*, September 1981. Reprinted by permission of the author.

180 "How to Complain When Your Toaster, Your VCR, or Your Banker Doesn't Do the Job" by Emily Card, *Ms.* Magazine, September 1986. Reprinted by permission of the author.

PAGE CHAPTER 12

191 From "More Letters from Papa" by John Welter, *Saturday Review*, January–February 1984. Reprinted by permission of the author.

196 "Letter to a Manufacturer" from *The Family Book of Humor* by H. F. Ellis.

200 Excerpt from *Please Don't Eat the Daisies* by Jean Kerr. Copyright 1954 by Jean Kerr. Reprinted by permission of Doubleday, a division of Bantam, Doubleday, Dell Publishing Group, Inc.

PAGE CHAPTER 13

211 "Atomic Courtesy" by Ethel Jacobson. Reprinted by permission of the author.

212   "Sonic Boom" Copyright © 1959 by John Updike. Reprinted from *Telephone Polls and Other Poems* by John Updike, by permission of Alfred A. Knopf, Inc.

217, From *Reader's Guide to Periodical Literature*, May 1988. Copyright ©
218   1988 by the H. W. Wilson Co. Reprinted by permission.

221   Marlene Martin, "The Menace and the Myth." *San Francisco Examiner & Chronicle*, July 18, 1982.

222   From "The shark: More threatened than threatening?" by Marlene Martin, *Sea Frontiers*, September–October 1985. Copyright © 1985 by The International Oceanographic Foundation. Reprinted by permission.

PAGE CHAPTER 14

240   "Test" by Rich Linder from *Inside English*, March 1985. Reprinted by permission of the author.

242   From *Unlimited Power: The New Science of Personal Achievement*. Copyright © 1987 by Anthony Robbins. Reprinted by permission of Simon & Schuster, Inc.

245   "The Nuclear-Winter Threat" by Thomas Levenson, *Discover*, January 1984. Copyright © *Discover*, 1984, Family Media, Inc. Reprinted by permission.

248   "All Riled Up About Ratings" by J. R. Reed and the chart "Ten Best . . . & Worst" from TIME, March 11, 1985. Copyright © 1985 Time Inc. All rights reserved. Reprinted by permission.

PAGE THE FINAL TOUCH: A HANDBOOK

262   William Zinsser, *On Writing Well: An Informal Guide to Writing Nonfiction*, Third Edition. New York: Harper & Row, 1985, pp. 121–122.

278   From *The Almanac of American Letters* by Randy F. Nelson. Copyright © 1981 by William Kaufmann, Inc. Reprinted by permission.

288   Excerpt from review of *I Know Why the Caged Bird Sings* by Robert Gross, *Newsweek*.

312   George Orwell, "Politics and English Language" in *Shooting an Elephant and Other Essays*. Orlando, Florida: Harcourt Brace Jovanovich, Inc., 1950.

316   John Martin and Michael Gordon, "Northeast Pacific Iron Distribution in Relation to Phytoplankton Productivity," *Deep Sea Research*, February 1988.

317   "Apartment House" by Gerald Raftery. Reprinted by permission of Paul Raftery.

The student essays appearing throughout this text are reprinted by permission of the authors.

INDEX